Dictionary of Living Thoughts of Leading Thinkers: a cyclopædia of quotations, etc.

S. Pollock Linn

DICTIONARY OF
LIVING THOUGHTS

OF

LEADING THINKERS

A

CYCLOPÆDIA OF QUOTATIONS

Designed for the use of the Senate, the Bar, the Pulpit,
and the Orator

BY

S. POLLOCK LINN, A.M.

NEW YORK
WILBUR B. KETCHAM
2 COOPER UNION

LIVING THOUGHTS.

———— ◆ ————

IDEAS go booming through the world louder than cannon. Thoughts are mightier than armies. Principles
have achieved more victories than horsemen or chariots.

Rev. Dr. W. M. Paxton.

———— ◆ ————

THOUGHT refuses to be stationary, institutions refuse
to change, and war is the consequence.

E. L. Youmans.

———— ◆ ————

TO be fossilized is to be stagnant, unprogressive, dead,
frozen into a solid. It is only *liquid currents* of thought
that move men and the world.

Wendell Phillips.

———— ◆ ————

IDEAS make their way in silence like the waters that,
filtering behind the rocks of the Alps, loosen them from
the mountain on which they rest.

D'Aubigné.

———— ◆ ————

LET an independent thinker show a fearless fidelity to his
convictions, and the shafts of bigotry and envy fall
helpless and harmless at his feet.

New York Tribune.

THE restless mind of man cannot but press a principle to the real limit of its application, even though centuries should intervene between the premise and the conclusion.

Henry Parry Liddon.

———◦◦◦———

THE force of ideas is never felt till they are voted down.

Theodore Tilton.

———◦◦◦———

GREAT thoughts
Stand up like church-spires 'mid village cots.

Bailey's Festus

———◦◦◦———

THE activity and soundness of a man's actions will be determined by the activity and soundness of his thoughts.

H. W. Beecher.

———◦◦◦———

GOD delights in true, earnest thinkers.

Dwight.

———◦◦◦———

PRESS on! for it is godlike to unloose
The spirit, and forget yourself in thought.

N. P. Willis.

———◦◦◦———

THE truth is, it is not the amount of thought which is poured in that gives wisdom, but the amount of *living*, creative mind and heart working on and stirred by what is so poured in.

F. W. Robertson.

———◦◦◦———

IN the end thought rules the world. There are times when impulses and passions are more powerful, but they soon expend themselves; while *mind*, acting constantly, is ever ready to drive them back and work when their energy is exhausted.

McCosh

A WORD in England is greater than a man in Italy. A thought in America is often greater than a cabinet in Europe.

Anon.

———◇———

IN place of the excess of verbal acquisition and mechanical recitation, we now need more *thinking about things;* in place of the passive acceptance of mere book and tutorial authority, we need more cultivation of independent judgment; and in place of much that is irrelevant, antiquated and unpractical in our system of study, there is needed a larger infusion of the *living* and *available* truth which belongs to the present.

E. L. Youmans.

———◇———

I DO not think that it is the mission of this age, or of any other age, to lay down a system of education which shall hold good for all ages. Let us never forget that the present century has just as good a right to its forms of thought and methods of culture as any former centuries had to theirs, and that the same resources of power are open to us to-day as were ever open to humanity in any age of the world.

Prof. Tyndall.

———◇———

THERE is an Arabian tale of a ship whose pilot unfortunately steered into the too close vicinity of a magnetic mountain. The nails were all attracted, the planks fell asunder, and total wreck ensued. So, many a man, sailing in the vessel of his belief, comes in contact with some system of philosophic or theological thought, which, like the magnetic mountain, draws out the connecting and riveting points of his faith, and his whole ship, himself sprawling among the severed timbers, lies scattered wide on the tossing sea.

Peter Bayne.

THE duty of man, as man, is *thought*. Pity and love may aid and cheer him, but, as sovereign worker in this world, his duty is governance, guidance—in a word, thought.

Peter Bayne.

———◦◦———

INTERESTING thoughts and feelings are the comets of the mind. They transit off. How can they be made fixed stars, and thus the mind's firmament become ever resplendent?

John Foster.

———◦◦———

THERE is such a thing as crystallized thought: the mind is, as it were, a cavern in which stalactites slowly form. Pendent they hang, small and great, massive and tender— sublime thoughts set in the perennial jewelry of poetic beauty. Let the torch of truth enter, and they will sparkle for ever with immortal lustre. Minds there are rich with stalactites of fadeless brilliancy.

Anon.

———◦◦———

LITERARY men converse with and write for literary men, and feel no necessity to translate their thoughts into the common, working-day language of ordinary life. Within the esoteric circle one dialect is spoken—without it, another; and thus speculation is unchecked by that constant reference to the common sense of mankind which, in freer countries, curbs its extravagance.

Aids to Faith.

———◦◦———

MAN is but a reed, the weakest in nature; but he is a reed which thinks. The universe need not rise in arms to crush him; a vapor, a drop of water, suffices to kill him. But were the universe to crush him, man would still be greater than the power which killed him; for he knows that he dies, and of the advantage which the universe has over him, the universe knows nothing.

Pascal.

—◆—

MODERN thought is so vague, and its expression so inadequate, that terseness, clearness and accuracy of thought and expression will always command attention.

N. Y. Ledger.

—◆—

EDUCATION is not learning; it is the exercise and development of the powers of the mind. There are two great methods by which this end may be accomplished: it may be done in the halls of learning, or in the conflicts of life.

Princeton Review.

—◆—

EDUCATION is the knowledge of how to use the whole of oneself. Men are often like knives with many blades; they know how to open one and only one; all the rest are buried in the handle, and they are no better than they would have been if they had been made with but one blade. Many men use but one or two faculties out of the score with which they are endowed. A man is educated who knows how to make a tool of every faculty—how to open it, how to keep it sharp, and how to apply it to all practical purposes.

Beecher.

—◆—

REMEMBER that much of knowledge is growth, not accumulation. The life that one is living in is the book that men more need to know than any other. Never outrun health; a broken-down scholar is like a razor without a handle. The finest edge on the best steel is beholden

to the services of homely horn for ability to be useful.
Keep an account with your brain. Sleep, food, air and
exercise are your best friends; don't cheat them or cut their
company. Don't fall into the vulgar idea that mind is a
warehouse, and education a process of stuffing it full of
goods. Don't think your mind to be a pickaxe, either,
with which a student delves like an Irishman digging for
ore. If you must have a figure, call it a sensitive plate, on
which Nature forms pictures. The more fine the surface
and sensitive the quality, the truer and better will be the
knowledge. Do not study for ideas alone, but train for
condition; get and keep a healthy brain, keep it fine, train
it to sharp and accurate impressions, give it lungs and
vigor, make it like a mirror before nature, or a daguerreo-
plate. Barton, don't mope! Be a boy as long as you live.
Laugh a good deal, frolic every day, keep up high spirits;
a low tone of mind is unhealthy. There is food and medicine in nerve. Quantity and quality of nerve mark the
distinctions between animals and between men, from the
bottom of creation to the top. Now, Barton, if you come
home with your cheeks sunken and your eyes staring out
of a hollow pit, I will disown you.

Wentworth's advice to Barton—Norwood.

———◦◇◦———

YOUNG men are subject to occasional and sometimes to
deep despondency, than which nothing is a severer test
of one's principles. Separated from the charities of life,
often held in anxious suspense, disconcerted in all their
plans, forsaken by those in whom they had trusted, or be-
trayed into the power of malignant men, their hearts are
often smitten by sorrow, and withered like grass. Then
evil, like an armed man, comes in upon them, when they
are lame and broken and incapable of playing the man.

A virtuous character was never formed under the prevailing influence of dejection and discouragement.

Dr. William Plumer.

———◦◦———

TWO worlds are ours—one creative of the other. There is the inner realm of thought, emotion and imagination, and there is the outward realm of practice, where thought, emotion and imagination take their investiture of flesh and matter, and pass into nature and history. In one we have them in their warmth and fusion, in the other we have them crystallized into fact. All radical changes in character begin with changes in the inner realm of thought and emotion. There we are moved upon by the powers that are above us; by the eternal spirit that lies on our soul like a haunting presence, giving us vision of celestial purity, bitter compunctions, sighs for a better state, and images that float down out of heaven through our fancies. But none of these are yet ours; they sometimes come without any agency of our own. Thus far they have wrought no change of character, for they have not yet passed under the action of a human will. Left to themselves, they are confused and indeterminate; they are appropriated by a distinct agency on our part, which consists of giving them a place by our own right arm among fixed and solid realities. The thoughts and emotions wrought in us by the Spirit of God are as yet foreign to us; they are heavenly treasures let down within our grasp. We grasp them by fixing them in the voluntary life, and they are ours for ever!

Edmund H. Sears.

———◦◦———

THIS world is a solemn fact; we are in it, passing through it; let us try to understand it, let us grapple with its mysteries, let us think much of its responsibilities, let us ponder the thoughts of the inquiring minds of past ages, let us prize all the light we have from man—from God, so that we may be guided aright amid its perils and changing experiences.

Rev. Dr. Alexander Reed, Philada.

————◦◦◦————

MEN'S proper business in this world falls mainly into three divisions:

1. To know themselves and the existing state of things they have to do with.

2. To be happy in themselves and the existing state of things.

3. To mend themselves and the existing state of things, as far as either are marred or mendable. Now men reverse all this. We have a general readiness to take delight in anything past, future, far off, or somewhere else, rather than in anything now, or near, or here, leading us gradually to place our pleasures principally in the exercise of the imagination, and to build all our satisfaction upon things as they are not.

Ruskin.

————◦◦◦————

MY friend, all speech and humor are short-lived, foolish, untrue. Genuine work done, what thou workest faithfully, that is eternal! Take courage, then; raise the arm, strike home, and that right lustily; the citadel of hope must yield to noble desire, thus seconded by noble effort.

Carlyle.

————◦◦◦————

THE greatest thing a human soul ever does in this world is to see something, and tell what it saw in a plain way. Hundreds of people can talk for one who can think, but thousands can think for one who can see. To see clearly, is poetry, prophecy and religion, all in one.

Ruskin.

NO class is, as a class, so long-lived as thinkers, especially earnest, joyous Christian students. Their powers remain unbroken to the end. They have inward stimulations in high objective aims, mental activity and sweet, perpetual joy, that of themselves tend most powerfully to prolong life.
                                                                            Dwight.

GENERAL scholarship presents one of its chief charms in the wider view which it furnishes of the great harmony of analogies prevailing in all sciences and knowledges, as constituting one vast sisterhood of mutually according witnesses that they all had a common origin in the will of one glorious Divine Being, and all have a common end in their benefits and uses to his creature—man!
                                                                            Dwight.

THE greatest beauties of art are those which are minutest, the greatest marvels of nature are those which are microscopic, and the greatest blessings of life are those momentary benefits the aggregate of which makes such a broad stream of bounty ever flowing unto all men from the heart of God. "He that is faithful in that which is least is also faithful in much." Nowhere is this more true than in the realms of scholarship. Nicety of knowledge is as essential an idea of a scholar as nicety of execution is of an artist.
                                                                            Dwight.

THAT proof of genius of which we so often hear—carelessness about trifles, while rejoicing in a vaulting, brilliant style of mind, in certain speculations or imaginative doctrines—is but a proof of a perverse heart, neglecting its duty because of its irksome details; or of a perverted

2

intellect to gain the desired result without heeding God's appointed law of work. Dwight.

———◦◦———

THE principles of Christianity have projected themselves into the civilization of this age with the fixedness with which a continent thrusts itself into the sea.
Dr. A. B. Miller.

———◦◦———

THERE are men whose independence of principle consists in having no principle on which to depend—whose free thinking consists not in thinking freely, but in being free from thinking, and whose common sense is nothing more than the sense that is most common.
Dr. M. W. Jacobus.

———◦◦———

ENNUI is the only other element necessary to be added in full strength to a deep, damning sense of guilt, to make a hell on earth within the soul itself. It extinguishes in its dark abyss every treasure and pleasure given to us from above. Anon.

———◦◦———

THERE is nothing that this age, from whatever standpoint we survey it, needs more, physically, intellectually and morally, than thorough ventilation.
Ruskin.

———◦◦———

THE fountain of perpetual youth in the heart has often been said to be poetry; it should rather be called thought—thought in whatever high, earnest form, but especially in those forms which are most full of activity without and gladness within. Anon.

ART is the application of knowledge to a practical end.
Sir John Herschel

I WILL oblige my daughters to marry for love.
Madame de Staël.

WRITE to me often, and write like a man.
Johnson to Boswell.

SMALL bodies with velocity have a greater momentum than large masses without it.
Lacon.

FASTING is the diet of angels, the food and refection of souls, and the richest and highest aliment of grace.
Lowth.

TIME creeps toward us with folded wings, but when 'tis past us, its wings seem to flap with speed.
Anon.

NO cosmetics, no arts of dress, no studied adjustment of light and shade, can adorn the human face or form like health. The perfection of all colors on earth is *flesh-color*, which blends them all in one in the mortal face of an immortal, and the perfection of that is seen only in the rosy tint of health.
Dwight.

MAN (from *meno*, to remember, to think), a rememberer, a thinker; *face*, from *facies*, *facio*, to make, because the face makes the individual appearance of any one man what it really is.
Dwight.

SKILL in composition is one of the last attainments of an educated mind; and therefore, when it appears in early youth, betrays at once its foreign origin.

Anon.

———◆◇◆———

THE great points to be gained by the true educator, in the character of all who drink inspiration from his heart and life, are such as these—elevation of thought, refinement, tenderness and delicacy of feeling, self-forget-fulness of aim, energy of purposes, and all pure, bright, joyous, religiousness of spirit.

Dwight.

———◆◇◆———

THE aristocracy of mind and heart is the only aristocracy that none wish to destroy.

Anon.

———◆◇◆———

THE earnest men are so few in the world that their very earnestness becomes at once the badge of their nobility; and as men in a crowd instinctively make room for one who seems eager to force his way through it, so mankind everywhere open their ranks to one who rushes zealously toward some object lying beyond them.

Dwight.

———◆◇◆———

THE closet and the study—these are the two corners of Eden still left to the world, and the two radiant points from which the light of heaven most streams out over all the earth.

Dwight.

———◆◇◆———

FEAR and Hope, the pale, trembling daughters of Mortality, will be lost in the overwhelming realities of futurity. Fear anticipates suffering, and Hope enjoyment, but where both are final, fixed and full, what place remains either for Hope or Fear. There is no hope like the hope of glory, and in heaven that will be realized. In heaven we can fear no change, and in hell no changes are to be feared.

Lacon.

———◇———

GOD always perfects his works from an elementary commencement by a regular method, and through succession of time. That is, he works by fixed law, and for this there appears this wise and benevolent reason, that if God should exercise his infinite power any otherwise, his working would be perfectly inscrutable to his intelligent creatures, and therefore to them a revelation of his power merely, and not of his wisdom.

Dr. A. A. Hodge.

———◇———

THE love principle is stronger than the force principle.

Dr. A. A. Hodge.

———◇———

I WILL pitch my tent here. A new state of things appals me.

Emerson.

———◇———

ÆSTHETICS is a heavenly ladder, where, like Jacob's, angels, pure thoughts and holy aspirations come from and go to God.

Augusta Evans.

———◇———

AS a nation we are intolerant of rest. If we have a brilliant man, we insist upon his always shining. We want our rose bushes to bloom all the year round, we would have our trees all bearing fruit, and our suns always shining. We kill three-fourths of our truly great men in the prime of life by expecting and exacting too much of them, and then call the legitimate result of our forcing system a dispensation of Providence.   Like the earth, minds must lie fallow at times.   Perpetual crops will exhaust any soil, and perpetual excitement will wear out any mind or body.

Waverley Magazine.

———◦◦◦———

THE shaping our own life is our own work.   It is a thing of beauty, it is a thing of shame, as we ourselves make it.   We lay the corner and add joint to joint, we give the proportion, we set the finish.   It may be a thing of beauty and of joy for ever.   God forgive us if we pervert our life from putting on its appointed glory!

Ware.

———◦◦◦———

IT is a sad thing when a man has either a reputation beyond his merit, or an ambition beyond his ability.

S. Beatty.

———◦◦◦———

I HAVE had the privilege of holding intercourse with only three whom I deemed great men.   One, the greatest, I think, Dr. Chalmers, ever rises up before my memory as a mountain, standing fair, and clear, and large.   The second, Hugh Miller, rises as a bold, rocky promontory, covered all over with numberless plants of wild, exquisite beauty.   The third, Bunsen, stretches out before me wide and lovely and fertile like the plains of Lombardy, which I had just passed through before visiting him.

McCosh.

———◦◦◦———

THE eternal idea of justice makes no one just, that of truth makes no one true, that of beauty makes no one beautiful; so the eternal law of right makes no one righteous.   All these standard ideas require a process or drill in the field of experience in order to become matured into character or to fashion character in the models they supply

Bushnell.

LIGHT, empty minds are ever running after trashy, superficial literature, just as the winds are ever flowing toward the place where the atmosphere is more rarefied.

Anon.

———◆◇◆———

POETS are creators, because recipients; they open their hearts wide to Nature, instead of going to her with views of her ready-made and second-hand. They come from her and give out what they have felt and what she said to them. So with Scripture—patient, quiet, long-revering listening to it—then suggestiveness.

F. W. Robertson.

———◆◇◆———

FAITH sustains the same relation to works that lightning does to thunder. Faith without works is dead—lightning without thunder is ineffective. Works evidence faith, so does thunder, lightning.

F. W. Robertson.

———◆◇◆———

I SAID fifteen years ago that Napoleon went up like a rocket and would come down like a stick; but I have waited fifteen years, and have come to the conclusion that there is no stick in that rocket.

G. F. Train.

———◆◇◆———

THE flowers within our reach we tread down without so much as even looking at them; the tiny exotic, which is far less beautiful, we covet because it is difficult of attainment.

Anon.

———◆◇◆———

PEOPLE hear a voice in the street and say, "It is only a child!" Only a child! My soul stands abashed and overwhelmed in the presence of these young princes of God, these sons and daughters of immortality, these voyagers eternity-bound. They have started out on a journey which will never end, but winding up among hierarchical splendors; yet upward bound for higher themes and loftier empires, for ever, for ever, or else pitching off the verge of a great night—deep, fathomless, irremediable, down for ever, for ever. By and by they shall have fleeter motion, by and by they shall take wings of light or darkness, by and by they shall come to thrones of honor or dungeons of despair; and while God lives and eternal ages go marching on, they will mount up steps of glory, shouting, "Hosanna! Hosanna!" or go down through labyrinths of disaster, crying, "Woe! woe!" Yet you say, "It is only a child, only a little hand, only a little foot, only a little heart—only a child."

Little Wanderers' Friend.

OH how hard it is to die, and not to be able to leave the world any better for one's little life in it!

Abraham Lincoln.

THE mystic cords of memory, stretching from every battle-field and patriot grave to every living heart and hearthstone all over the land, will yet swell the chorus of the Union, when again touched, as surely they will be, by the better angels of our nature.

Lincoln's First Inaugural.

THERE are many ways of living down shame and sorrow. They may be lived down in secret, without sympathy, or openly with love. They may be lived down with the terror of cowards, or with honest courage. They may be lived down with craven fear of the world's opinion, or the comfort which comes from the lips of generous friends. At the worst, they may be lived down under cruel obloquy, till that time comes when the wicked and the weary alike find rest. **Live It Down—a novel.**

———◇———

THE rainbow of peace now hangs like a flag of victory on the rear of the cloud of war. **Beecher**

———◇———

LET God do his work. **Last words of Robertson.**

———◇———

GAY, giddy, happy Paris, where life is a pastime, and the only reality death. **Erring yet Noble.**

———◇———

FORCE, force, everywhere force! we ourselves a mysterious force in the centre of that. There is not a leaf rotting on the highway but has force in it; how else could it rot? **Carlyle.**

———◇———

BETTER be in shame now than at the day of judgment. **Mohammed.**

———◇———

THAT great mystery of Time, were there no other, the illimitable, silent, never-resting thing called time, rolling, rushing on, swift, silent, like an all-embracing ocean-tide, on which we and all the universe swim like exhalations, like apparitions, which are and then are not; this is for ever very literally a miracle—a thing to strike us dumb, for we have no word to speak about it. **Carlyle**

ETERNAL silence is the duty of a man.

Carlyle.

————◆————

CONGRESS is like a ball on a fountain. It will rise just as high as the popular impulse lifts it. The popular impulse at this moment is sufficient to lift it to impartial suffrage.

Tilton, 1866.

————◆————

SAID Tilton of Miss Anna E. Dickinson: "Her eyes are a sufficient proof of the immortality of the soul."

————◆————

THE truly illustrious are they who do not court the praise of the world, but perform the actions which deserve it.

Tilton.

————◆————

DESPONDENCY is ingratitude—Hope is God's worship.

Beecher.

————◆————

I DO not wonder that ungodly men are repelled by the porcupine Christians, bristling all over with the sharp quills of prejudice, bigotry, censoriousness, exclusiveness and all manner of unlovely things. I personally have come in contact with more than one porcupine Christian of both sexes.

Dr. F. T. Brown.

————◆————

MR. BANCROFT'S pompous and elaborate introduction to his eulogy of Lincoln reminds us of Carlyle's figure of half a cubic inch of soap made up, with the aid of a brush and a little water, to a puncheon of lather. Its leading thought is neither new nor happily developed.

N. Y World

I HAVE seen it stated that while the dance was progressing at a large ball in Moscow, the air became heated, the room very warm, and when the windows were lowered the cool currents rushed in, condensing the vapors of the room and causing a miniature snow-storm, the flakes falling and lighting on the cheeks and breasts of beauty. How untimely it seemed! What a strange scene at a royal ball! But have we not seen similar phenomena in the moral world? God often sends us cold currents of his wrath, which sweep across the sky of our hopes, distilling the vapors of our joy, and chilling our very life with freezing storms worse than hail and tempest.

Anon.

THERE is hypocrisy in the carnal life no less than in the religious. Men often appear worldly, when, in fact, they are sick of the world and thinking much of religion, and men often appear religious when they are sick of religion and are greatly in love with the world.

S. Beatty.

THE commander says Rest! and the weary soldier stacks his arms; so will God give his people eternal rest, and they shall stack their arms in heaven.

Rev. Nivlock.

AROUND the Son of God men and things take their places. Him they must serve, whether they will or no.

Dr. A. A. Hodge.

DR. JOHNSON turned upon one of his flatterers once and addressed him thus: "Sir, you have but two topics—yourself and me. I am sick of both!"

THE praise of God in the sanctuary no more belongs exclusively to the choir than the railway-track belongs exclusively to the locomotive. The track is for the locomotive, but only that it may draw the train of cars behind it. When it switches the congregation off on a side track and leaves it there, and takes exclusive possession of the King's highway of praise, it becomes an unmitigated nuisance.

Dr. F. T. Brown.

———◦◇◦———

STYLE is the gossamer on which the seeds of truth float through the world.

Bancroft

———◦◇◦———

COULD we see when and where we are to meet again, we would be more tender when we bid our friends good-bye.

Ouida.

———◦◇◦———

COULD we follow people home and see them in the privacy of their own chambers, when the green curtains are down, we would see much anguish that is carefully concealed from the world.

Ouida.

———◦◇◦———

BE polished, but solid. We cannot polish any matter that is not solid. We cannot polish boultry, but we can polish ebony. We cannot polish pumice-stone, but we can polish marble. We cannot polish lead, but we can polish gold.

Ouida.

———◦◇◦———

COLERIDGE cried, "Great God! how glorious it is to live!" Rénan asks, "O God, when will it be worth while to live?"

Ouida.

TO become educated we must learn to observe. Observation gives us facts, data; from this we rise to deduction; then we generalize and make universal application. This heightens and straightens both our reason and imagination.

N. Y. World.

———◇———

IT is our hearers who inspire us.

Vinet.

———◇———

THAT which we call the spirit of the age is seldom a definite and comprehensive thing, like a sequential system; it is a fleeting cloud-picture, in which the beams of light fall apart ere they hardly have completed their image. All these varying colors do form the representation of an age, and when blended they constitute its distinct though evanescent expression.

Hagenbach.

———◇———

HE who when goodness is impressively put before him, exhibits an instinctive loyalty to it, starts forward to take its side, trusts himself to it—such a man has faith, and the root of the matter is in such a man. He may have habits of vice, but the loyal and faithful instinct in him will place him above many that practice virtue.

Ecce Homo.

———◇———

WE ought to be just as tolerant of an imperfect creed as we are of an imperfect practice. Everything which can be urged in excuse for the latter may also be pleaded for the former. If the way to Christian action is beset by corrupt habits and misleading passions, the path to Christian truth is overgrown with prejudices, and strewn with fallen theories and rotting systems, which hide it from our view. It s quite as hard to think rightly as it is to act rightly, or even to feel rightly, and as all allow that an error is a less culpable thing than a crime or a vicious passion, it is monstrous that it should be more severely punished; it is monstrous that Christ, who was called the friend of publicans and sinners, should be represented as the pitiless enemy of bewildered seekers after truth.

Ecce Homo.

———◦◦◦———

IT is doubtless needful that popular theology, which, like everything else, tends to settle down into mere formulas, should thus be shaken up from time to time, and measured and adjusted by its eternal standards.

Gladstone on Ecce Homo.

———◦◦◦———

THIS is the age of subjectivity, and each one must see with his own eyes, and comprehend with his own understanding, and examine with his own judgment, all things in the political, literary and religious world. Each one has a special creed, a separate theology, a treasury of inner experience and views differing from those of any one else. This depends a great deal upon natural constitution, the degree of culture and the personal experience of the individual. And yet, while each one should prize and develop his own personality and individuality, even subjectivity may be abused. It may be carried to a point at which the bonds of fraternity may be severed, the general welfare impaired, the higher authority which ought to rule over all personal thought be put in peril.

Hagenbach

———◦◦◦———

IDOLATRY is the grand theme of prophets. They hate and fight it, as did Isaiah—Luther.

Carlyle.

ART is based on a strong sentiment of religion. It is a profound and mighty earnestness; hence it is so prone to co-operate with religion. Art is a severe business—most serious when employed in grand and sacred objects. The artist stands higher than art, higher than the object. He uses art for his purposes, and deals with the object after his own fashion. Goethe.

THERE are but few notes in music, but few letters in the alphabet, but few axioms in mathematics, but few elementary substances in nature. So there are but a few solid principles in the moral and intellectual world, which lie back of everything, and which govern every operaticn of thought and emotion. Dr. M. W. Jacobus.

FORMALISM is the symptom that death is come nigh. No more immoral act can be done by a humane creature, for it is the beginning of all immorality, or rather it is the impossibility henceforth of any morality whatsoever: the innermost moral will is paralyzed thereby—cast into fatal, magnetic sleep. Carlyle.

AS astronomy had its Kepler, who subjected the eccentric orbits of the planets to definite laws, and Newton who explains these laws by one embracing generalization, so sociology has its Comte, who has not only demonstrated the scientific character of social phenomena, but explained the law which governs their development, who has not only recognized that there is an organic evolution working all historical phenomena, but explained the character of this evolution and its invariable mode of operation.
Edinburgh Review, April 1868.

THE true system of Redemption is in the Scriptures, inseparable from the facts, just as the true theory of astronomy has been from the creation with the stars in the sky, whether mankind read them aright or not. The theologian, like the astronomer, is nothing more than the interpreter who observes the facts, who gradually reads the system in the facts, and who teaches to others precisely what he has read in the book, neither more nor less.

Hodge on the Atonement.

———◇———

A TRULY great man's actions are works of art. Nothing with him is extemporized or improvised. They involve their consequences, and develop themselves along with the events that gave them birth.

Guesses at Truth.

———◇———

THE future is ever before us. Our faces are directed toward it, and we are journeying on. God so made us that, whether we will or not, we are constrained to look onward to what is before us. The present does not satisfy us. Our ideal, whatever it be, lies further on.

Rev. E. H. Gillett.

———◇———

AS rivers generally spring from high mountains, so knowledge and moral power rise and are ever nourished from the heights of humanity.

Guesses at Truth.

———◇———

NO character can become complete without trial and suffering. Edmund Burke once said to Fox, in the English Parliament, "Obloquy is a necessary ingredient of all true glory · calumny and abuse are essential parts of triumph."

Guesses at Truth.

A JUDICIOUS reticence is hard to learn, but it is one of the great lessons of life. Chesterfield.

———◆◇◆———

AT last we will all have to start on that dark, perilous journey. We must all die, and go out beyond the air and up through the stars. Rev. A. A. Hodge, D.D.

———◆◇◆———

THERE is and can be no other rule of social life than to allow intercourse to be regulated by elective affinity; that is, to let those who are conscious of congeniality with each other associate to such a degree and on such terms as they shall find mutually satisfactory. Pittsburg Gazette.

———◆◇◆———

THE great idea of the nineteenth century, running through all fiction, poetry, philosophy and theology, is, the equality of all men in the sight of God. Monarchies are being limited, the oppressed are being freed, the masses are being granted and protected in their rights, the wicked pressure is being lifted from woman, intelligence and freedom are being universally diffused, and all men, white and black, rich and poor, are being taught their unlimited right to life, Liberty and the pursuit of happiness. London Spectator.

———◆◇◆———

YOUNG man! suppose you were to "take stock" of yourself to-night, where would you be? You are not as respectable as you were a year ago! Gough.

———◆◇◆———

LET a broken man cling to his work. If it saves nothing else, it will save him. Beecher.

3

BEAUTY whatever the moral nature behind it, is and must for ever be, essentially aristocratic. It attracts more than the average share of love and homage. The democratic element is therefore instinctively arrayed against it. But nature here is invincible, and neither democracy nor mediocrity can make a pretty woman plain or an ugly one pretty. What remains, therefore, is to make the fatal gift as uncomfortable to the possessor as possible, and such is the way of the unhandsome world.

Round Table.

———◇———

THE great secret of success in life is, for a man to be ready when his opportunity comes.

Disraeli to the young men of Liverpool.

———◇———

SOMETHING noble, something good, something pure, something manly, something godlike, is knocked off a man every time he gets drunk or stoops to sin through forgetfulness of God.

Gough.

———◇———

OUR moods are lenses coloring the world with as many different hues.

Emerson.

———◇———

IT is a part of my religion never to hurt any man's feelings.

W. D. Howard, D.D.

———◇———

REPUBLICAN liberty has its dangers as well as its advantages. The less the masses feel of outward force and of the compulsion of secular power, the more they need the control of religion and of moral principles.

Guesses at Truth.

I WOULD rather be a prince among preachers, than to be the foremost crowned head of Europe.

Rev. S. J. Wilson, D.D.

———◦◦◦———

WE hear of the province of government, as if it had any other province than to subserve the wishes of the people. Constitutions are only the expression of the will of the people at the time they are framed, and are liable to be altered whenever the public good may demand. But a constitution should be changed only in the way it prescribes for its own alteration and amendment.

N. Y. World.

———◦◦◦———

IF, rejecting all that is merely accidental, we look at the essential characteristics of the Whig and the Tory, we may consider each of them as the representative of a great principle essential to the welfare of nations. One is, in an essential manner, the guardian of liberty, and the other of order. One is the moving power, and the other is the steadying power, of the state. One is the sail, without which society would make no progress, the other the ballast, without which there would be small safety in a tempest.

Macaulay.

———◦◦◦———

MOUNTAINS never shake hands. Their roots may touch, they may keep together some way up, but at length they part company and rise into individual, isolated peaks. So it is with great men; at first they grow up together, seeming to be animated by the same spirit—to have the same desires and anticipations, the same purposes and ends. But after a while the genius of each begins to show itself and to follow its own bent. They separate and develop more and more; and those who, when young, worked in concert, stand alone in their old age. But if mountains do not shake hands, neither do they kick each other.

Guesses at Truth.

———◦◦———

THAT most valuable faculty of intellectual man, the judgment, the enlightened, impartial, unbiased judgment, must be kept in perpetual activity, not only in order to ascertain that the cause be good, but to determine the degree of importance in any given case, that we may not blindly assign an undue value to an inferior good.

Hannah More.

———◦◦———

A RIGHT view of a man's fundamental character is essential to the right understanding and estimate of his acts.

Martensen.

———◦◦———

PROSE is the work-day dress in which truths do secular duty. Poetry is the robe, the royal apparel, in which truth asserts its divine origin. Prose is truth looking on the ground, eloquence is truth looking up to heaven, poetry is truth flying upward toward God.

Beecher's Norwood.

———◦◦———

THE very habit of using words which belong to a higher state of feeling and experience than we ourselves have attained to, deadens the sense of truth and causes a dismal rent in the soul.

Guesses at Truth.

———◦◦———

THE greatest homage we can pay to truth is to use it.

Emerson

———◦◦———

ALL truth undone becomes unreal.

Robertson.

THE secret of influence is will, whether good or bad.

Robertson.

———◇———

No MAN can ever rise above that at which he aims.

A. A. Hodge, D.D.

———◇———

JONATHAN EDWARDS, when a boy, wrote in his journal, "Resolved to live with all my might while I do live."

———◇———

MY race is infinite, but I am never to stand still in the course.

Schleiermacher.

———◇———

IN these days nothing is counted so proper as property.

Anon.

———◇———

AN English paper, wishing to say that Mr. Disraeli is a liar, says he is "conspicuously inexact."

———◇———

THE truest style of eloquence, secular or sacred, is practical reasoning animated by strong emotion.

Anon.

———◇———

ELOQUENCE is the transference of thought and emotion from one heart to another, no matter how it is done.

Gough.

———◇———

ELOQUENCE does not require mellifluous words and euphonious sentences. It is often found in rough, uncouth garb, just as the lightning often gleams from rugged thunder-clouds.

Gough.

ELOQUENCE is a gift. It cannot be learned, and should be used for God and the right. It places man under an awful responsibility.   **Gough.**

---◆◇◆---

NO elaboration of rhetoric, no oratorical culture, which ignores the spontaneous emotions of an honest, fearless, loving heart, can produce eloquence. Would you rule men from the rostrum, from the bar, or from the sacred desk? Let no devil cheat you out of your conscience; let no callous critic shame you out of your honest emotions. For what is eloquence but truth in earnest? the mind's best words spoken in the mind's best moments. When truth gets full possession of a man's conscience, when all his sensibilities are aroused and his sympathies in full play, when the soul becomes luminous until the interior light and glow blaze out through every loop and crevice, when from head to foot the whole man becomes the beaming, burning impersonation of truth,—then is he honestly, naturally, irresistibly eloquent.

Theo. Cuyler's Address to the Princeton Students.

---◆◇◆---

DAVID wailing over his self-ruined darling, Absalom; Paul pleading before Felix until the guilty man paled to the color of his marble throne; Martin Luther stretching up to the full height of his manhood in those words: "Here I stand, I cannot otherwise, God help me. Amen;" Patrick Henry, sounding the key-note to Bunker Hill in "Give me liberty, or give me death!" Whitefield depicting the perils of a lost soul on the verge of the pit, until the plumes on duchesses' head-dresses quivered, and Chesterfield cried out, "Good God! he is gone!" Kossuth sounding the requiem of his dead nationality; and Alexander Duff pronouncing his sublime farewell to the heathery hills of Scot-land,—these men were eloquent, not by special inspiration of the head, but by overpowering inspiration of the heart. The burning soul kindled the lips, and the baptism of eloquence came in the form of a fiery tongue. The loftier the emotion, the more impressive the utterance of the orator. The same law applies to eloquence that applies to hydro-statics. If the jet is to be thrown to a great height in the public fountain, the spring that feeds the fountain must have a lofty birth-place on the mountain-side. The grandest achievements of eloquence have been reached when the orator has received the fullest celestial baptism of love— when self has been swallowed up in the glory that surrounds the cross of Calvary.

Theo. Cuyler's Address to the Princeton Students.

SPEAKING against time has become one of the fine arts.

Charles Sumner.

NOTHING gives more of sympathy to the voice than real goodness.

Bautain.

READ the best authors on their strongest points.

Prof. (now Gen.) Fraser.

INSTRUCTION ends in the school-room, but education ends only with life. A child is given to the universe to educate.

Robertson.

TRUTH is only got at by assaulting and laying low the surroundings that throw it out of proportion and hide it from view.

Bishop Butler.

IF you cannot bring your condition to your mind, bring your mind to your condition.

Dr. M. W. Jacobus

———◦◦◦———

ADHESIVENESS is a great element of success. Genius has glue on his feet, and will take hold of a marble slab.

S. J. Wilson, D.D.

———◦◦◦———

THOSE who have finished by making all others think with them, have usually been those who began by daring to think for themselves.

Colton.

———◦◦◦———

THE most manifest sign of wisdom is continued cheerfulness.

Montaigne.

———◦◦◦———

THE drying up a single tear has more
   Of honest fame than shedding seas of gore.

Byron.

———◦◦◦———

BE thou as chaste as ice, as pure as snow, thou shalt not escape calumny.

Shakespeare.

———◦◦◦———

A VULGAR man is captious and jealous—eager and impetuous about trifles. He suspects himself to be slighted, and thinks everything that is said meant for him.

Chesterfield.

———◦◦◦———

MEN of great parts are often unfortunate in the management of public business, because they are apt to go out of the common road by the quickness of their imagination.

Swift.

BUY what thou hast no need of, and ere long thou shalt sell thy necessaries.

Franklin.

———◇———

WITH many readers brilliancy of style passes for afflu- ence of thought; they mistake buttercups in the grass for immensurable gold mines under the ground.

Longfellow.

———◇———

IT sounds like stories from the land of spirits
If any man obtain that which he merits,
Or any merit that which he obtains.

Coleridge.

———◇———

ACCOMPANY your own flag throughout the world, under the protection of your own cannon.

Daniel Webster.

———◇———

LOOK not mournfully into the past; it returns no more: wisely improve the present, and go forth into the shadowy future without fear and with a manly heart.

Longfellow.

———◇———

KEEP thy spirit pure from worldly taint by the repellant strength of virtue.

Philip Bailey.

———◇———

BE what your friends think you are; avoid being what your enemies say you are; go right forward and be happy.

Brick Pomeroy.

———◇———

ALWAYS do what you are afraid to do.

Emerson.

AUTHORSHIP is, according to the spirit in which it is pursued, an infamy, a pastime, a day-labor, a handicraft, an art, a science, a virtue. .

Schlegel.

WHEN an author has a number of books out, a cunning hand will keep them all spinning, as Signor Blitz does his dinner-plates, fetching each one up as it begins to wabble, by an advertisement, a puff, or a quotation.

Holmes.

AN author, after writing a book, does nothing for a few months but look around and drink in generally.

Holmes.

AN author's first novel is naturally drawn to a great extent from his own personal experience, but the moment he goes out of his personality, he must have creative power as well as the narrative art and the sentiment, in order to tell a living story; and this is rare.

Holmes.

SOCRATES calls beauty "a short-lived tyranny;" Plato, "divinity taking outlines and colors;" Theophrastus, "a silent cheat;" Theocritus, "a delightful prejudice;" Corneades, "a solitary kingdom;" Domitian said that "nothing was more grateful;" Aristotle affirmed that "beauty was better than all the letters of recommendation in the world;" Homer, that 'twas "a glorious gift of nature," and Ovid calls it "a favor bestowed by the gods."

Anon.

IF you ever saw a crow with a king-bird after him, you will get an image of a dull speaker and a lively listener.

Holmes.

THE bigot is like the pupil of the eye—the more light you put upon it the more it will contract.

Holmes

———◇———

BUILD thee more stately mansions, O my soul,
As the swift seasons roll!
Leave thy low-vaulted past!
Let each new temple, nobler than the last,
Shut thee from heaven with a dome more vast,
Till thou at length art free,
Leaving thine outgrown shell by life's unresting sea.

Holmes

———◇———

A PAGE digested is better than a volume hurriedly read.

Macaulay.

———◇———

A MAN can never be a true gentleman in manner until he is a true gentleman at heart.

Dickens.

———◇———

HAPPINESS is the congruity between a creature's nature and its circumstances.

Bishop Butler.

———◇———

I AM so much a utilitarian that I prefer the useful to the useless.

Sir W. Hamilton.

———◇———

THE price of Liberty is eternal vigilance, and the price of wisdom is eternal thought.

Frank Birch.

———◇———

ROUSE thee, heart!

Bailey's Festus.

I ALWAYS believed in life rather than books. I suppose every day of earth, with its hundred thousand deaths and something more of births—with its loves and its hates, its triumphs and defeats, its pangs and blisses has more of humanity in it than all the books that were ever written put together. I believe the flowers growing at this moment send up more fragrance to heaven than was ever exhaled from all the essences ever distilled.   Holmes.

———◦◦◦———

BOOKS are at once our masters and our servants. They have a silent independence, an unchanging voice, a calm declaration of truths as they will. But they are unobtrusive. They wait for our moods and leisure. They are never jealous if we neglect them, nor quarrelsome when we are familiar. They wait upon us in youth, in manhood and in old age with a vivacity that time never chills, and an instructiveness that repetition never wearies. Books gradually lose their inert and dead form, and become to us like persons that have pulse and articulate voice. We feel more intimately acquainted with authors two hundred years dead than we do with our daily companions. A book is better for weariness than sleep—for cheerfulness, than wine. It is often a better physician than the doctor, a better preacher than the minister, a better sanctuary than a drowsy church.
                Pittsburg Christian Advocate.

———◦◦◦———

DISCUSSION is the very bulwark of truth, the only safeguard against the imperfections of the human mind, the only chastiser of extravagance, the only antagonist of dogmatism, the only hand-post that points us perpetually along the path of moderation, which is most commonly the path of truth. The little mind that looks upon the contending sects around it is scandalized, and says with

Pilate, in a jest, " What is truth?" without ever intending to listen for a reply; but the more expanded intellect sees in these same struggles of human thought, the gradual yet sure unfolding of the whole great system of religious truth, from the germs that lie before it in the Word or around it in the world.

Morell.

———◦◦◦———

I do not ascribe these modes of reasoning to the obtuseness of the last speaker, but to his great perspicacity. He sees but too keenly the tendency or course of an argument or fact, and sets out to meet it in advance.

Alexander Campbell.

———◦◦◦———

THE mattock will make a deeper hole in the ground than lightning.

Horace Mann.

———◦◦◦———

THE eloquence of Daniel Webster was the majestic roar of a strong and steady blast pealing through the forest; but that of Henry Clay was the tone of a godlike instrument, sometimes visited by an angel-touch, and swept anon by all the fury of the raging elements.

E. L. Mageon.

———◦◦◦———

IN truth, what is it that leads us to attach the value we do attach to intellectual labor and achievement? Not the mere practical result of those engagements, nor the mere labor in itself considered; but the emotion, the sentiment, the moral power connected with it, and by which it is prompted, animated and rewarded. Within the entire circle of our intellectual constitution we value nothing but emotion; it is not the powers, or the exercise of the powers, but the fruit of those powers in so much feeling of a lofty kind as they will yield. Now that toward which we are con-stantly tending as our good, that which we rest in when it is attained as sufficient, is that which shall be ultimate, and shall survive whatever has been mediate, or contributory, or accessory. Everything short of the affections of the soul is a means to an end, and must have its season; it is temporary, but the affections of the soul are the end of all, and they are eternal. Let the universe perish or be changed, the soul shall live.

Isaac Taylor.

———◇———

THE uses of mediocrity are for every-day life, but the uses of genius, amidst a thousand mistakes which mediocrity never commits, are to suggest and perpetuate ideas which raise the standard of the mediocre to a nobler level. There would be far fewer good men of sense if there were no erring dreamers of genius.

Bulwer.

———◇———

THE foot-ball at Rugby and the regatta at Eaton, bowling at Harrow and cricket at Westminster, succeeded by all those invigorating exercises in constant practice at Oxford and Cambridge, give to England the most elegant and able-bodied scholars in the world.

E. L. Magoon.

———◇———

TIE down a hero, and he feels the puncture of a pin; throw him into battle, and he is almost insensible to gashes. So in war, impelled alternately by hope and fear, stimulated by revenge, depressed by shame or elevated by victory, the people become invincible. No privation can shake their fortitude, no calamity break their spirit.

John C. Calhoun

INTEMPERANCE wipes out God's image and stamps it with the counterfeit die of the devil; intemperance smites a healthy body with disease from head to heel, and makes it more loathsome than the leprosy of Naaman or the sores of Lazarus; intemperance dethrones man's reason, and hides her bright beams in the mystic clouds that roll round the shattered temple of the human soul, curtained with midnight.

Gough.

———◦◦———

A SOLDIER oughtn't to grunt!

Gen. Jackson.

———◦◦———

OUR religion should be carried into everything. It should go with us to the farm and the factory; to the counting-house and the court-house; into the sick chamber not only, but into the senate-chamber; with the mariner it should ride the stormy sea, and with the miner descend into the bowels of the earth; it should sit with the artist in his studio, with the teacher in his school-room, with the lawyer in his office; it should go with the physician to his patients and the artisan to his shop; it should stand with the salesman behind the counter and with the clerk at his desk; it should be carried into our pleasures, and by no means be absent from our politics.

Rev. Dr. W. D. Howard, Pittsburg.

———◦◦———

YOUNG men! let the nobleness of your mind impel you to its improvement. You are too strong to be defeated, save by yourselves. Refuse to live merely to eat and sleep. Brutes can do these, but you are men. Act the part of men. Prepare yourselves to endure toil. Resolve to rise; you have but to resolve. Nothing can hinder your success if you determine to succeed. Do not waste your time by wishing and dreaming, but go earnestly to work. Let nothing discourage you. If you have but little time, improve that little; if you have no books, borrow them; if you have no teachers, teach yourself; if your early education has been neglected, by the greater diligence repair the defect. Let not a craven heart or a love of ease rob you of the inestimable benefit of self-culture. Labor faithfully, labor fearlessly, and look to God, who giveth wisdom and upbraideth not, and you shall reap a harvest more valuable than gold or jewels.

Rev. Dr. W. D. Howard, Pittsburg.

THE vastness of the visible universe, so far as it actually comes within our means of knowledge, may be taken as a sort of image of the vastness of that range of intellectual and moral existence of which the visible universe is the platform.

Isaac Taylor.

OF law there can be no less acknowledged than that her seat is the bosom of God, her voice the harmony of the world; all things in heaven and earth do her homage—the very least as feeling her care, the greatest as not exempt from her power; all of them admire her as the mother of their peace and joy.

Richard Hooker.

LAW, according to the Duke of Argyll, is "order produced by contrivance for a purpose by will," and such a definition must be maintained everywhere by controversy. "How will you explain the Christian miracles by contrivance?" exclaims the theologian, or "how can you reduce to order the eccentricities of free-will?" adds the metaphysician. "Show us clear proof of purpose in the apparent want of ingenuity in Nature, and how do you know that it required a will to originate species on the globe?" inquires the naturalist. These are the principal questions discussed with great fairness and honesty by the duke.

Contemporary Review

———◦◦◦———

THE same progress of philosophy that materializes spirit also spiritualizes matter. We lose nothing in giving up the old ideas of immateriality, if we still hold that matter is cunning enough to produce consciousness, thought, affection and will. Names are of no consequence. If the latest thinkers choose to call the thing that manifests these phenomena, "nervous fluid," or "ether," or "force," or "tissue," under the play and vibration of a combination of forces, I do not see in this language any danger of our losing our old-fashioned souls. Matter or dynamic machinery that is capable of *personality* is very likely to have also the faculty of *immortality*.

J. H. Noyes—Letter to N. Y. World.

———◦◦◦———

YOU see I am not mincing matters, but avowing nakedly what many scientific thinkers more or less distinctly believe. The formation of a crystal, a plant or an animal is in their eyes a purely mechanical problem, which differs from the problem of ordinary mechanics in the smallness of the masses and the complexity of the process involved. Here you have one half of our dual truth; let us now glance at the other half. Associated with this wonderful mechanism of the animal body we have phenomena no less certain than those of physics, viz., the facts of consciousness, but between which and the mechanism we discern no necessary connection. . . . . I hardly imagine that any

4

profound scientific thinker who has reflected upon the sub
ject exists who would not admit the extreme probability
of the hypothesis, that for every act of consciousness,
whether in the domain of sense, of thought or of emotion, a
certain definite molecular condition is set up in the brain—
that this relation of physics to consciousness is invariable,
so that given the state of the brain, corresponding thought
or feeling might be inferred.   But how inferred?   It is at
bottom not a case of logical inference at all, but of empiri-
cal association. . . . . Granted that a definite thought and
a definite molecular action in the brain occur simultaneously,
we do not possess the intellectual organ, nor apparently any
rudiment of the organ, which would enable us to pass by a
process of reasoning from the one phenomenon to the other:
they appear together, but we do not know why.   Were our
minds and senses so expanded, strengthened and illuminated
as to enable us to see and feel the very molecules of the
brain; were we capable of following all their emotions, all
their groupings, all their electric discharges, if such there
be; and were we intimately acquainted with the corresponding state of thought and feeling, we should be as far as ever
from the solution of the problem—"How are these physical
processes connected with the facts of consciousness?"   The
chasm between the two classes of phenomena could still remain intellectually impassable.   Let the consciousness of
love, for example, be associated with a right-handed spiral
motion of the molecules of the brain, and the consciousness
of *hate* with a left-handed spiral motion.   We should then
know when we love that the motion is in one direction, and
when we hate that the motion is in the other; but the
"why" would still remain unanswered.

In affirming that the growth of the body is mechanical,
and that thought, as exercised by us, has its correlative in
the physics of the brain, I think the position of the material-

ist stated, as far as that position is a tenable one. I think the materialist will be able finally to maintain this position against all attacks; but I do not think, as the human mind is at present constituted, that he can pass beyond it. I do not think he is entitled to say that his molecular groupings and his molecular notions explain everything. In reality, they explain nothing. Prof. Tyndall.

THE laws of nature were not appointed by the great Law-giver to baffle his creatures in the sphere of conduct, still less to confound them in the region of belief. As part of an order of things too vast to be more than partly under-stood, they present, indeed, some difficulties which perplex the intellect, and a few also, it cannot be denied, which wring the heart. But on the whole they stand in har-monious relation with the human spirit. They come visibly from one pervading Mind, and express the authority of one enduring Kingdom. Argyll.

WE listen willingly to the physiologist when he gives us an analysis of the machinery of our bodies, when he traces out all the ropes and pulleys by which motion is con-veyed from nerve to nerve, from limb to limb, from the resolution of the brain to the action of the hand. But it is quite another thing if he declares that his analysis ex-hausts the subject—that mind is nothing but nerve force, and mental movements nothing but the rapid coursings of nerve-currents; that, in short, our nature cannot be proved to contain any spiritual element which is distinct from the material and subject to entirely different laws. "The scientific mind," says even Prof. Tyndall, "can find no repose in the mere registration of sequences in nature. The further question intrudes itself with resistless might—

Whence comes sequence? What is it that binds the consequent with the antecedent in nature? The truly scientific mind never can attain rest until it reaches the forces by which the observed succession is produced." But, admitting this, we venture to say that it is not within the range of science to conduct us to the final answer. A law of nature is but a formula for expressing the sequence which it has no power to originate. A force of nature is itself but a medium and an instrument, and has no claim to be regarded as a cause. We can appreciate the great conceptions by which these forces have been elucidated, and can admire the beauty of the system which connects the various chains of sequence under the uniformity of "correlation" and "continuity;" but all these discoveries only prepare the way for a still more absorbing question, which intrudes itself with still more resistless might: "What is the first cause which set all this array of force in motion, and which guides it through the complicated counterplay of nature? What ultimate agent poised the stars and fixed the equilibrium of the universe, and adjusted and still controls the complexities of its interbalanced forces?" To this far more engrossing question Science leads the way, but can supply no answer. It must leave the mystery unsolved and insoluble, unless it submits as a learner to be taught of God.

Contemporary Review, Sept., 1867.

——◇——

WE often speak of material forces as if we could identify any kind of force with matter. But this is only one of the many ambiguities of language. All that we mean by a material force is a force which acts *upon* matter, and produces *in* matter its own appropriate effects. We must go a step farther, therefore, and ask ourselves, What is force? and this Science cannot tell us.

Contemporary Review, Sept. 1867

FORCE has no inherent life or power in itself, except as vitalized and sustained by the energy of God.

Contemporary Review, Sept., 1867.

———◦———

THE name Jesus is the secret grip, the magic watchword and countersign of the Christian brotherhood.

Dr. M. W. Jacobus.

———◦———

EVERYTHING is heaving and great events are pending, and it is hard to study Genesis when all is now Revelation.

Dr. M. W. Jacobus.

———◦———

MATERIALISTS have so spirited away God that to many it is now immaterial where he is.

Dr. M. W. Jacobus.

———◦———

A SELF-SUSPICION of hypocrisy is a good evidence of sincerity.

Hannah More.

———◦———

IT is only people that have lost their own self-respect who imagine that others are slighting and endeavoring to injure them.

Mrs. M. S. C.

———◦———

WE must tramp upon our feelings when principle is at stake.

S. J. Wilson, D.D.

———◦———

EVERY man truly lives so long as he acts his nature or some way makes good the faculties of himself.

Sir Thomas Brown.

———◦———

PUT not your trust in money, but put your money in trust.

Holmes.

THE world is generally ready to deride men of one idea, even when it is perhaps unconsciously entering into their labors. A man thoroughly in earnest in any great work must always be more or less the butt of ridicule. But by and by, when this concentration of purpose has hewn down all obstacles, and arrives in sight of its ultimate object, the link between it and current opinion is suddenly restored, and the whole world is ready to prostrate itself and do homage to the man of one idea.

London News

———◇———

I LIKE egotists.

Ballentine

———◇———

OUR modern music is little better than brilliant noise, which rather irritates than soothes the nerves.

N. Y. Herald.

———◇———

MY lord, a classical education has given you unlimited command of all beautiful figures of speech. Masks, hatchets, rocks and vipers, dance through your mind in all the mazes of metaphorical confusion. These, my lord, are the glowing companions of a disturbed imagination, the melancholy madness of poetry without its inspiration.

Junius' Letters.

———◇———

REAL republicanism is stern and severe; its essence is not in form of government, but in the omnipotence of public opinion which grows out of it.

Holmes.

———◇———

REVOLUTIONS never turn back, but they sometimes make very acute angles.

Anon.

PITTSBURG is the Vulcan of the North, the forger of the thunderbolts of war; she stands a power felt in every department of the government, and recognized by it as of vital importance in its present struggle for existence.

Pittsburg Post, 1863.

———◇———

EACH of us has his special label for a particular position, and by it we steadily and regularly, even though sometimes struggling against it ourselves or though struggled against by others, fall into our appropriate places. Neither are we to attribute all this to a fatal necessity. We are not blindfolded, shackled, manacled and led captive by an inexorable fate or irresistible power, except as our condition is necessarily determined by antecedent causes, which are themselves mostly in our power, or in the power of those who have the controlling influence of our early years—those years fraught with the conditions of a future necessity.

Varro.

———◇———

DO you want an image of the human will, or the self-determining principle, as compared with its pre-arranged and impassable restriction? A drop of water imprisoned in a crystal; you may see such an one in any mineralogical collection. One little fluid particle in the crystalline prism of the solid universe.

Holmes.

———◇———

GREAT natural advantages are seldom combined with great acquired ones, because thay render the labor requisite to attain the last superfluous and irksome. It is only necessary to be admired, and if we are admired for the graces of our persons, we shall not be at much pains to adorn our minds.

Magoon

THERE is no credit in knowing how to spell, but posi tive disgrace in being ignorant on that point. So there can be no credit in doing right, while it is infamous to do wrong.

G. F. Train.

THE world usually pushes a man the way he makes up his mind to go. If going up, they push him up; if going down, they push him down—gravitation, however, making the speed greater on the decline.

G. F. Train.

WHEN a man asks your advice, he generally wants your praise.

Chesterfield.

A GENIAL enthusiasm is to the body of an argument what the breath of the Almighty was to the yet un-vitalized Adam.

Magoon.

SILENCE and reserve suggest latent power. What some men think has more effect than what others say.

Chesterfield.

THEY who live most by themselves reflect most upon others, and he who lives surrounded by the million never thinks of any but the one individual—himself. We are indeed so linked to our fellow-beings that, were we not chained to them by action, we are carried to and connected with them by *thought*.

Bulwer.

HER coldness of manner was like the snow on the side of the volcano.

Bulwer

SOCIETY is a strong solution of books. It draws the virtue out of what is best worth reading, as hot water draws the strength of tea-leaves.

Holmes.

———◆———

IN national armories we sometimes see large quantities of martial implements curiously arranged in fantastic forms. How much more impressive they would be if seen glittering in quick motion on the field! and how much more potent would be their use when grasped by well-disciplined legions rushing to the final charge! A single weapon wielded by a chivalrous and resolute hero would be more effective than the holiday show of all the martial weapons in repose on earth.

Magoon

———◆———

ALAS for those that never sing,
But die with all their music in them !

Holmes.

———◆———

THE great boast of polished life is the delicacy and even the generosity of its hostility ; that principle which forbids us to attack the defenceless, to strike the fallen or to mangle the slain, and enjoins us, in forging the shafts of satire, to increase the polish exactly as we add to their keenness or their weight.

Chesterfield.

———◆———

HOLLOW trees are always the stiffest, but the mightiest oak, if sound, can bend. The more exalted a man is by station, the more powerful should he be by kindness. There is no policy like politeness, since a good manner often succeeds where the best tongue has failed. Politeness is most useful to inspire confidence in the timid and encourage the deserving.

Magoon.

GENTLENESS is not weakness. A mind that is addicted only to fawning and flattery will never honor truth and duty by an allegiance based on principle and adorned by true nobleness of spirit. Such an unsubstantial character can no more be made to assume the aspect of real politeness than a sponge or a fungus of any sort can be polished like a diamond or gold. Lead may be heavy enough for many useful purposes, but it is too unsubstantial and worthless to be coined into the currency of a nation; and so of the public men it symbolizes—they are too stupid to be trusted, and too uncouth to be admired. True greatness is always sympathetic and generous.

Magoon.

———◦◦◦———

THE moon—the flatterer of decay.

Bulwer.

———◦◦◦———

SAD-EYED workers!

George Eliot.

———◦◦◦———

NOTHING sharpens the arrow of sarcasm so keenly as the courtesy that polishes it; no reproach is like that we clothe with a smile and present with a bow.

Chesterfield.

———◦◦◦———

DOUBT-AWAKING Science!

Atlantic Monthly.

———◦◦◦———

MEN cling to what they see through, like an insect to a pane of glass.

G. F. Train.

———◦◦◦———

THE man that wants to see me is the very man I want to see.

Payson.

HEAVEN is not to be expected in this world. External circumstances go but a little way toward making us happy. The relief which we receive in our afflictions and distresses has often more real pleasure in it than we experience in our greatest prosperity. **Dr. A. Alexander.**

———◦◦◦———

THE deep undertone of the world is sadness—a solemn bass, occurring at measured intervals and heard through all other tones. Ultimately, all the strains of this world's music resolve themselves into that tone; and I believe that, rightly felt, the cross, and the cross alone, interprets the mournful mystery of life, the sorrow of the Highest—the Lord of Life,—the result of error and sin, but ultimately remedial, purifying and exalting. **Robertson.**

———◦◦◦———

LET us be thankful for the pangs by which God brings us to himself. **Anon.**

———◦◦◦———

HOPE, though your sun is hid in gloom,
  And o'er your careworn, wrinkled brow
Grief spreads his shadow—'tis the doom
  That falls on many now. **Anon.**

———◦◦◦———

THE men that hope little are the men that go on working. **Beecher.**

———◦◦◦———

AS a man upon a battle-field will receive a mortal hurt, and scarcely know that he is struck, so I, when I was left alone with my undisciplined heart, had no conception of the wound with which it had to strive. **David Copperfield**

IT is those invisible, subtle strokes at the unseen centres of hope and courage that are hard to bear.

Chronicles of Carlingford.

———◦◦◦———

EXPERIENCE is a fine word for suffering.

Hannah More.

———◦◦◦———

WE wrangle with Providence, and call our wrangling reason; we rush upon God's mysteries, and tear ourselves against the appointments of his throne, and then because we bleed, complain that he cruelly mocks our understanding.

Bushnell.

———◦◦◦———

IN this world God's people are under "the weeping willows of banishment."

Spurgeon.

———◦◦◦———

SAD things in this life of breath
　Are truest, deepest, sweetest,
Tears bring forth the richness of our nature,
As rains sweeten the smelling brier.

Anon

———◦◦◦———

EACH in his hidden sphere of joy or woe,
　Our hermit-spirits dwell and range apart:
Our eyes see all around, in gloom or glow,
Hues of their own fresh borrowed from the heart.

Anon

———◦◦◦———

OUR life was but a battle and a march;
　And, like the wind's blast, never resting, homeless,
We stormed across the war-convulséd earth.

Wallenstein.

AT the end of life a man finds himself rich, not so much by his fortunes as by his misfortunes. The Persians had a vase of glass which when empty was colorless, but when filled with wine, flashed forth many rare pictures. So a bosom empty of a heart of pain makes a lustreless life, but a bosom in which a heart bleeds reveals hidden virtues.

Tilton.

BEWARE of desperate steps—the darkest sky,
Live till to-morrow, will have passed away.

Cowper.

UNDER the pressure of melancholy and despondency, individual tastes and preferences die away; but as surely as they die, so surely, as long as man lives, will they revive again. It is not, therefore, in such moods that momentous decisions should be made, yet it is in such moods that too often they are so.

Bulwer.

THEY who can catch at happiness on the bright surface of things imagine they can secure it, such as it is, with less risk and more certainty; they who dive for it in the waters of deeper feeling, if they succeed, bring up pearls and diamonds, but if they sink they are gone for ever.

Mrs. H. B. Stowe.

Some faces show
The last act of a tragedy in their regard,
Though the first scenes be wanting.

Mrs. Browning.

AFTER all, the joy of success does not equal that which attends the patient working.

Augusta Evans.

MELANCHOLY is God's visitation upon an idle mind; his mode rather of scourging such an one back again to his duty; for the way of escape from any trouble in life is duty coupled with trust in God.   Dwight.

————•◦•————

IT was a saying of Aristotle, that all noble-minded men are inclined to sadness. It is not merely the feeling that their own lot is a hard one which oppresses them; it is something more—it is their inward sympathy and consciousness of participation in the sufferings of the human race to which they belong.   Guesses at Truth.

————•◦•————

THERE are many phases through which the soul must go before it can attain even that approximation to the divine which is possible on earth. We cling to prop after prop; we follow longingly whichever of earth's beautiful and blessed things seems most to realize that perfect ideal which we call happiness. Of these joys the dearest, the truest, the most satisfying is that which lifts us out of ourselves, and unites us in heart and soul—ay, and intellect, too, for the spirit must find its mate to make the union perfect —with some other human being. This blessed bond we call love. But the chances of fortune come between us and our desires; the light passes, and we go on our way in darkness. There are times when we must stand alone, and see earth's deepest and most real joys float by like shadows. Alas! we can but stretch out our arms toward that Infinite which alone is able to fill the longings of an immortal spirit. Then, with our wounded souls lying naked and open before the Beholder of all, we look yearningly toward the eternal and divine life, complete, unchangeable, and cry, with solemn, thankful voice, "O God! thy fullness is sufficient for me; O God! thy love is an all-boundless store."   Anon.

MUCH that we select and smile upon and follow with adulation in the common walks of life, never passes the sacred threshold of the heart. We admire the gay. They make our melancholy sweeter by contrast when we retire within ourselves. We pursue them. We take them to our hearts—to the outer vestibule of our hearts, and if they are gay only, they are content with the homage we pay them there. But the chamber within is meanwhile lonely. It aches with its desolation. The echo of the mirthful admiration without jars upon the mournful silence within.

N. P. Willis.

----◦◦----

SELF-ABANDONED, relaxed and effortless, I seemed to have laid me down in the dried-up bed of a great river; I heard a flood loosened in remote mountains. I felt the torrent come: to rise I had no will—to flee I had no strength. I lay faint, longing to be dead. One idea only still throbbed life-like within me—a remembrance of God; it begot an unuttered prayer; these words went wan· dering up and down in my rayless mind, as something that should be whispered, but no energy was found to express them: "Be not far from me, for trouble is near, there is none to help." It was near, and as I had lifted no petition to heaven to avert it, as I had neither joined my hands, nor bent my knees, nor moved my lips, it came in full, heavy swing; the torrent poured over me. The whole consciousness of my life lorn, my love lost, my hope quenched, my faith death-struck, swayed full and mighty above me in one sullen mass. That bitter hour cannot be described. In truth, "the waters came into my soul; I sunk into deep mire. I felt no standing. I came into deep waters, the floods overflowed me."

Jane Eyre

B UT mine is now a humbled heart,
    My lonely pride is weak as tears;
No more I seek to stand apart,
    A mocker of the rolling years.

Alexander Smith

———◦•◦———

W HAT is Blondin's rope to the narrow, uncertain
    bridge which ever and anon appears before us in the
road of life? What are the yeasty waters of that green
river to the deep and dark tide which awaits our fall from
the single strand that spans it? The audience of the
world is looking on at our passage, and few among them
care for our danger or are interested in our success. Yet
there are some—some hearts are beating high, some tearful
eyes are strained to watch our progress, some breaths
come quickly as we move on, and some fervent prayers are passionately offered up for our safety. Ye cannot broaden the bridge: it hangs poised by the hand of
Destiny from shore to shore. Alone and unsupported must
we cross, and the shades of night gather around before we
reach the friendly foothold beyond. We dare not look
back, we cannot turn back; we must go on and never tarry
an instant. Let us chalk our soles well, then, and show to
others, more timid, more thoughtless, that the frail pathway may be securely trod. Nay, more; let us hew out the
pure, white, friendly rock we know of, and make surer the
unknown, unfamiliar, inexperienced soles of our brethren
with it, that they may travel on erect and fearless.

Atlantic Monthly.

———◦•◦———

WE bury love;
Forgetfulness grows over it like grass:
That is a thing to weep for, not the dead.

Alexander Smith.

AND he who throws the dice of destiny,
  Though with a sportive and unthinking hand,
Must bide the issue, be it life or death.
One path is clear before us.   It may lead
O'er perilous rocks, cross lands without a well,
Through deep and difficult chasms; but therein
The whiteness of the soul is kept, and that,
Not joy nor happiness, is victory.

Alexander Smith

———◦◦———

    PLEASURE, naked to the waist,
With high-flushed cheeks and loose, disheveled hair,
Flung herself 'cross his path; she clasped his knees;
He saw her beauty, and he was undone.

Alexander Smith.

———◦◦———

    How this mad old world
Reels to its burning grave, shouting forth names
Like a wild drunkard at his frenzy's height;
And they who hear them deem such shouting fame!

Alexander Smith

———◦◦———

'TIS not for me, ye heavens! 'tis not for me,
  To fling a poem like a comet out, far-splendoring
The sleepy realms of night.

Alexander Smith

———◦◦———

MEN and women make their own beauty or ugliness.
  Bulwer speaks in one of his novels of a man "who
was uglier than he had any business to be," and, if we could
but read it, every human being carries his life in his face,
and is good-looking, or the reverse, as that life has been
good or evil.   On our features the fine chisels of thought
and emotion are eternally at work.

Alexander Smith.

5

THERE is a certain even-handed justice in Time: for what he takes away he gives us something in return. He robs us of elasticity of limb and spirit, and in its place he brings tranquillity and repose, the mild, autumnal weather of the soul. He takes away hope, but he gives us memory, and the settled, unfluctuating atmosphere of middle age is no bad exchange for the stormful emotions, the passionate crises and suspenses of the earlier day.

Alexander Smith.

YOUTH is the time for action—middle age for thought In youth, red-handed, red-ankled, with songs and shoutings, we gather in the grapes; in middle age, under our own fig tree, or in quiet gossip with a friend, we drink the wine free of all turbid lees. Youth is a lyrical poet—middle age is a quiet essayist, fond of recounting experiences, and of appending a moral to every incident. In youth the world is strange and unfamiliar, novel and exciting; everything wears the face and garb of a stranger; in middle age the world is covered over with reminiscences as with a garment; it is made homely with usage, it is made sacred with graves. And in middle age, too, provided the man has been a good and an extraordinarily happy one, along with the mental tranquillity there comes a corresponding sweetness of the moral atmosphere. He has seen the good and the evil that are in the world, the ups and the downs, the almost general desire of the men and the women therein to do the right thing if they could but see how, and he has learned to be uncensorious and humane, to attribute the best motive to every action, and to be chary of imputing a sweeping, cruel blame. He has a quiet smile for the vainglorious boast, a feeling of respect for shabby-genteel virtues, and a pity for threadbare garments proudly worn. *He* would not be satirical for the world. He has no finger of scorn to point at anything under the sun. He has a hearty amen for every good wish, and in the worst cases he leans to a verdict of not proven. And along with this blandness and charity, a certain grave, serious humor—a smile on the lip and a tear in the eye—is noticeable frequently in middle-aged persons. Pity lies at the bottom of it, just as pity lies unsuspected at the bottom of love. It is a crocus growing out of a child's grave. Hawthorne and Dickens know how to paint it.

Alexander Smith.

THERE is a peculiar beauty about godly old age—the beauty of holiness. Husband and wife who have fought the world side by side, who have made common stock of joy or sorrow, and become aged together, are not unfrequently found curiously alike in personal appearance, in pitch and tone of voice, just as twin pebbles on the beach, exposed to the same tidal influences, are each other's *alter ego.*

Alexander Smith.

THE beautiful are never desolate:
Some one always loves them—God or man.
If man abandons, God takes them.

Bailey's Festus.

THE blossom cannot tell what becomes of its odor, and no man can tell what becomes of his influence and example, that roll away from him and go beyond his ken in their perilous mission.

Beecher.

NOT for art, not for truth, not for God will we give up our ease. We will only give it up for money, and that to purchase future ease.

Round Table.

REVOLUTION may change the face of nature and sweep nations from the earth; custom and habit and exterior circumstance may change and pass away; but the inner life of man, with all its joy and hope and love and sorrow and care, remains the same in every nation and in every age—intensely active and grand and interesting.

Bulwer.

———◆———

ROB genius of its confidence, of its lofty self-esteem, and you clip the wings of the eagle; you domesticate, it is true, the wanderer you could not hitherto comprehend, in the narrow bounds of your household affections; you abase and tame it more to the level of your ordinary judgment—the walled-in and petty circumference of your little and commonplace moralities; but you take from it the power to soar, the hardihood which was content to brave the thunder-cloud and build its eyrie on the rock, for the proud triumph of rising above its kind, and contemplating with a closer eye the majesty of heaven.

Bulwer's Disowned

———◆———

IN the years I've changed,
  Wild and far my heart hath ranged,
And many sins and sorrows now
Have been on me avenged.
But to you I've been faithful,
Whatever good I lacked,
I loved you, and above my life
Still hangs that love, intact
You love the trembling rainbow,
I the reckless cataract;
Still I love you, Barbara!

Alexander Smith

A STILL small voice spake unto n e,
  "Thou art so full of misery
Were it not better not to be?"
Then to the still small voice I said,
Let me not cast in endless shade
What is so wonderfully made.

Tennyson.

———◦◦———

STRONG in the goodness of his cause, with his back to
  the throne of God and his foot on the rock of truth, a
man can stand against the world.

Guthrie.

———◦◦———

WHERE truth and right are concerned, we must be firm
  as God.

Guthrie.

———◦◦———

WE live in this world only for the opinions of the good
  and noble.   How crushing it must be to occupy with
them a position of ambiguous respect!

Col. E. K. Kane.

———◦◦———

ONLY with silence as their benediction
      God's angels come,
When in the shadow of a great affliction
    The soul sits dumb.

Anon

———◦◦———

I DON'T like these cold, precise, perfect people, who, in
  order not to speak wrong, never speak at all, and in
order not to do wrong, never do anything.

Beecher.

———◦◦———

SPEECH is the highest species of action.

Zachos.

ORATORS are manufacturers of phrases.

Napoleon.

———◇———

WHATEVER is popular deserves attention.

Thackeray.

———◇———

EXCEPTIONAL women ought to have exceptional rights.

Anna E. Dickinson.

———◇———

WOMEN who can reign in monarchies ought to vote in republics.

G. F. Train.

———◇———

THE only way to get along in the world these days is to be as tough as possible. If people see they can annoy you, they will never let you have any peace.

Rev. W H. Goodrich, Cleveland, O.

———◇———

THE *Tribune* and the *Herald* make opinions: the authorities at Washington obey them.

Wendell Phillips.

———◇———

AFTER all, the strongest sentiment on this continent is nationality—love of country, glory in the Revolution and Declaration of Independence, reverence for Washington and the founders of our Constitution. Cut an American into a hundred pieces and boil him down, and you will find him all Fourth of July.

Wendell Phillips.

———◇———

WE can be generous and liberal in our views, without being loose and latitudinarian. Truth is many-sided, and no dogmatic system contains it all.

Dr. Rylance of Chicago.

THE true pilot is the man who navigates the bed of the ocean even more than its surface.

Victor Hugo.

———◆◆———

THE most perfect thing in the world is a woman's temper, but I am bound to say I have seen some tempers better than others.

Henry Vincent.

———◆◆———

POCK-MARKED with pistol-shots!

Vincent's description of Cromwell's Soldiers

———◆◆———

TO seize the universal in the particular is the highest wisdom.

William E. Channing, D. D.

———◆◆———

A MAN too full of sentiment is like an overflowing fountain—he soon forms a puddle round him.

Norwood.

———◆◆———

AMID all the changes that are going on around us, I believe that nothing true or good will ever perish.

Anon.

———◆◆———

WHEN, oh when shall we learn that loyalty to Christ is tested far more by the strength of our sympathy with truth than by the intensity of our hatred of error! I will tell you what to hate. Hate hypocrisy, hate cant, hate intolerance, oppression, injustice, hate Pharisaism; hate them as Christ hated them, with a deep, living, god-like hatred. But do not hate *men* in intellectual error. To hate a man for his errors is as unwise as to hate one who, in casting up an account, has made an error against himself.

F. W. Robertson.

NEVER does a man know the force that is in him till some mighty affection or grief has humanized the soul.

F. W. Robertson.

———

A SILENT man is easily reputed wise. The unknown is always wonderful. A man who suffers none to see him in the common jostle and undress of life easily gathers round him a mysterious veil of unknown sanctity, and men honor him for a saint.

F. W. Robertson.

———

ON sympathy the final awards of heaven and hell are built; attraction and repulsion, the law of the magnet. To each pole all that has affinity with itself; *to* Christ all that is Christlike—*from* Christ all that is not Christlike—for ever and for ever.

F. W. Robertson.

———

THE serene, silent beauty of a holy life is the most powerful influence in the world, next to the might of the Spirit of God.

Beecher.

———

WHAT martial music is to marching men,
Should song be to humanity.

Alexander Smith.

———

OVER the lodge of a college at Oxford, England, there is said to be a sun-dial on which these words are engraven, "Pereunt et Imputantur," the hours perish and are imputed. They perish, and yet are to be accounted for.

Rev. E. H. Gillett.

———

OUR duties to others ought to be continually looked at from their stand-point.

Essays on Social Subjects.

HAVE you ever seen those marble statues in some public square or garden which art has so finished into a perennial fountain that through the lips or through the hands the clear water flows in a perpetual stream, on and on and on for ever; and the marble stands there—passive, cold, making no effort to arrest the gliding water? It is so that time flows through the hands of men—swift, never pausing, till it has run itself out; and there is the man petrified into a marble sleep, not feeling what it is which is passing away for ever. It is so, brethren, just so, that the destiny of nine men out of ten accomplishes itself, slipping away from them, aimless, useless till it is too late.

F. W. Robertson.

TO a docile mind which is watching for a disclosure of the Divine Will, there is often an overpowering reciprocity of evidence which leaves no room for a doubt. One stands as in the focus of an amphitheatre of mountains, in which one hears from all sides the reverberations of a single voice.

Austin Phelps.

CENSURE and criticism never hurt anybody. If false, they can't hurt you unless you are wanting in manly character; and if true, they show a man his weak points and forewarn him against failure and trouble.

Gladstone.

THE circumstances of the world are so variable that an irrevocable resolution is almost a synonymous term for a foolish one.

W. H. Seward.

EPICURIANISM—the sparkling Sadduceeism of Greece.

Princeton Review.

NOT what we *think* or *say*, but what we *do*, will have its effect upon the world. Let, then, the thinker do and the doer think.

Rob Roy McNulty.

———◆———

THE most foolish of all errors is, that clever young heads think that they lose their originality when they recognize the truth which has already been recognized by others.

Goethe.

———◆———

ONE can neither protect nor arm himself against criticism. We must meet it defiantly, and thus gradually please it.

Goethe.

———◆———

CLEVER people are the best encyclopædias.

Goethe.

———◆———

WHEN I hear people talk of liberal ideas, I always wonder how we are deceived by the sound of words. An idea is not at liberty to be liberal. Let it be mighty, apt, conclusive in itself, that it may fulfill its own purpose to be productive. A notion is still less at liberty to be liberal. It has an entirely different purpose. We must seek for liberality in sentiments, for they are the living heart. But sentiments are very seldom liberal, because they spring immediately from the strictest—*i. e.*, most illiberal—relationships and necessities of our own personality.

Goethe.

———◆———

MAINTAIN the place where thou standest.

Goethe.

———◆———

THE weak man or woman who stoops to whine over neglect and poverty, and the snarls of the world, gives the sign of his or her own littleness.

Adah Isaacs Menken.

THERE is a political force in ideas which silently renders protestations, promises and guarantees, no matter in what good faith they may have been given, of no avail, and which makes constitutions obsolete. Against the uncontrollable growth of the anti-slavery idea the truth was forced to contend.

Draper.

THE remorseless Past stood ever near, breathing through the broken chords of life its never-ending dirge.

Adah Isaacs Menken.

STRENGTH—the sorrow-born.

Adah Isaacs Menken.

O GOD! have mercy on the souls of men who are false to their earthly love and trust!

Adah Isaacs Menken.

OH I am sick of what I am—of all
Which I in life can ever hope to be!
Angels of light, be pitiful to me.

Anon.

SORROWS are often like clouds, which, though black when they are passing over us, when they are past, become as if they were the garments of God, thrown off in purple and gold along the sky.

H. W. Beecher.

ROMANISM makes the relation of the believer to Christ depend on his relation to the Church, while Protestantism makes the believer's relation to the Church depend on his relation to Christ.

Rev. Frothingham of N. Y.

THE sympathetic-ink remains colorless and invisible, so long as the paper upon which it has been used is cold, but becomes of a fine blue or green when the paper is warmed; and before the hidden beauty of some men's natures can be revealed they must be thrown into the heated furnace and made to pass through the fiery trial of affliction, but no fiery furnace can be made hot enough to scorch a man into despair so long as there stands by him the form of one like unto the Son of God.

Anon.

———◦◦◦———

FAITH is the Christian consciousness at rest. Morality is the Christian consciousness in motion.

Rev. Frothingham of N. Y.

———◦◦◦———

THE greatest element of criticism is taste.

Sainte Beuve.

———◦◦◦———

A MAN'S happiness and success in life will depend not so much upon what he has or upon what position he occupies, as upon what he is, and the heart he carries into his position.

Prof. S. J. Wilson.

———◦◦◦———

LIBERTY, equality, fraternity; these are not the mere catch-words of the politician—they are the watch-words of the race.

Prof. M. W. Jacobus.

———◦◦◦———

EVERY glass of beer carries in it a remorseful yesterday and a dread to-morrow.

George Alfred Townsend

———◦◦◦———

WHENEVER a man has once done a deed, it stands fixed for ever and for ever.

Beecher.

IF the Republicans in America are successful in the coming election, it will be on account of their candidate and in spite of their platform; if the Democrats succeed, it will be on account of their platform, and in spite of their candidate.

London Review

———◇———

IT was the conservatism of Republicanism that nominated Grant, and the radicalism of Democracy that nominated Seymour.

Round Table

———◇———

DEEP-SEEING love.

Ruskin.

———◇———

ONLY my heart to my heart shall show it,
Or I walk desolate day by day.

Jean Ingelow.

———◇———

CONSCIENCE, true as the needle to the pole, points steadily to the pole-star of God's eternal justice, reminding the soul of the fearful realities of the life to come.

Rev. E. H. Gillett.

———◇———

MAN has wondrous impulses toward futurity, which, like the instinctive flight of birds before their actual migration, betoken his destiny to another clime. In earnest communion with ourselves we become conscious of our own eternity.

Alger.

———◇———

WE have but one life here, and that is very precious to us. Nor to us alone; a human life is in itself a precious thing, and no soul in which the sense of humanity dwells can see a life thrown away without a deep uprising sorrow.

Bibliotheca Sacra.

THE dove, cleaving in free flight the thin air, whose resistance it feels, might imagine that her movements would be far more freer and rapid in airless space.

Kant.

THERE is an underlying character in men, and in their acts, of which they are themselves often unconscious, but which may prove, in the end, of momentous import. So there is an underlying character in sects and parties, often of more consequence than anything that they profess or do. The creed and the reasoning of a philosophical or theological school frequently presupposes principles not announced, but, on the contrary, disowned and scorned, which are yet, in reality, adopted and enthroned, and are sure to work their way forth into public acts and into acknowledged authority.

Bibliotheca Sacra.

IN the next life I hope to suffer till I learn the mastery of myself and keep the conditions of my higher life. Through the Red Sea of pain I will march to the Promised Land, the Divine Ideal guiding from before, the Egyptian Actual urging from behind.

Theodore Parker.

THE child, through stumbling, learns to walk erect. Every fall is a fall upward.

Theodore Parker.

REMORSE is the pain of sin.

Theodore Parker.

THE greatest men have been those who have cut their way to success through difficulties.

F. W. Robertson,

A MAN behind the times is apt to speak ill of them, on the principle that nothing looks well from behind.

Holmes.

———◦◦———

SUBLIMITY tabernacles not in the chambers of thunder, nor rides upon the lightning's flash, nor walks upon the wings of the wind; but it is man's spirit up there in its lofty aspirings, yoking itself with the whirlwind, riding upon the northern blast, scattering bounty all around it on its upward, wondrous, circling way.

Gough.

———◦◦———

I REMEMBER reading in a fairy tale that a whole city was in one night changed to stone. There stood a war-horse, with nostrils distended, caparisoned for the battle. There stood the warrior, with his hand of stone on the cold mane of that petrified horse. All is still, lifeless, death-like, silent. Then the trumpet's blast is heard ringing through the clear atmosphere. The warrior leaps upon his steed, the horse utters the war-neigh and starts forth to the battle, and the warrior, with his lance upraised, rides on to victory. Now, young man, put the trumpet to your lips, blow a blast that shall wake the dead stocks and stones, and on, on, upward to victory over all evil habits and evil influences surrounding you.

Gough's Lecture on Habit.

———◦◦———

THERE is not, in my opinion, a more pleasing and trium-phant consideration in religion than this—of the per-petual progress which the soul makes toward the perfection of its nature, without ever arriving at a period in it. To look upon the soul as going on from strength to strength; to consider that she is to shine for ever with new accessions of glory and brighten to all eternity; that she will be still adding virtue to virtue, and knowledge to knowledge,—carries in it something wonderfully agreeable to that ambition which is natural to the mind of man. Nay, it must be a prospect pleasing to God himself, to see his creation for ever beautifying in his eyes, and drawing nearer to him by greater degrees of resemblance. Methinks this single consideration of the progress of a finite spirit to perfection will be sufficient to extinguish all envy in inferior natures and all contempt in superior. That exalted angel which now appears as a god to a human soul knows very well that the period will come about in eternity when the human soul shall be as perfect as he himself now is; nay, when she shall look down upon that degree of perfection as much as she now falls short of it. It is true the higher nature still advances, and by that means preserves his distance and superiority in the scale of being; but he knows that how high soever the station is of which he stands possessed at present, the inferior nature will at length mount up to it, and shine forth in the same degree of glory. With what astonishment and veneration, therefore, may we look into our souls, where there are such hidden stores of virtue and knowledge, such inexhausted sources of perfection. We know not yet what we shall be, nor will it ever enter into the heart of man to conceive the glory that will be always in reserve for him. The soul, considered with its Creator, is like one of those mathematical lines that may draw nearer to another for all eternity without a possibility of touching it; and can there be a thought so transporting as to consider ourselves in these perpetual approaches to Him who is not only the standard of perfection, but of happiness

Spectator.

———◦◦◦———

THE universe is the realized Thought of God.

Carlyle.

LIKE dim curtains, painted with shapes of terror, of gloom and of weird grandeur, that hang round a dusky hall waving fitfully in the faint light, these questions concerning the mysterious and the Infinite hang round my mind, filling it with solemn shadow. I look on them as on mystic hieroglyphics, but when I ask their secret they remain silent as Isis. I ever turn away, saying in baffled pride, I will compel your answer in eternity, yet always turn again, fascinated by their sublime mystery and stung by their calm defiance. **Peter Bayne.**

———◦◦◦———

MAN'S actions here are of infinite moment to him, and never die or end at all. Man, with his little life, reaches upward high as heaven—downward low as hell; and in his threescore years of time holds an eternity fearfully and wonderfully hidden. **Carlyle.**

———◦◦◦———

HERE stretches out of sight, out of conception even, this vast Nature, daunting, bewildering, but all penetrable, all self-familiar, an unbroken unity; and the mind of man is a key to the whole. He finds that the universe, as Newton said, "was made at one cast;" the mass is like the atom—the same chemistry, gravity and condition. The asteroids are the chips of an old star, and a meteoric stone is a chip of an asteroid. As language is in the alphabet, so is entire Nature—the plan of all its laws—in one atom. The good wit finds the law from a single observation—the law and its limitations and its correspondences—as the farmer finds his cattle by a footprint. "State the sun and you state the planets, and conversely." While its power is offered to his hand, its laws to his science, not less its beauty speaks to his taste, imagination and sentiment.

6

Nature is sensitive, refining, elevating. How cunningly she hides every wrinkle of her inconceivable antiquity under roses and violets and morning dew! Every inch of the mountains is scarred by unimaginable convulsions, yet the new day is purple with the bloom of youth and love. Look out into the July night, and see the broad belt of silver flame which flashes up the half of heaven, fresh and delicate as the bonfires of the meadow-flies. Yet the power of numbers cannot compute its enormous age—lasting as space and time, embosomed in time and space; and what are they—time and space? Our first problems, which we ponder all our lives through, and leave where we find them; whose outrunning immensity, the old Greeks believed astonished the gods themselves; of whose dizzy vastitudes all the worlds of God are a mere dot on the margin; impossible to deny, impossible to believe. Yet the moral element in man counterpoises the dismaying immensity, and bereaves it of terror.

Emerson.

—◦◦—

MATTER, power, spirit, each points to the other, and each finds in the other its fulfillment. But spirit is the root of all things—the invisible creator of nature—eternally the same, while the creature is ever undergoing fresh changes. Spirit is uncreated and self-existent. Nature and all in it exists and perishes, and satisfies only so far as spirit reveals itself therein. Nature is the garb of spirit, sometimes seen in rags, sometimes clothed in the royal garments of majesty. But nature is never more than a covering, a form, a type, a perishable image of an imperishable Being. Only Spirit and Revelation are real. Matter and force, life and act, have only value and significance because therein spirit makes itself known and develops its eternal existence. Man even is dust, and nothing without spirit.

Schenkel.

SCIENTIFIC skeptics say that in the laws of nature there is manifested no free overruling will; they regard these laws as the expression of an irrational necessity. But so nature would be blind—the creature of chance without a plan. But are not, on the contrary, the laws of nature indicative of a plan and object in the highest degree? They are unchangeable because they need no improvement, because they are perfect. They are perfect because the product of the most perfect reason and the highest design. Because God is unchangeable, therefore, also, are the laws of nature unchangeable. But this unchangeableness is not the stillness of death—it is the fullness of life. Yea, in the laws of nature themselves is revealed the living, divine Spirit, and the regulations of the world are the expressions of His attributes and purposes. Therefore nature does not speak to us in the inarticulate language of irrational elements, but in the speech of divine wisdom. Her phenomena and laws are the expression of all-wise Will, whose purposes we revere even when they remain hidden from our finite understanding. Therefore we are not afraid of the results of scientific inquiries, that they will shake the faith of God. Superficial, not deep, investigations are dangerous to religion. The less the inquirer finds himself able to explain this world from nature, the more will he find himself forced to recognize a supernatural first cause; the more unsatisfactory materialism is in a scientific point of view, the more indispensable the belief in spirit. The world is the temple of the living God: God is the eternal, infinite spirit, from everlasting to everlasting. The world is a temple of his glory and goodness, the mountains are the pillars of his power, the streams the veins of life, the sea the womb of renewal, the sun the source of life, the stars the emblems of the boundlessness of creation. Religion and reason equally point to the belief in the indissoluble union of God and the world, in which spirit is the being of nature—nature its outward form. The supernaturalism of spirit by no means disturbs the unity of the world; a visible and invisible world belong to the necessary order of this union.

London Journal of Sacred Literature.

———◦◦———

SCIENCE has robbed us of the old heaven up among the stars—the heaven of the Bible and of childhood. She has unroofed the imposing temple under whose dome of spangled azure David sang and the whole procession of primitive saints reverently trod. She has left us no firmament to support God's throne, and his footstool has become a flying, whirling ball. She has taken us down to the ancient sheol and lo! instead of souls, there is nothing there but seething chemicals and centres of gravitational and magnetic attraction. The going forth of morning and evening no more rejoices; it is only an optical illusion, produced by the diurnal revolution of the earth. To ascend into heaven now and twelve hours hence is to go in diametrically opposite directions. The deeper you descend into hell, the higher you go into the heaven of your antipodes. The world has no longer top or bottom. Up and down are become provincialisms, meaningless to all who take comprehensive views of things. We ourselves are but microscopic animalculæ, clinging to a grain of sand, which eddies its little round in the obscurest corner of the great cosmos of nature. Our heaven is gone, our old hell, our biblical picture of creation, the significance of natural evil, our own central position and importance in the universe of being. Science has robbed us of all these things, and Science must bring them back. Can she do it? Is there to come a time when the rainbow shall again be the seal of a divine covenant, and not an illustration of the laws of optics? Is there to come a time when we shall be able, without scientific compunction, to call the peopled sky heaven, and, with the simple souls of old time, pry to descry in the remotest spaces the hearth-fires of the holy— the ne er-darkened tabernacles of the angels, "the faire folde" of God? Can Science rehallow the vast temple she has so ruthlessly, so utterly desecrated? Can she again fill it with the hush of awful presences, the sanctity of a divine habitation? Will she ever be able to cast out the buyers and sellers, the whole herd of scientific speculators, which she has introduced, and re-invest the dismantled altars with their original sacredness?

Bibliotheca Sacra, Oct., 1863.

WHATEVER may be the surprises of the future, Jesus Christ will never be surpassed. His worship will grow young without ceasing, his legend will call forth tears without end, his sufferings will melt the noblest hearts; all ages will proclaim that, among the sons of men, there is none born greater than Jesus. Ernest Renan.

THE myriad members of the starry archipelago are peopled with orders of intelligent beings, differing from our race even as the planets differ in magnitude and physical structure; and as feeble fancy struggles to grasp and comprehend the ultimate destiny of the countless hosts of immortal creatures, to which our earthly races, with their distinct, unalterable types, are but as one small family circle amid clustering worlds, we can but reverently worship the God of revelation who can "bind the sweet influences of Pleiades or loose the bands of Orion."

Augusta Evans.

THE stony lips of geology assert that our globe is growing old; thousands of generations have fallen asleep in
the bosom of mother Earth, the ashes of centuries have
gathered upon the past, are creeping over the present; and
yet, in the face of catacombs and mummies and mouldering monuments chiseled in the infancy of the human race,
Mathematics unrolls her figured scroll and proclaims that
time has but begun. It will take eighteen million years
for the starry universe to revolve around the central sun.

Augusta Evans.

———◦◦———

INFIDEL philosophers have placed in hostile attitude
against Christianity geology from below, and from the
altitudes of the upper firmament, astronomy; then from the
mysteries of the human spirit attempts have been made to
discover some spell by which to disenchant the world of its
confidence in the Gospel of Christ. From lecture-rooms
of anatomy the lessons of materialism have been inculcated
for the purpose of ridiculing religion and expelling it from
the earth. Others attempt to associate the doctrines of
phrenology with their denial of the Christian revelation, as
if there were any earthly connection between the form of
the human skull and the truth or falsehood of religion.
But Christianity carries with it an evidence which is unas-
sailable, and which places it beyond the reach of external
violence. It is not the hammer of the geologist that can
break this evidence. It is not the sword of the warrior nor
pen of the infidel critic, let him be poet or historian, that
can mutilate or deface it. It is not the telescope of the
astronomer that can enable us to descry in it any character
of falsehood. It is not the knife of the anatomist that
can show us the alleged rottenness which lies at its core.
It is not by a dissecting of metaphysics that the mental
philosopher can probe his way to the secret of its insuffi-

ciency, and make exposure to the world of the yet unknown flaw which vitiates the proof of the Christian faith. All these sciences have at one time or another cast their missiles at the stately fabric of our faith, but they have all fallen harmless and impotent at its base.

Anon.

———◦✦◦———

TO-DAY the great question that is stirring men's hearts to their very depths is, Who is this Jesus Christ? His life is becoming to us a new life, as if we had never seen a word of it. There is round about us an influence so strange, so penetrating, so subtle, yet so mighty, that we are obliged to ask the great heaving world of time to be silent for a while, that we may see just what we are and where we are. That influence is the life of Jesus Christ. We cannot get clear of it; we hear it in the tones of joy— we feel it stealing across the darkness of sorrow; we see it where we least expect it. Even men who have traveled farthest from it seem only to have come round to it again; and while they have been undervaluing the inner worth of Jesus Christ, they have actually been living on the virtue which came out of his garments here.

Ecce Deus.

———◦✦◦———

JESUS! How does the very word overflow with exceeding sweetness, and light and joy, and love and life; filling the air with odors, like precious ointment poured forth; irradiating the mind with a glory of truths in which no fear can live; soothing the wounds of the heart with a balm that turns the sharpest anguish into delicious peace; shedding through the soul a cordial of immortal strength! Jesus! the answer to all our doubts, the spring of all our courage, the earnest of all our hopes, the charm omnipotent against all our foes, the remedy for all our weakness

the supply of all our wants, the fullness of all our desires!
Jesus! melody to our ears, altogether lovely to our sight,
manna to our taste, living water to our thirst, our shadow
from the heat, our refuge from the storm, our pillar of fire
by night, our morning star, our sun of righteousness.
Jesus! at the mention of whose name every knee shall
bow and every tongue confess. Jesus! our power; Jesus!
our righteousness; Jesus! our sanctification; Jesus! our
redemption; Jesus! our elder brother—our blessed and
only Redeemer. Thy name is the most transporting theme
of the Church, as they sing going up from the valley of
tears to their home on the mount of God: thy name shall
ever be the richest chord in the harmony of heaven where
the angels and the redeemed unite their exulting, adoring
songs around the throne of God and the Lamb. Jesus!
thou only canst interpret thy own name, and thou hast done
it by thy works on earth and thy glory at the right hand
of the Father.   Dr Bethune.

----◦◇◦----

CHRIST was the great spiritual regenerator of the race.
He was not a poet, orator, warrior, statesman, artist;
and yet think what he has done! With a mind divinely
clear and serene, he saw, at once too, through all sham
right to the heart of everything; and his kingdom is in the
heart of things—in the hearts of men. It works and sub-
dues by love. It is spiritual, and it has changed the world.
Let men account for this wonderful change since Christ!
What did it? How came it, if Jesus Christ be not what
he claimed to be—the Son of God, the Saviour of the world!
We need not discuss details—how account for this great
fact—the spiritual regeneration of the world—of millions
of trusting hearts by Christ, whom we worship upon our
knees!   Frances Cobbe.

CHRIST while a child, setting the stars of heaven, the city of Jerusalem, the shepherds of Judea, the sages of the East and the angels of God in motion, attracting the best elements of the world, and repelling the evil, presents a contrast which brings together the most opposite yet not contradictory things, and is too deep, too sublime, too significant to be the invention of a few illiterate fishermen.

Schaff.

———◦◦———

FOR a number of men to fabricate such a book as the New Testament would be more incredible than that it should contain the account of a real life. No Jewish writers assumed the tone, none expressed the morality of the Gospel. It has such striking marks of truth, such unmistakable marks that the writers of such books would be a greater wonder than their hero. It is no invention of men.

Rousseau.

———◦◦———

COMING to Jesus is the desire of the heart after him. It is to feel our sin and misery, to believe that he is able and willing to pardon, comfort and save us, to ask him to help us, and to trust in him as in a friend. To have just the same feelings and desires as if he were visibly present, and we came and implored him to bless us, is to come to him, though we do not see his face nor hear his voice. Repenting sinner! your very desire for pardon, your prayer, " Jesus, save me, I perish," this is coming to him.

Newman Hall.

———◦◦———

IF Protestantism has failed, then Christianity has failed; for Protestantism is the purest and best form Christianity has yet assumed. I know of nothing more *catholic* than Christianity.

Rev. Dr. Northrup of N. Y.

JESUS CHRIST pours out a doctrine beautiful as the light, sublime as heaven, and true as God.

Theo. Parker.

———◦◦◦———

> But here was one,
> Faultless though compassed with infirmity,
> In human weakness sinless, who had stooped
> Lower than angelhood in might, but dwarfed
> In uncreated goodness infinite.
> The loftiest seraphim; no stern recluse
> As his forerunner; but the guest and friend
> Of all who sought him, mingling with all life
> To breathe his holiness on all.　No film
> Obscured his spotless lustre.　From his life
> Truth limpid without error flow'd.　Disease
> Fled from his touch.　Pain heard him, and was not.
> Despair smiled in his presence.　Devils knew,
> And trembled.　In the omnipotence of faith
> Unintermittent, indefectible.
> Leaning upon his Father's might, he bent
> All nature to his will.　The tempest sank,
> He whispering, into waveless calm.　The bread,
> Given from his hands, fed thousands and to spare.
> The stormy waters, or the solid rock,
> Were pavement for his footsteps.　Death itself
> With vain reluctances yielded its prey
> To the stern mandate of the Prince of life.

Bickersteth.

———◦◦◦———

ONCE united to Christ by a living faith, and we can look upon the condemning law as canceled by our surety; we can look upon death as robbed of its sting, and the grave as robbed of its victory.

Christian at Work

CHRISTIANITY is the most practical thing, the most immediately and substantially important thing, in the universe. Visionary! fanciful! impractical! the occupation of dreamers, enthusiasts and fanatics! Aha! Did I not tell you that we need *elevation?* How can any, how dare any, prate thus of our faith? Hearken to the truth; if we need health, it is perfect health, and that for ever! If we need genius, it is perfect genius, and that for ever! If we need learning, it is perfect learning, and that for ever! If we need eloquence or pleasure or fame or power or wealth or rank or office, whatever we need, it implies constitutional and conditional perfection, and that for ever!

Let me speak for you—one voice for humanity. I need a perfect body to contain, identify and obey my soul. I need a perfect home, I need a perfect government, I need a perfect society, I need perfect employment, I need the fullness of eternal life with God in heaven, I need the attainment of my true destiny to stand, as a perfect man, before the perfect God, acknowledged as his child, his image and his heir. The Son of God knew this need, and therefore became the Son of Man, that he might supply it.

Rev. T. H. Stockton, Chaplain of H. R.

———◦◦◦———

THIS is no mere martyr dying for the truth, no mere man just "reeling out of life;" no mere example of the Perfect Man, to show men how to die, no mere theatrical display of the method of the divine government; it is God manifest in the flesh, dying for the sins of the world; it is the Eternal Son, in the likeness of sinful flesh, offering himself up as a substitute and surety for his own people; it is the Lamb of God taking away the sin of the world. His death is vicarious; it is not for himself, but for others.

Ecce Deus-Homo.

CHRIST'S death was not caused by the physical pain of the crucifixion, for just as he died he cried with a loud voice of triumph. But the separation of his soul and body was his own voluntary act! He had power to lay down his life, and power to take it again; his humanity was not descended from Adam by ordinary generation, but, being miraculously formed by the Holy Ghost, was exempted from the death penalty of the law. He gave his life a ransom for many. He was the eternal High Priest, who slew and offered the victim, and he himself was the victim. The whole story of his death loses its consistency the moment you deny the voluntary act of the High Priest in offering the sacrifice.

Ecce Deus-Homo.

———◦◦◦———

IN the very centre of history, pure and perfect pain, on account of sin, is endured—that spiritual pain by means of which the past is remitted, the development of sin retracted and removed. On the cross the new Adam offered up himself—the principle of self—that cosmical principle from which the kingdoms of this world derived all their false glory—a principle which stirred even in him, though it never became actual sin.

Bishop Martensen.

———◦◦◦———

CULTIVATE deep solemnity of manner. It is a message from the Infinite and Eternal God that you have to deliver. How solemn the thought! It forbids all flippancy of speech and levity of manner.

Hints to Evangelists.

———◦◦◦———

WHAT men call virtue is a name and a dream unless it be planted deep in the blood of the Redeemer.

F. W. Robertson

THE dark possibility of being cast away must have a subjective validity and power in the consciousness even of the regenerate man, who experiences the hidden power of sin in the prevailing conflict of life, stern and unceasing, and who, under the sense of his own weakness, cannot but tremble for and mistrust himself.

Bishop Martensen.

CHRIST'S death was not simply the world's example; it was the world's sacrifice. He died not merely as a martyr to the truth. His death is the world's life!

F. W. Robertson.

IF Christ could have been ignored, he would have been ignored in Protestant Germany, when Christian faith had been eaten out of the heart of that country by the older Rationalism. Yet scarcely any German thinker of note can be named who has not projected what is termed a Christology. The Christ of Kant is the Ideal of Moral Perfection, and as such, we are told, he is to be carefully distinguished from the historical Jesus, since of this Ideal alone, and in a transcendental sense, can the statements of the orthodox creed be predicated. The Christ of Jacobi, is a Religious Ideal, and worship addressed to the historical Jesus is denounced as sheer idolatry, unless beneath the recorded manifestation the Ideal itself be discerned and honored. According to Fichte, on the contrary, the real interest of philosophy in Jesus is historical and not metaphysical; Jesus first possessed an insight into the absolute unity of the being of man with that of God, and in revealing this insight he communicated the highest knowledge which man can possess. Of the late Pantheistic philosophers, Schelling proclaims that the Christian theology is probably in error when it teaches that at a particular mo-

ment of time God became incarnate, since God is external
to all time, and the incarnation of God is an eternal fact
But Schelling contends that the man Christ Jesus is the
highest point or effort of this eternal incarnation, and the
beginning of its real manifestation to men. None before
him in such a manner has revealed to man the Infinite.
And the Christ of Hegel is not the actual incarnation of
God in Jesus of Nazareth, but the symbol of his incarnation in humanity at large. Fundamentally differing as do
these conceptions in various ways from the creed of the
Church of Christ, they nevertheless represent so many
efforts of non-Christian thought to do such homage as is
possible to its great object; they are so many proofs of the
interest which Jesus Christ necessarily provokes in the
modern world, even when it is least disposed to own his
true supremacy.   Liddon's Bampton Lectures.

————◇◇◇————

THE interest of modern criticism centres in Him who is
ever most prominently and uninterruptedly present to
the eye of faith. The popular controversies around us tend
more and more to merge in the one great question respecting our Lord's person; that question, it is felt, is bound up
with the very existence of Christianity, and a discussion
respecting Christ's person obliges us to consider the mode
of his historical manifestation; so that his life was probably never studied before, by those who practically or
avowedly reject him so eagerly as it is at this moment.
For Strauss he may be no more than a leading illustration
of the applicability of the Hegelian philosophy to purposes
of historical analysis; for Schenkel he may be a sacred
impersonation of the anti-hierarchical and democratic temper, which aims at revolutionary Germany; Ewald may
see in him the altogether human source of the highest
spiritual life of humanity; and Rénan, the semi-fabulous

and somewhat immoral hero of an Oriental story, fashioned
to the taste of a modern Parisian public. And what if you
yourselves are even now eagerly reading an anonymous
writer, of far nobler aim and finer moral insight than these,
who has endeavored, by a brilliant analysis of one side of
Christ's moral action, to represent him as embodying and
originating all that is best and most hopeful in the spirit
of modern philanthropy, but who seems not indisposed to
substitute for the creed of his Church only the impatient
proclamation of his Roman judge?

Ay, though you salute your Saviour in Pilate's words,
Behold the Man! at least you cannot ignore him; you cannot resist the moral and intellectual forces which converge
in our day with an ever-increasing intensity upon his sacred
person; you cannot turn a deaf ear to the question which
he asks of his followers in each generation, and which he
never asked more solemnly than now: "Whom say men
that I, the Son of Man, am?"

Liddon's Bampton Lectures.

THEY who believe may, by reason of the very loyalty
and fervour of their devotion, so anxiously and eagerly
watch the fleeting, earth-born mists which for a moment
have threatened to veil the face of the Sun of Righteousness, as to forget that the true weal and safety of the soul
is only assured while her eye is persistently fixed on his imperishable glory. They who have known the aching misery
of earnest doubt may, perchance, be encouraged, like the
skeptical apostle, to probe the wounds with which from age
to age error has lacerated Christ's sacred form, and thus to
draw from a nearer contact with the Divine Redeemer the
springs of a fresh and deathless faith, that shall win and
own in him to all eternity the unclouded presence of its
Lord and God.

Liddon's Bampton Lectures.

IN regard to religious truth there will be no uncertain
    sound uttered within these walls. What is proclaimed
here will be the old truth which has been from the beginning; which was shown in shadow in the Old Testament; which was exhibited fully in the New Testament, as
in a glass; which has been retained by the one catholic Church
in the darkest ages; which was long buried, but rose again
at the Reformation; which was maintained by the grand
old theologians of Germany, Switzerland, England and
Scotland, and is being defended with great logical power in
the famous theological seminary with which this college is
so closely associated. But over this massive and clearly-
defined old form of sound words I would place no theological doctor—not Augustine, not Luther, not Calvin, not
Edwards—but another and far fairer face, lifted up that it
may draw all eyes toward it—"Jesus, at once the author
and the finisher of our faith."

Dr. McCosh's Inaugural at Princeton

———◆———

THE New Testament does homage to the Old, just as the
    rising sun sheds back a radiance on the horizon whence
it rose, whilst at the same time it pours the flood of day
upon the skies. The New Testament supplies the master-
key that unlocks the holy hieroglyphics of the dimmer
revelation—characters which before were undecipherable
and unintelligible—just as the inscriptions which have been
traced on the Sinaitic rocks, and on the monuments disem-
boweled from the ruins of mighty Nineveh, were, in effect,
lost to us until the cipher was found out by which they
could be read and interpreted, but then unfolded all their
hidden treasures of hoary knowledge and sepulchred
wisdom.

It pleased God to treat his Church in the primitive

economy as we treat our offspring in their early days. He placed the infant Church under an infant system of education, and taught her more through the eye than through the ear. He surrounded her with emblems and symbols, the material but majestic language of an initiatory and imperfect dispensation. At the same time these emblems and symbols were fraught with glorious import, big with the unsearchable riches of grace. And now that we look back upom them from the vantage-ground of evangelic elevation, what an exhaustless treasury of divine wisdom, and what an exuberant storehouse of magnificent illustration, do we find in those memorials of the past! How beautifully, for instance, does the Epistle to the Hebrews unlock the glorious prefigurations contained in what, but for such development, might have been deemed the cumbrous, unmeaning ritual and ceremonial of the ancient Jews. But laid open and irradiated by that epistle, all is befitting, significant and grand. Now the high priest, with his vestment, his mitre and his breastplate; now, the divers washings and the sundry purifications, and the ever-recurring and interchanging offering; now, the sin-offering and the trespass-offering and the offering of incense; now, the offering of the first green ears, and the wave-offering, and the heave-offering,—all these are seen to have been images and adumbrations of the glorious realities of the Gospel, foreshadowing all the noblest hopes and blessed consolations of the people of God.

Rev. Hugh Stowell, M. A., on the Glory of the Old Testament.

——◦◦·——

NO man can conceive aright of the glory of the Old Testament who has not studied deeply—earnestly, prayerfully studied—that marvelous epistle in which we behold how the Gospel lights up the Law and how the Law

7

illustrates and magnifies the Gospel. There we learn that
clearer and juster conceptions of the Gospel may be formed
by looking back to its types in the Law than can be obtained by looking at it simply in itself and by itself. Just
as when examining some exquisite and curiously furnished
castings you may frequently get a better and fuller idea of
their ingenuity and perfection by scrutinizing the moulds
in which they were cast than you can by dwelling exclusively on the mouldings themselves. Who would make
light of that hemisphere of revelation—the Old Testament—
which is thus gemmed with stars that beam so benignly on
the dark pathway of the pilgrim of faith as he journeys
forward to another?

Rev. Hugh Stowell, M. A., on the Glory of the Old Testament.

——◦◦◦——

THE Old Testament Scriptures are essentially one with
the New; both are so compacted that the latter may be
said to rest upon the former, since the former are pregnant
with types and shadows which find their realization in the
latter. The Old Testament is the New Testament concealed, and the New Testament is the Old Testament revealed. The Old Testament is rich in promises, and replete
with holy records of the heart and lovely exemplifications
of grace, which continue fresh and fragrant as ever. It
furnishes us with narratives the most touching and histories
the most impressive, fitted to bring truth down to the commonest understanding, as well as to bring it home to the
heart of every child. It presents us with the most instruc-
tive and marvelous commentary on the human heart, revealing all its depths and tracing all its intricacies. It, and
it alone, discloses the providential rule of God over nations—
how he deals with them even as he does with individuals,
according to their works, allotting them their retribution in

this world, because there can be no national retribution in the world to come. What if the New Testament crowns the Old, as the noontide crowns the morning? Shall we therefore contemn the blessed dawn? Is not the day all one? Is it not throughout an effulgence from the Sun of Righteousness?

Rev. Hugh Stowell, M. A., on the Glory of the Old Testament.

————◦◦————

GUARD against favoritism in the Word of God. Take the Bible as a whole. Reverence every part of it. The more your mind is enlarged to grasp and come in contact with revelation as a whole, the more will your tone of piety be healthy, and the more will your principles be fixed, broad and firm.

Keep closer and yet closer to your Bibles. There is one thing that will stand, whatever fall; one thing that will not be consumed, whatever may be burnt up; and that is the Word of God! Less and less, therefore, rest your faith on human authority, on creeds or councils or hierarchs or church authority, or anything extraneous to the Bible; but dig deep and build firm on the rock of inspiration, that your faith may not stand in the wisdom of man, but in the power of God. There it will stand, fixed and calm, upheld by the Spirit of God, and though divines may controvert one another, and theological theories come into collision, and though men's minds may be driven to and fro, like leaves of the forest when moved by the wind, and though many may be " ever learning and never coming to the knowledge of the truth," you shall know the truth, and of whom you have learned the truth, and on what foundation it reposes, and thus and there a sweet serenity shall pervade your souls.

Rev. Hugh Stowell, M. A., on the Glory of the Old Testament.

I THINK I hear the song, "Lift up your heads, O ye gates: and be ye lifted up, ye everlasting doors, that the King of glory may come in." The bars of massy light are all unloosed; the pearly gates are all wide open flung; and as he passes through, mark you, the highest joy which swells his soul is that he has opened those gates, not for himself—for they were never shut on him—but that he has opened them for sinners. It was for this, indeed, he died; and it is for this that he ascends on high, that he may "open the kingdom of heaven for all believers." See him as he rides through heaven's streets! "Thou hast ascended up on high; thou hast led captivity captive; thou hast received gifts of man." Ah! but hear the refrain—for this is the sweetest note of all the hymn— "Yea, for the rebellious, also—yea, for the rebellious, also, that the Lord God might dwell among them." The scattered gifts of his coronation, the lavish bounties of his ascension, are still for sinners. He is exalted on high—for what? To give repentance and remission of sins. He still wears upon his breastplate the names of sinners; upon his hands and upon his heart does he still bear the remembrance of those sinners; and every day for the sinner's sake he doth not hold his peace, and for the sinner's sake he doth not rest, but cries unto God until every sinner shall be brought safely home.   **Spurgeon.**

THE very existence of *atheism*, however defiantly proclaimed or studiously practiced, is now scarcely believed in. *Pantheism*, that wicked absurdity which splinters God into fragments and vitalizes and deifies every atom with independent thought and consciousness, is repugnant to common sense, and would not live an instant did it not captivate that resistless passion of man's impetuous heart for the beautiful, the weird and the heroic. The *development theory*, which would exalt mud into man, and dust into deity, has long since been ridiculed into merited obscurity. *Rationalism*, or rather *irrationalism*, drifts a chilling, glittering iceberg on the surging ocean of thought, freezing the life-currents of trust and hope. *Materialism*, which ignores the supernatural—the very spinal column and nervous system of God's universe—tracing the origin of everything to the portentous collision of corporeal particles of matter, is destructive to religion, inimical to poetry and fatal alike to every lofty conception and immortal aspiration of the soul. To those who adopt such a theory the universe is a mere blind machine, moved by a mysterious and relentless fate, with no other explanation than the fact of its existence, whose destiny is shrouded in eternal gloom, and whose entire meaning is exhausted by a scientific description of its various parts! These are they who, with the Bible in their hands and the splendor of creation before their eyes, hold that matter can think and create, that order is the result of chance, that life, beautiful, splendid and momentous, is a mere phenomenon, soon to disappear for ever; who would shiver every touch, blot out every remembrance, congeal every affection, and wrest the universe from the God it proclaims.

Anon.

THE atonement made by Christ for the sin of man is not to be regarded as the procuring cause of God's love, but as its result and manifestation. It was the eternal love of the Father that caused the incarnation and atoning work of the Son. The atonement is the highest proof possible of the love of the Father as well as of the Son. The method, however, of the atonement is indicative of forensic justice as well as of redeeming mercy.

Wright on the Divine Fatherhood

THE Son of God is the central power of the universe, animating and conserving all existence, upon which faith lays hold for life and support.

Henry Vincent.

CHRIST is more than the ideal of virtue, more than the religious genius of the world.

Bushnell.

OH it were a nobler triumph of the modern pulpit to see men of strong principles and self-controlling wisdom gathering round them the most boisterous elements of our social atmosphere, conducting the lightnings with which its darkest thunder-clouds are charged, and showing to the nation they have saved that the preaching of the cross is still the power of God.

Beecher

HEATHENISM was the seeking religion, Judaism the hoping religion. Christianity is the reality of what Heathenism sought and Judaism hoped for.

Luthardt.

SAY what men may, it is doctrine that moves the world. He who takes no position will not sway the human intellect. Logical men, dogmatic men, rule the world. Aristotle, Kant, Augustine, Calvin—these are names that instantly suggest systems, and systems that are exact, solid, and maintain their place from century to century.

Prof. Shedd.

THE higher the sphere of life, the more fully does it hold good that particular individuals must be many things to many men, as Aristotle, Leibnitz, Shakespeare, Beethoven, Calvin, Napoleon.

Martensen.

MORE precious is it to trace the earnest throbs of the most wounded heart than to live among those human machines to whom existence is one daily round of dullness and frivolity. Looking on these, youth, with its bursting tide of soul and sense, shrinks back aghast: "Let me not be as these! Rather let my pulses swell like a torrent, pour themselves out and close; let heart and brain work their work, even to the perishing of both; be my life short like a weaver's shuttle, but let it be a life full, strong, rich, perchance a day only, but one of those days of heaven which are as a thousand years."

Anon.

———◦◦———

FOR two ends only is renown precious: for ambition's sake and for love's. I have neither. Life seems now made not for happiness, but for worthy toil. I stand in the world's vineyard, not as a joyful gatherer of fruit, but as a laborer, patient and active, yet looking toward the day's close as toward its chiefest joy.

Anon.

———◦◦———

TIES of blood do not necessarily constitute affection. The world, ay, even the best and truest part of it, is a little mistaken on this point. The parental or fraternal bond is at first a mere instinct, or, viewed in its highest light, a link of duty; but when, added to this, comes the tender friendship, the deep devotions which spring from sympathy and esteem, then the love is made perfect, and the kindred of blood becomes a yet stronger kindred of heart. But unless circumstances, or the nature and character of the parties themselves, allow opportunity for this union, parent and child, brother and sister, are as much strangers as though no bond of relationship existed between them.

Anon.

THERE is nothing I despise more than to hear a person raking up and exaggerating the errors of another's past life, no matter how good he may now be, or how nobly he may be doing his life's work—errors which have long been bitterly repented of and corrected; errors which God has forgiven, for which Jesus has atoned, and against the repetition of which the man is ever on his guard; errors which have disciplined the man, by an experience never to be forgotten, to have charity and forgiveness when he sees them in others, weak, frail, passionate as himself. It is just as if we were to be constantly reminding all the beautiful butterflies that they were once ugly caterpillars! There is such a thing as reformation. God can change an erring man's heart and life, and this he does often suddenly though radically, and it is not the spirit of the meek and forgiving One to be ever remembering and enlarging upon the errors of another's past, that forgets the faults and sins of self, and heightens and colors the defects and weaknesses of others.

Anon.

----◆----

THE worst kind of vice is advice.

Coleridge.

----◆----

FAITH is the substance of things hoped for, as it gives these things a substance or subsistence in the mind, by substantiating and realizing them to the mind and impressing them upon the heart. It is likewise the evidence of things not seen, as it applies the evidences of their reality to the mind, and makes them as evident and real to the soul as if they were visible things. When a person truly believes, the Gospel is written in and upon the heart, engraven upon the spirit of the mind, so as to become the principle of his actions and affections.

Cases of Conscience.

WE are only safe when we can see the cross of Jesus clearly cut and sharply defined against the sky of our eternal destiny.

Anon.

———◦◦———

THE Scythians of old used to strike the cords of their bows at feasts, to remind themselves of danger.

Bancroft.

———◦◦———

STRATAGEMS in war and love are only honorable when successful.

Bulwer.

———◦◦———

VAST as is the conclusion of a world of sinners redeemed, atoned for, reconciled, the premise that Jesus crucified is truly God more than warrants it.

Henry Parry Liddon.

———◦◦———

NOR, most assuredly, is any the least and lowest act of sacrifice destined to perish. It thrills on in its undying force through the ages; it kindles, first in one, and then in another unit of the vast company of moral beings, a new devotion to truth, to duty, to man, to God.

Henry Parry Liddon.

———◦◦———

FOR one there is who has silently advanced through time from the beginning. Bloody ages—brilliantly splendid epochs—are merely dissimilar chambers, through which he has advanced, silently, calmly, becoming more and more distinct through the twilight veil, until he has reached the period on the threshhold of which he now stands—contemplated by many with rapture, by many with fear. And if it is asked where is this form before whom thrones totter, crowns fall off and earthly purples grow pale, the reply is— Man, man in his original Truth—man formed in the image of God.

Fredrika Bremer.

THE only way in which to fit a people for self-government is to entrust them with self-government.

Macaulay.

———◆◇◆———

LOGIC is the anatomy of thought.

Locke.

———◆◇◆———

WORDS are not essential to the existence of thought—only to its expression.

Dugald Stewart.

———◆◇◆———

THINKING is the talking of the soul with itself.

Plato.

———◆◇◆———

MUSIC is the inarticulate speech of the heart, which cannot be compressed into words, because it is infinite.

Wagner.

———◆◇◆———

A MAN'S collective dispositions constitute his character.

Atwater.

———◆◇◆———

STATEMENT is argument.

Shedd.

———◆◇◆———

I LIKE to see a young man have a good opinion of himself. It is like a florid style—he will soon get over it.

Dr. McClintock.

———◆◇◆———

GENERAL ideas are generally wrong.

Dr. M. W. Jacobus.

———◆◇◆———

I AM but an atom, but an atom in a solid, God-governed world, where truth is mightiest. Insignificant as I am, the universe were incomplete without me.

Anon.

WE have no reason to fear that the poor and unfortunate will ever receive too much attention, either at home or abroad.

Mrs. E. C. Stanton.

————◇————

IT is remarkable with what Christian fortitude and resignation we can bear the suffering of other folks.

Dean Swift.

————◇————

THOSE who marry intend as little to conspire their own ruin as those who swear allegiance; and as a whole people is to an ill government, so is one man or woman to an ill marriage.

John Milton.

————◇————

A CONDITION requiring the continuance of marriage, notwithstanding a change in the feelings of the parties, is absurd, shocking and contrary to humanity.

Jeremy Bentham.

————◇————

MARRIAGE having this peculiarity, that its objects are frustrated when the feelings of both parties are not in harmony with it, should require nothing but the declared will of either party to dissolve it.

Alexander Humboldt.

————◇————

THE Divine chemistry works in the subsoil.

Hawthorne.

————◇————

MONSIEUR, when a wife's nature loathes that of the man she is wedded to, marriage must be slavery; against slavery all right thinkers revolt; and though torture be the price of resistance, torture must be dared; though the only road to freedom be through the gates of death, those gates must be passed, for freedom is indispensable.

Charlotte Bronte.

THE subject of marriage is usually discussed as if the interests of children were everything, those of grown persons nothing.

John Stuart Mill.

———•◇•———

THE flattest substances have some carbonic acid in them.

Gail Hamilton.

———•◇•———

AT last my very dreams were administrative.

M. Thiers.

———•◇•———

PRINCIPLE is to a man what a free constitution is to a nation; without that principle or that free constitution, the one may be for the moment as good, the other as happy, but we cannot tell how long that goodness and happiness will continue.

Bulwer.

———•◇•———

I DID not *fall* into love—I *rose* into love.

Bulwer.

———•◇•———

IT is peculiarly American not to be satisfied with anything.

Beecher.

———•◇•———

LIKE a drum, the city rolls out the sound of its industry, mustering the youth of all nations with great haste to its ranks.

Beecher.

———•◇•———

LOVE is carnalized by disappointment.

Fowler.

———•◇•———

MAKE it the interest of others to be your friends. Command honors, as well as bestow them.

Dr Samp'e

IT is a matter of the simplest demonstration that no man can be really appreciated but by his equal or superior.

Ruskin.

———◦◦◦———

IF a man has not such control of his feelings as to make his feelings control his will, then he is but half educated.

Ruskin.

———◦◦◦———

THE more we study human nature, the less we think of men—the more of man.

Tilton

———◦◦◦———

A MAN'S call to the ministry consists in his ability to preach Christ and the willingness of the people to hear him.

Dr. Tyng.

———◦◦◦———

DEAN SWIFT once preached to an audience of tailors from the text, " A remnant shall be saved."

Shedd.

———◦◦◦———

THE true and proper stimulant for the intellect is truth. There is no sin in being excited by truth. There is no mental injury in such excitement. Hence, buy the truth and sell it not.

Shedd.

———◦◦◦———

WE love flattery, even when we see through it, and are not deceived by it, for it shows that we are of importance enough to be courted.

Emerson.

———◦◦◦———

SHAKESPEARE, with all his genius, failed to create any great religious character.

Atlantic Monthly.

WHEN another's egotism offends us, it is generally be cause he tramps on the toes of our own egotism.

Dr. A. A. Hodge.

THE righteous and the wicked are separated by a gulf of fire.

Austin Phelps.

CHARACTER, good or bad, has a tendency to perpetuate itself.

Dr. A. A. Hodge.

JUST to think of a science of the stars preaching that there is no God!

Rev. David Riddle, D.D.

THE world is made up of complemental forces and com pensating influences.

Round Table.

THE Grecian sculptors could cut the marble like snow.

Emerson.

PRAYER is not overcoming God's reluctance; it is laying hold of his highest willingness.

Trench.

I HAVE always dreaded to provoke reason, but never in dividuals.

Mirabeau.

HE bore his heart as high as his head.

Timon on Mirabeau.

HOW often have I lamented that his powers should have wanted the influence of an unsullied reputation!

Dumont on Mirabeau.

O LIBERTY! how many crimes have been committed in thy name!

Madame Roland.

———◆◆———

VICE stings us even in our pleasures, but Virtue consoles us even in our pains.

Colton.

———◆◆———

THE cross of Christ is the measure of the love of God to us, and the measure of the meaning of man's existence.

F. W. Robertson.

———◆◆———

WE lose time by Remorse.

F. W. Robertson.

———◆◆———

RELIGION has only calm, sober, perhaps monotonous pleasures to offer at first. The deep rapture of enjoyment comes in after-life, and that will not satisfy the young heart. Men will know what pleasure is, and they drink deep, keen delight, feverish enjoyment—that is what you long for—and these emotions lose their delicacy and their relish, and will only come at the bidding of gross excitements. The ecstasy which once rose at the sight of the rainbow in the sky, or the bright brook, or the fresh morning, comes languidly at last only in the crowded midnight room, or the excitement of commercial speculation, or beside the gambling-table, or amidst the fever of politics. It is a spectacle for men and angels when a man has become old in feeling and worn-out before his time.

F. W. Robertson.

———◆◆———

IN the subtle alchemy of Hope the slightest possibilities are ever transmuted into golden probabilities and inevitable certainties.

Round Table.

MEN are usually tempted by the devil, but an idle man positively tempts the devil.

Spanish Proverb.

———◦◦◦———

IN heaven hands clasp for ever.

Greek Proverb.

———◦◦◦———

LET us bear our trials as the Alps bear up the snow and ice by which they are covered; let us stand, in the strength of Christ, against trouble as the hills stand against the winds and the waves.

Dr. Seiss.

———◦◦◦———

THERE are men whose consciences, somehow, get entangled with their nervous system, so that they cannot think an evil thought without torture.

Greyson Letters.

———◦◦◦———

A MAN living amid the advantages and activities of the nineteenth century is a condensed Methusaleh.

Dr. Chapin.

———◦◦◦———

TRUTH is by its very nature intolerant, exclusive, for every truth is the denial of its opposing error.

Luthardt.

———◦◦◦———

WHERE is the glory in spending one's life in trying to preserve the political balance of Europe? The salvation of one human soul is worth more than the advancement in civilization of the entire human race.

Ruskin.

———◦◦◦———

MY heart is cracking with impatience.

Shakespeare.

MY sky is dark and lowering, and seems to be closing around me like a grave. I tunnel through the days in total darkness.

Edgar Allen Poe.

———◦◦◦———

ENERGY of will depends upon depth of emotion.

Martensen.

———◦◦◦———

SELF-RESPECT will do to begin with, but self-abnegation is the only consummate virtue.

Round Table.

———◦◦◦———

ONE thing only in this world always depends upon ourselves, and that is the resolution to do what is in accordance with right reason. Here is virtue. Here also is the only true happiness possible to man.

Descartes.

———◦◦◦———

WHAT! rest, ease here! in the ministry or in Christian work! There is no rest here. Now is the time for battle, for work! Heaven will be our rest. Now is the time for steady, prudent, arduous, unflinching effort.

D. L. Moody.

———◦◦◦———

LIFE is like a city full of crooked streets.

Anon.

———◦◦◦———

SORROWS humanize our race. Tears are the showers that fertilize the world.

Jean Ingelow.

———◦◦◦———

WHAT shall we say of flowers—those banners of the vegetable world—which march in such various and splendid triumph before the coming of its fruits.

Argyll.

THEY are poor
That have lost nothing; they are poorer far
Who, losing, have forgotten; they most poor
Of all who lose and wish they might forget.

Jean Ingelow.

———◦◦◦———

REAL friendship is of slow growth. It seldom arises at first sight. Nothing but our vanity will make us think so. It never thrives unless engrafted upon a stock of known and reciprocal merit.

Chesterfield.

———◦◦◦———

NEVER seem to affect the character in which you wish to shine. Modesty is the only sure bait when you angle for praise. By modesty I do not mean timidity and awkward bashfulness. On the contrary, be inwardly firm and steady. Know your own value, but take care to let nobody discover that you know it. Whatever real merit you have, other people will discover, and people always magnify their own discoveries, as they lessen those of others.

Chesterfield.

———◦◦◦———

MYTHOLOGY is religion growing wild.

Schelling.

———◦◦◦———

WHEN Augustine was asked what God was doing before he created the world, he replied, "Preparing punishment for people who ask indiscreet questions.

Saisset.

———◦◦◦———

THINGS do not melt quietly into the peace of the kingdom of God. There is a crash of ruin and a wine-press of the wrath of Almighty God, and a lake that burns with fire and brimstone.

Progress of Doctrine in the New Testament—Bernard

A SEARED conscience is like a tympanum without resonance.

Theo. Cuyler.

———•◦•———

GOD leads Nature by the hand; she walks in his statutes, keeping his judgments and doing them, moved to obedience by no will but His.

Anon.

———•◦•———

THERE are passages in Shakespeare that burst upon the mind like splendor from heaven.

Carlyle.

———•◦•———

THE memory is never responsible for what the attention never gives it in charge.

Anon.

———•◦•———

TIME, which deadens hatred, secretly strengthens love.

Richter.

———•◦•———

ONE clairvoyance on earth is certain, and that is the clairvoyance of love.

Anon.

———•◦•———

COUNT that day lost whose low, descending sun Sees at thy hand no worthy action done.

Mosaics of Life.

———•◦•———

TO never rest is the price paid for our greatness. Could we rest, we must become smaller in soul. Whoever is satisfied with what he does has reached his culminating point—he will progress no more. Man's destiny is to be not dissatisfied, but for ever unsatisfied.

F. W. Robertson.

THE tendency of philosophy has been to throw back the personal being farther and farther from the time when every branch and stream was believed a living power, to the period when "principles" were substituted for this belief; then "*laws;*" and the philosopher's God is a law into which all other laws are resolvable.

F. W. Robertson.

LIFE outweighs all things if Love lies within it.

Goethe.

THIS is ever the way in religious perplexity; the unsympathizing world taunts or misunderstands. In spiritual grief, they ask, Why is he not like others? In bereavement, they call your deep sorrow unbelief. In misfortune, they comfort you, like Job's friends, by calling it a visitation. Or, like the barbarians at Melita, when the viper fastened on Paul's hand, no doubt they call you an infidel, though your soul be crying after God.

F. W. Robertson.

HE whom society has restored realizes the possibility of restoration to God's favor; the man whom society will not forgive nor restore is driven into recklessness.

F. W. Robertson.

INNOCENCE apprehends the approach of evil by the instinctive tact of contrast; guilt, by the instinctive consciousness of similarity.   F. W Robertson.

No sensible person ever made an apology.

Emerson,

WHAT I don't see
   Don't trouble me;
And what I see
Might trouble me,
Did I not know
That it must be so.

Goetn .

THE rarest attainment is to grow old happily and grace·
fully.

L. M. Child.

THERE is even a happiness
   That makes the heart afraid.

Thomas Hood.

NEVERTHELESS, I confide the whole matter to Providence, and shall endeavor so to live that the world
may come to an end at any moment without leaving me at
a loss to find a foothold somewhere else.

Hawthorne.

WE live in deeds, not years; in thoughts, not breaths;
   In feelings, not in figures on a dial:
We should count time by heart-throbs. He must lives
Who thinks most, feels the noblest, acts the best.

Bailoy's Festus.

ALL persons are not discreet enough to know how to take
things by the right handle.

Cervantes.

THE hand that rocks the cradle rules the world.

Anon,

THE fate of the child is always the work of his mother.

Napoleon

————◦◦◦————

BE *noble;* and the nobleness that lies
In other men *sleeping,* but never *dead,*
Will rise in majesty to meet thine own.

Anon.

————◦◦◦————

THE one prudence in life is concentration.

Emerson.

————◦◦◦————

ONLY what we have wrought into our characters during
life can we take away with us.   Humboldt.

————◦◦◦————

To live in hearts we leave behind is not to die.

Thomas Campbell.

————◦◦◦————

THE voices that spoke to me when a child are now speaking through me to the world.

Bishop Simpson.

————◦◦◦————

CHRISTIANITY feels herself equal to the task of conquering the world.   Bishop Simpson.

————◦◦◦————

YOUNG man! you are a stumbling-block to your companions: you have power over them; you are going to
ruin, and they are following you.   Bishop Simpson.

————◦◦◦————

A GREAT deal depends upon a man's *courage* when he
is slandered and traduced.   Weak men are crushed by
detraction, but the brave hold on and succeed.

H. S. Stevens, Esq., Cleve'and, O.

WHEN the world *frowns* we can face it, but let it *smile,* and we are undone.

Bulwer.

———◇◇———

ALL our trials and disappointments finally bring to us a reward, even in this world, in increased usefulness and happiness. Whatever cloud may for a moment envelop a deserving man, it is sure to pass away and leave him shining forth at last with steady and cloudless light.

Hon. R. C. Parsons, Cleveland, O.

———◇◇———

PRIZE respect more than affection.

William E. Channing, D. D.

———◇◇———

FEW persons have sufficient wisdom to prefer censure, which is useful to them, to praise, which deceives them.

La Rochefoucault.

———◇◇———

GOD made the country and man made the town.

Cowper.

———◇◇———

O HEAVEN! were man
But constant, he were perfect: that one error
Fills him with faults.   Shakespeare.

———◇◇———

HE that loves to be flattered is worthy o' the flatterer.

Shakespeare.

———◇◇———

THE brave abroad fight for the wise at home.

Dryden.

———◇◇———

TRUTH cannot long be concealed: she will burst the doors of her imprisonment and flash her splendors on the world.

Bulwer.

LEAVE your place in the world for ten minutes, and when you come back somebody else has taken it; but when you leave the world for good, who remembers that you had ever a place even in the parish register?

Bulwer.

———◦◦———

TRUTH fears nothing but concealment.

Guizot.

———◦◦———

IF poets sing to the young, and the young hail their own interpreters in poets, it is because the tendency of both is to idealize the realities of life, finding everywhere in the real a something that is noble and fair, and making the fair yet fairer and the noble nobler still.

Bulwer.

———◦◦———

PUBLIC gossip is sometimes the best security for the ful fillment of private engagements.

Bulwer.

———◦◦———

STRIKE! but hear me.

Themistocles.

———◦◦———

A DEMOCRAT goes to the Declaration of Independence to learn what rights he has, and then to the Constitution to see what rights he has surrendered.

Henry Clay Dean.

———◦◦———

THE negro question is the Gulf Stream in our politics.

Wendell Phillips.

———◦◦———

TRUTH is the apostle before whom every cowardly Felix trembles.

Wendell Phillips.

THE negative part of a conversation is often as important as its positive.

Theodore Winthrop.

———◇◇———

BUT if it was ordained!

Grace Greenwood.

———◇◇———

MAN'S best powers point him Godward.

Spurgeon.

———◇◇———

ALL liking has its grounds in likeness.

Dr. A. A. Hodge.

———◇◇———

DO thoroughly whatever work God may give you to do, and cultivate all your talents besides. If God does not utilize these talents in this world, he will in the next.

Dr. A. A. Hodge.

———◇◇———

A PANIC of memory.

Haven.

———◇◇———

SMILES are the language of love.

Anon

———◇◇———

THE cannon-ball passing through a four-feet bore receives its direction for the whole range; so the soul in child-hood receives its direction for eternity.

Anon.

———◇◇———

THE truer we become, the more unerringly we know the *ring* of truth.

F. W. Robertson.

———◇◇———

SELF-RESPECT has more self-reliance than self-assertion.

Round Table.

THIS proposition looks fair, but its fallacy becomes apparent under the first steady look.

Biblical Repository.

———◦◦◦———

ALL thine own on earth,
Beloved, and in glory all thine own.

Bickersteth.

———◦◦◦———

GOD bless thee!—God be blessed for thee!

Bickersteth

———◦◦◦———

HEAVEN can attest that I fought bravely when the heavy blows fell fast.

Adah Isaacs Menken.

———◦◦◦———

LET the worldly-minded enjoy their fashionable parties and amusements : I have grand times here in my study.

Rev Dr. W. D. Howard.

———◦◦◦———

MY greatest sorrows are those of my own heart. Outward troubles serve rather to steady than to disconcert me.

Rev. George Paull.

———◦◦◦———

WE must not only pray for God to save particular persons, but we ourselves must use means to reach these same persons, and then pray God to bless the means.

Anon.

———◦◦◦———

UNTIL the ladies have recognized, or refused to recognize, a man's merit, his social position is not yet determined.

Saturday Review.

———◦◦◦———

THINGS that never happen are often as much realities to to us in their effects as those that are accomplished.

Dickens

ANOTHER stately cypress has been planted, in the will of God, by the pathway of our nation's destiny. Upon its branches let us mutely hang our funereal garlands, moistened with our tears.

Marshall Swartzwelder, Esq., on the death of Lincoln.

———◦◦———

MAN is, in a sense, supernatural, because he works on the chain of causes and effects from without the chain.

Bushnell.

———◦◦———

TONES are the cadences which emotion gives to thought.

Herbert Spencer.

———◦◦———

THE world thinks more of condition than of character.

Bushnell.

———◦◦———

MEN brave enough to repent.

Bayne.

———◦◦———

THE theatre is the illumined and decorated gateway to ruin.

Dr. P. D. Gurley on the death of Lincoln.

———◦◦———

THE greatness of melancholy men is seldom strong and healthy.

Bulwer.

———◦◦———

WHEN General Lee heard of Stonewall Jackson's wound, he said, "He is better off than I am. He has lost his *left* arm, but I have lost my *right* one."

Pollard.

———◦◦———

OLD truths are always new to us, if they come with the smell of heaven upon them.

John Bunyan

WHEN Mr. Sumner said, ten years ago, that freedom was rational, and slavery sectional, all the world but Massachusetts laughed, for slavery sat upon a throne and gave evidence of power, and declared that her sceptre should be borne to Bunker Hill.

Tilton.

POETS are all who love—who feel great truths and tell them.

Bailey's Festus.

TAKE your stand, unswerving, heroic, by the altar of truth, and from that altar let neither sophistry nor ridicule expel you.

Henry Vincent.

THE literature of any age is but the mirror of its prevalent tendencies.

The Nation.

THE educated clergyman has an unwritten liturgy in his own cultivated and pure taste, which he is at perfect liberty to vary with times and circumstances.

Shedd.

THE gratitude of the lowly is precious.

Gen. Howard.

THE heart must be pure to be fearless.

Anon.

TRUE nobility is exempt from fear.

Shakespeare.

THE worth of anything
Is just as much as it will bring.

Anon

I NEVER knew a genius yet who did not carry about him, either in face or person, or in a certain inexplicable grace of manner, the patent of nobility which Heaven has bestowed upon him.

The Ogilvies.

———o———

INDIFFERENCE wilts!

Mrs. Craig.

———o———

ALL is but lip-wisdom which wants experience.

Sir Philip Sydney.

———o———

WHEN our hatred is too keen, it places us beneath those we hate.

La Rochefoucault.

———o———

WE sow many seeds to get a few flowers.

Anon.

———o———

WE cannot all be cabin-passengers in the voyage of life. Some must be before the mast.

Anon.

———o———

SPEAK the truth by all means; let it fall upon the hearts of men with all the imparted energy by which the spirit gives it power; but speak the truth in love, and, perchance, it may subdue them by its winsome beauty, and prompt their acknowledgment that it is altogether lovely.

Rev. William Morley Punshon.

———o———

YOUNG man! where is your mark on the nineteenth century?

Dr. S. J. Wilson.

———o———

MINISTERS are like trees—they do not bear to be often transplanted.

Anon.

THE whole universe of God will crumble to pieces before God will overlook or despise one single tear of genuine repentance.

Judge McWilliams.

———◦◊◦———

HE knocked at each one
Of the doorways of life, and abode in none.

Lucile.

———◦◊◦———

PRINCIPLES are very important, but they need to be adorned by the graces to render them attractive.

Anon.

———◦◊◦———

BE not hasty to cast off every aspersion that is cast on you. Let them alone for a while, and then, like mud on your clothes, they will rub off of themselves.

Dr. Murray.

———◦◊◦———

ANALYSIS is the great characteristic of the present age.

J. G. Hoyt.

———◦◊◦———

RELIGIOUS excitement is to the steady influence of Christian principle as is the scarlet flush of fever to the uniform glow of health.

Dr. Murray.

———◦◊◦———

IT would require an infinite intelligence to project a successful lie.

Dr. Burt.

———◦◊◦———

How to get bored is the object of all civilization.

Theodore Winthrop.

———◦◊◦———

I WANT to keep alive my head in my heart.

Doddridge.

THE Bible, diamond-like, casts its lustre in every direction; torch-like, the more shaken the more it shines;
herb-like, the more pressed the sweeter its fragrance.

Anon.

———◦◦◦———

HELL is as ubiquitous as condemning conscience.

Robertson.

———◦◦◦———

DID I ever tell you, among the affecting little things one
is always seeing in these battle-fields, how, on the
ground upon which the battle of Bull Run was fought, I
saw pretty, pure, delicate flowers growing out of the empty
amunition-boxes, and a wild rose thrusting up its graceful
head through the top of a broken Union drum, which
doubtless sounded its last charge in that battle, and a cunning, scarlet verbena peeping out of a fragment of an exploded shell, in which strange pot it was planted? Wasn't
that peace growing out of war? Even so shall the beautiful and graceful ever grow out of the horrid and terrible
things that transpire in this changing but ever-advancing
world. Nature covers even the battle-fields with verdure
and bloom. Peace and plenty spring up in the track of
devouring campaigns, and all things in nature and society
shall work out the progress of mankind.

George Alfred Townsend.

———◦◦◦———

THE flowers of rhetoric are only acceptable when backed
by the evergreens of truth and sense. The granite
statue, rough hewn though it be, is far more imposing in its
simple and stern though rude proportions, than the plaster-
cast, however elaborately wrought and gilded.

Macaulay.

———◦◦◦———

PIETY sat with tearful eye by the side of Patriotism.

Rev. Herrick Johnson on the Christian Commission.

TO return thanks for the operation of the Spirit of God in the conversion of sinners is the most delightful part of a minister's duty.   Christmas Evans.

———◦◦◦———

WHEN men get loose in their theology,
   The screws are started up in everything.
                                            Bitter Sweet.

———◦◦◦———

I HAVE never known the winter's blast,
   Or the quick-lightning, or the pestilence,
Make nice distinctions when let slip
From God's right hand.   Bitter Sweet.

———◦◦◦———

THAT man has lived to little purpose who has not learned that what the great world pities, and its teachers disallow, even though mixed with tokens of weakness, is many times deepest in truth and closest to the real sublimities of life and religion.   Bushnell.

———◦◦◦———

WHEN the lofty palm tree of Teilan puts forth its flowers, the sheath bursts with a report that shakes the forest; but thousands of other flowers of equal beauty open in the morning, and the very dew-drops hear no sound; even so many souls do blossom in mercy, and the world hears neither whirlwind nor tempest.   Spurgeon.

———◦◦◦———

FOR a few brief days in May the orchards are white with blossoms. They soon turn to fruit, or else float away, useless and wasted upon the idle breeze. So it will be with your present feelings. They must be deepened into decision or be entirely dissipated by delay.
                                        Theodore Cuyler.

POETICAL divines of real genius are so rare that we should thank God for the few. Why should poetry, the highest and noblest of the arts, be banished from theology? Has not God joined them together in the first and last chapters of the Bible? Has he not identified poetry with the very birth of Christianity, in the angelic hymn, as well as with its ultimate triumph, in the hallelujahs of the countless hosts of the redeemed?

Schaff

———◇———

THEOLOGY and Philosophy, in their boldest flights and nearest approaches to the vision of truth, unconsciously burst forth in the festive language of poetry, and poetry itself, in its highest and noblest forms, is transformed into worship of Him who is the eternal source of the true, the beautiful and the good.

Schaff.

———◇———

THE poetic instinct turns whatever it touches into gold.

Holland.

———◇———

POETRY, and its twin sister, Music, are the most sublime and spiritual arts, and are much more akin to the genius of Christianity, and minister far more copiously to the purposes of devotion and edification than Architecture, Painting and Sculpture. They employ word and tone, and can speak thereby more directly to the spirit than the plastic arts by stone and color, and give more adequate expression to the whole wealth of thought and feeling.

Schaff.

———◇———

ARCHITECTURE is a handmaid of devotion. A beautiful church is a sermon in stone, and its spire a finger pointing to heaven.

Schaff.

9

CALVINISM has always had an ennobling influence upon human character, and has done much to promote human liberty.   Schaff.

———◦◦———

CALVINISTIC doctrine is traced back in a line of fire to Augustine and Paul.   Dr. S. J. Wilson.

———◦◦———

THE essential guilt of suicide is unbelief—despair of God's love and goodness.   F. W. Robertson.

———◦◦———

A MAN'S daily conduct prevails to stamp his character with the impression of truth. Quietly does the clear light, shining day after day, refute the ignorant surmise or malicious tale which has thrown dirt on a pure character.
                                                       Anon.

———◦◦———

MEMORY seizes the passing moment, fixes it upon the canvas, and hangs the picture on the soul's inner chambers for her to look upon when she will.
                          Haven's Mental Philosophy.

———◦◦———

THE flesh of animals who feed excursively is allowed to have a higher flavor than that of those who are cooped up. May there not be the same difference between men who read as their taste prompts and men who are confined in cells and colleges to stated tasks?   Boswell.

———◦◦———

IN the Mammoth Cave, where the light of day never enters, the fish are eyeless, having lost their organ of sight from long disuse, but the slave in his captivity, enveloped in worse than cavern darkness, and shut out from all the privileges which a man formed in the image of God has a right to enjoy, has retained his capacity for liberty, education and religion.

Rev. Dr. Bittenger, Sewickley, Pa.

———————

I WAS never happy till I gave up trying to be a great man, and was willing to be nobody.

Payson.

———————

A CHRISTIAN'S spirituality will depend as much upon his work as his work upon his spirituality.

Chalmers.

———————

WALK the sea-shore, and you will see all around you the fragments of broken wrecks—here a spar, there a torn sail; wherever you turn some evidence of disaster and loss, and beyond all you will hear the great, roaring, surging ocean, heaving and tossing in its boundless expanse; and as we walk the shore of the sea of life we see all around us the wrecks of broken hopes, broken plans, broken families and broken hearts, and beyond all we hear the roaring, surging ocean of existence, heaving and sighing in its boundless mystery and might.

Rev. Stuckenberg, Pittsburg, Pa.

———————

IF, then, Protestantism has done anything toward restoring the purity of the apostolic Church—if it has taught that God only is to be invoked and worshiped, and that no creature is to be deified—if it has held up the Word of God instead of a self-constituted priesthood—if it has recognized in every follower of Christ a friend and brother, and has stoutly maintained that religion is a thing of the heart and life, not of empty and gaudy externals,—then it is *not* a fail ure, and any man who asserts that it is, has not only need of more gospel, but need of more sense. I tell you it is not every man who could find out that Protestantism is a fail·ure. If it is so, may it keep on, and may we have a greater failure than we have ever yet seen.

Rev. Dr. Northrup in reply to Dr. Ewer of N. Y.

———◦◦◦———

THE command that the waters should be gathered was the command that the earth should be sculptured.

Ruskln.

———◦◦◦———

I READ Shakespeare, Wordsworth, Tennyson and Cole·ridge for views of man to meditate upon, instead of theological caricatures of humanity; and I go out into the country to feel God; dabble in chemistry to feel awe of him; read the life of Christ to understand, love and adore him; and my experience is closing into this—that I turn with disgust from everything but Christ. A sublime feeling of a presence comes upon me at times, which makes inward solitariness a trifle to talk about.

F. W. Robertson.

———◦◦◦———

IT is said that often, under favorable circumstances, men on board a vessel a hundred miles from shore hear the ringing of church-bells on placing their ears in the focus of the mainsail; and so as the Christian sails on the ocean of life, often, under favorable circumstances, is the music of heaven wafted to his ears, cheering him with sweet hopes of a happy home beyond the deep.

Anon.

———◦◦◦———

WHO will speak the solvent word for all these problems?

Emerson.

AN apt quotation is as good as an original remark.

Proverb

I SHALL sink
As sinks a stranger in the crowded streets
Of busy London; some short bustle's caused
A few inquiries, and the crowd close in,
And all's forgotten!

Anon.

THE Turks tell their people of a heaven where there is sensible pleasure, but of a hell where they shall suffer they don't know what. Christians quite invert this order; they tell us of a hell where we shall feel sensible pain, but of a heaven where we shall enjoy we can't tell what.

Selden.

WINTER is the time for reflection, for reformation and improvement. People who live in tropical countries are deficient in manliness of character.

Horace Bushnell.

THERE is a broad distinction between character and reputation, for one may be destroyed by slander, while the other can never be harmed save by its possessor. Reputation is in no man's keeping. You and I cannot determine what other men shall think and say about us. We can only determine what they *ought* to think of us and say about us, and we can only do this by acting squarely up to our convictions.

Holland.

THEY fell in obedience to the laws.

Epitaph on Leonidas and his Spartans

WE do not feel our own moral deformity. We are like those animals in creation which are vile and loathsome to our senses, but are not so to themselves, nor yet to one another. Their loathsomeness is their nature, and they do not perceive it. Our corruption is part and parcel of ourselves, and at our best we have but a feeble comprehension of its intensity.

Rev. Ryle.

THERE are men who always look at things through the spectacle of books. It is as though a number of eyes were set in a row, like boys playing at leap-frog, each hinder one having to look through all that stands before it, and hence seeing nature, not as it is in itself, but refracted and distorted by a number of more or less disturbing media.

Guesses at Truth.

ONE of the first things a soldier has to do is to harden himself against heat and cold. He must inure himself to bear sudden and violent changes of temperature. In like manner they who enter into public life should begin by dulling their sensibilities to praise and blame. We must turn our back on the one—we must face the other. We must keep a firm footing, and beware of being lifted up, remembering that this is the commonest trick by which wrestlers throw their antagonists.

John Bright.

MUSICAL! how much lies in that. A musical thought is one spoken by a mind that has penetrated into the innermost heart of the thing, detected the inmost mystery of it—namely, the melody that lies hidden in it, the inward harmony of coherence which is its soul, whereby it exists and has a right to be in this world. All inmost things, we may say, are melodious, naturally. utter themselves in song.

The meaning of song goes deep. Who is there that in logical words can express the effect music has on us? A kind of inarticulate, unfathomable speech which leads us to the edge of the Infinite, and lets us for moments gaze into that.

Carlyle.

———◦◦———

THE true reformer is the *seminal* reformer, not the *radical.* And this is the way the Sower, who went forth to sow his seed, did really reform the world, without making any open assault to uproot what was already existing.

Guesses at Truth.

———◦◦———

WE talk of faculties as if they were distinct, things separable; as if a man had intellect, imagination, fancy, etc., as he has hands, feet and arms. This is a capital error. We hear of a man's intellectual and moral natures as if these were divisible and existed apart. This is a necessity of language: at bottom these divisions are but names. Man's soul, his spiritual nature, is essentially one and indivisible.

Carlyle.

———◦◦———

ALL that a man does is physiognomical of him. You may see how a man would fight by the way in which he sings; his courage or want of courage is visible in the word he utters, in the opinion he has formed, no less than in the stroke he strikes. He is *one,* and preaches the same self abroad in all those ways.

Carlyle.

———◦◦———

DARTING, frisking, singing life.

Bushnell.

———◦◦———

MEN err not so much in prompt action as in hasty judgment.

Louis Napoleon.

NATURE is a revelation of God. Art is a revelation of man. Art means power; it is the power of man's soul working outward. Art pre-exists in nature, and nature is reproduced in art. What we call miracles of art are not so to those who create them. They are natural and easy to them.

Longfellow.

———

"HOW well that point was put!" said Dean Swift when he once heard a man express an opinion in conformity with his own.

———

OLD Sam Johnson once said to Boswell that a woman speaking in public always reminded him of a dog walking on two legs. The wonder with him was, not that the dog did it well, but that he did it at all.

———

AS Washington Irving was walking down Broadway, New York, one day, his attention was drawn to a picture labeled, "Christus Consolatus" (Christ the consoler), hanging in a window. He shed tears, inquired for the artist, purchased the picture and kept it in his room till death. So when the Spirit of God opens our eyes to see Christ as he is, let us weepingly take him to our hearts and keep him there till death, when he will lift us to his throne to reign with him for ever.

Independent.

———

PRACTICAL wisdom acts in the mind as gravitation does in the material world—combining, keeping things in their places, and maintaining a mutual dependence amongst the various parts of our system. It is for ever reminding us where we are and what we can do, not in fancy but in real life. It does not permit us to wait for dainty duties, pleasant to the imagination, but insists upon our doing those which are before us.

E. P. Whipple.

———◦◦———

Do to-day thy nearest duty.

Goethe.

———◦◦———

BEHOLD eighty-three years passed away! What cares! what agitation! what anxieties! what ill-will! what sad complications! and all without other result except great fatigue of body and mind, and disgust with regard to the past, and a profound sentiment of discouragement and despair with regard to the future.

Talleyrand, the night before he died.

———◦◦———

MANY of our cares are but a morbid way of looking at our privileges.

Walter Scott.

———◦◦———

THE world does not require so much to be informed as reminded.

Hannah More.

———◦◦———

WE live in an age when, as Pope said of that in which he wrote, "it is criminal to be moderate."

Hannah More.

———◦◦———

THEMISTOCLES declared that the trophies of Miltiades prevented him from sleeping.

Hannah More.

———◦◦———

THERE is no temptation so great as not to be tempted at all.

Hannah More.

WEALTH has now all the respect paid to it which is due only to virtue and to talent, but we can see what estimate God places upon it, since he often bestows it upon the meanest and most unworthy of all his creatures.

Dean Swift.

———◇◇———

THE apprehension of a misfortune or calamity may prove its cause. **Draper.**

———◇◇———

DOUBT is the accusing attorney in the Court of Truth.

Anon.

———◇◇———

WHERE is the crime of turning a few ounces of blood from their natural channels?

Hume on Suicide.

———◇◇———

THERE is some hope of a man's conversion so long as he is capable of loving something besides himself.

Charles Phillips.

———◇◇———

EVERY age, like the seed, is at one and the same time the product of combined influences of the past and the germ of life for the future. **McCosh.**

———◇◇———

POVERTY is the sixth sense.

German Proverb.

———◇◇———

HE is a wise man who always knows what to do next.

Proverb.

HANG it! how I like to be liked, and what I do to be liked!

Charles Lamb.

———◆◆———

ATHEISTIC liberty is the worst kind of tyranny.

Prof. C. E. Stone, D.D.

———◆◆———

RELIGION is the dream of the human soul.

Feuerbach.

———◆◆———

NOT only strike while the iron is hot, but make it hot by striking.

Cromwell

———◆◆———

WE should endeavor to forgive injuries and bury them in love.

Dr. Watts.

———◆◆———

PEOPLE who are so very good, and are never so much as justly angry and irritable, and don't stand up for themselves, them our Lord God soon takes to himself.

Walpurga.

———◆◆———

THE little dissatisfaction which every artist feels at the completion of a work forms the germ of a new work.

Auerbach.

———◆◆———

THERE is no beautiful intercourse unless one feels oneself regarded with favor.

Auerbach.

———◆◆———

LOVE me, and tell me so sometimes!

Gail Hamilton

———◆◆———

THE metaphor is a kind of syllogism.

Aristotle.

I DON'T believe that the way to make a man love heaven is to disgust him with earth. Let us love all that is bright and beautiful and good in this world.

Beecher.

WHATEVER is practically important to religion or morals may at all times be advanced and argued in the simplest terms of colloquial expression. From the pulpit, perhaps, no other style should at any time be heard, for the pulpit belongs to the poor and uninstructed.

Isaac Taylor.

TRUE liberty consists only in the power of doing what we ought to will, and in not being constrained to do what we ought not to will.

Jonathan Edwards.

THE union of believers to Christ, their common Head, and, by means of the influence they derive from him, their union to each other, may be illustrated by the *load-stone*. It not only attracts the particles of iron to itself by the magnetic virtue, but by this virtue it unites them one among another.

Dr. James Alexander.

THE stoutest timber stands on Norwegian rocks, where tempests rage, and long, hard winters reign. The muscles are seen most fully developed in the brawny arm that plies the hammer. Even so, the most vigorous and healthy piety is that which is ever active in a busy world, which has difficulties to battle with, which has its hands full of good works, which has neither time nor room for evil, but, aiming at great things for God and man, promptly dismisses temptation with Nehemiah's answer: "I have a great work to do, therefore, I cannot come down."

Bishop McIlvain.

PREACHING may be compared to lightning, of which it is said there are three kinds—the flash, the zigzag and the slant. The flash looks brilliant, lights up the sky, and people gaze at it with wonder. The zigzag is here, and there, and everywhere, darting from cloud to cloud without any apparent object or effect. But the slant sends the bolt right down to the earth, and rives the gnarled oak, and is mighty through God to the pulling down of strongholds.

Enoch Pond, D.D.

LITERATURE is the immortality of speech.

Schlegel.

I BELIEVE in heart-earnestness. Deep feeling is contagious. Words poured forth from burning hearts are sure to kindle the hearts of others. A tear-drop is a very little thing, and yet it is a thing of power. Hearts that can stand everything else are often melted by a tear. Let the heart palpitate in every line and burn in every word.

Enoch Pond, D.D.

A WATCH without a mainspring is no better than a rock for keeping time. So a man without religion, without a heart-purpose, a moving and a directing power, is not much in a life where nothing is so much needed as object-action. Our acts are selfish trifles, valueless ciphers, but when placed after Christ they become resistless.

Dr. Bethune.

WE have seen the Senator from Massachusetts occupy one whole day in picking these arrows out of his body, and to judge from the length and seriousness of his occupation, he might be supposed to have been stuck as full of them as the poor fellow whose transfixed effigy on the first leaf of our annual almanacs attracts the commiseration of many children.

Thomas H. Benton on Webster's Reply to Hayne.

———◦◦◦———

THERE are immense rocks—boulders—so nicely poised on a mere point that a little force will set them in motion, while the strength of many hands cannot bring them to rest. So the deepest emotions are often awakened by the most trivial occurrences. A word, a tone of voice, a smile, or a tear may move the soul from its rest, and nothing but His voice who calmed the sea of Galilee can again restore its serenity.

Archbishop Trench.

———◦◦◦———

POLITICAL convulsions, like geological upheavings, usher in new epochs of the world's progress.

Wendell Phillips.

———◦◦◦———

THE Union, like ancient Israel, may be symbolized by the burning bush that Moses saw encircled with flames yet unconsumed.

Boston Watchman and Reflector.

———◦◦◦———

WE seldom think how much we owe our first love.

Goethe.

———◦◦◦———

THE path of duty in this world is not all gloom or sadness or darkness. Like the roads of the South, it is hedged with everbloom, pure and white as snow. It is only when we turn to the right hand or the left that we are lacerated by piercing thorns and concealed dangers.

Rev. James Kerr

———◦◦◦———

THE conscious water saw its God and blushed.

Richard Crashaw

THERE are necessities in our hearts which nothing human can supply; passions, which nothing human can either satisfy or control; desires, which nothing human can either subdue or gratify; powers, which nothing human can either adequately excite or occupy; and oh, there are sorrows, deep sorrows, which will not be assuaged; wounds which, if the balm that is in Gilead cannot heal, must fester for evermore; sins, far beyond the reach of all skill but that of the great Physician of souls. Will you risk that skill, my brother? Will you ask him to remember Calvary, and then to pity you? This is his proposal which has gone out into all the world and the sound thereof to every creature. Dr. Breckinridge.

———◇———

THE severe competitions for subsistence and wealth which characterize every large city is a terrible ordeal for any human being to pass through. George Peabody.

———◇———

HE is wise who knows the sources of knowledge—who knows who has written and where it is to be found. Dr. A. A. Hodge.

———◇———

WE sometimes think the world is going back, but it is because we are going ahead too fast, just as things appear when we are whirling on in the cars. Dr. S. J. Wilson.

———◇———

THE public mind is educated quickly by *events*—slowly by *arguments*. N. Y. World.

———◇———

CONTINUANCE in sin but increases the probabilities of perpetuated impenitence. David H. Riddle, D.D.

THE reflex action of transgression on the mind is spiritual blindness, on the heart, spiritual hardness, and on the will, spiritual bondage.　　　　　　Rev. A. A. Hodge, D.D.

———◦◦◦———

EDUCATION is the cheap defence of nations.
　　　　　　Edmund Burke.

———◦◦◦———

AN obstinate man does not hold opinions, but they hold him; for when he is once possessed with an error, it is like a devil, only cast out with great difficulty. He delights most of all to differ in things indifferent. He is resolved to understand no man's reason but his own, because he finds no man can understand his but himself. His opinions are like plants that grow upon rocks, that stick fast though they have no rooting. The more inconsistent his views are, the faster he holds them, otherwise they would fall asunder of themselves; for opinions that are false ought to be held with more strictness than those that are true, otherwise they will be apt to betray their owners before they are aware.
　　　　　　Bishop Butler.

———◦◦◦———

MANNER eludes all seizure. There is no chemistry which can capture the singing of Patti, the acting of Jefferson, the reading of Dickens, the oratory of Gough, and pass them down in glass jars for the inspection of future ages.　　　　　　New York Independent.

———◦◦◦———

WENDELL PHILLIPS is an orator of calm, sparkling, conversational grace, of restrained intensity, of insuperable poise, of universal culture, who, showing the high art of achieving great results by the simplest means, conducts his audience not by a steady flame, but by a succession of lightning flashes; crowds long processes of reason-

ing into an epigram; abashes political selfishness by a classical jest; punctures stately reputations with the diamond
point of a fatal epithet; and, with no more apparent effort
than that of audible breathing, utters the word which becomes the battle-cry of an epoch.

New York Independent.

THEODORE PARKER was voracious rather than vera-
cious; often rude, and careless; often false, always unre-
liable. In denunciative eloquence, sarcasm and scorn and
abhorrence, he was certainly among the first of men. Nor
was he wanting in that nobler eloquence which makes the
beauties of the natural world its instruments, and stirs the
soul with sublime joys; or even in that other, higher yet,
which appeals directly to the moral nature, awakens its
intuitions and its passions and benevolent desires. But the
highest sphere of all seems to have been above his reach,
and those tender and solemn views of God and man which
come through the knowledge of the truth as it is in Jesus,
earnest as death, sweet and blessed as heaven, we do not
find in Mr. Parker's writings.

Bibliotheca Sacra.

A ROOM without pictures is like a room without windows. Pictures are loopholes of escape to the soul,
leading to other scenes and other spheres. Pictures are
consolers of loneliness; they are books, they are histories
and sermons, which we can read without the trouble of
turning over the leaves.

Downing.

FLOWERS are not trifles, as we might know from the
care God has taken of them everywhere. Not one un-
finished, not one bearing the marks of a brush or pencil.
Fringing the eternal borders of mountain ranges, gracing

10

the pulseless beat of the gray old granite, everywhere they are harmonizing. Murderers do not ordinarily wear roses in their buttonholes. Villains seldom train vines over their cottage doors. **Presbyterian Banner.**

MUSIC and flowers are evangels of purity and faith, redolent of God, if we but unlock our hearts to their ministry; and the man or woman who is impervious to their subtle, spiritualizing influences may feel assured that there is something essentially wrong in his or her organization or habits of life. **Augusta Evans.**

PHILOSOPHY is the science of realities.

Emerson.

THE great face was so sad, so earnest, so longing, so patient. There was a dignity not of earth in its mien, and in its countenance a benignity such as never anything human wore. It was stone, but it seemed sentient! If ever image of stone thought, it was thinking. It was looking toward the verge of the landscape, but looking at nothing—nothing but distance and vacancy. It was looking over and beyond everything of the present, and far into the past. It was gazing over the ocean of time, over lines of century-waves, which, farther and farther receding, closed nearer and nearer together, and blended at last into one unbroken tide, away toward the horizon of a remote antiquity. It was thinking of the wars of departed ages— of the empires it had seen created and destroyed—of the nations whose birth it had witnessed, whose progress it had watched, whose annihilation it had noted—of the joy and sorrow, the life and death, the grandeur and decay of five thousand slow revolving years. It was the type of an attribute of man—of a faculty of his heart and brain. It was Memory—Retrospection, wrought into visible, tangible form. All who know the pathos there is in memories of days that are accomplished and faces that have vanished, albeit only a trifling score of years gone by, will have some appreciation of the pathos that dwells in these grave eyes that look so steadfastly back upon the things they knew before History was born, before Tradition had being— things that were and forms that moved in a vague era that even Poetry and Romance scarce knew of—and passed one by one away, and left the stony dreamer solitary in the midst of a strange, new age and uncomprehended scenes! The Sphynx is grand in its loneliness—it is imposing in its magnitude, it is impressive in the mystery which hangs over its story. There is that in the overshadowing majesty of this eternal figure of stone, with its accusing memory of the deeds of all ages, that reveals to one something of what he shall feel when he stands at last in the awful presence of God. **Mark Twain's Description of the Sphynx.**

———•◦•———

THERE are recollections as pleasant as they are sacred and eternal. There are words and faces and places that never lose their hold upon the heart. They may be words that we seldom hear amid the whirl and competition of life, faces that we may never see on earth again, places that we are but seldom permitted to revisit; but they were once the scenes, the associates, the joy of our life; they had a controlling influence in training our aspirations and in shaping our destinies, and they can never be wholly forgotten. The flight of years cannot sully their innocence nor diminish their interest, and eternity will preserve them among the dearest reminiscences of earth. We may meet and love other faces, we may treasure other words we may have other joys, we may mingle in other scenes and form other associations, but these old familiar faces and these dear old familiar scenes remain invested with a fadeless beauty, sacred in their exemption from oblivion and decay.

Anon.

———•◦•———

MAY peace and harmony ever be with us, and may our great Ruler in heaven ever guide us.

A Benediction.

———•◦•———

You assume that I assume.

W. C. Falconer.

———•◦•———

RHETORICAL grace is to composition and delivery what female figures are to history-pictures. However exquisite the color-expression, heroical the forms and full of majestic action, the result will but feebly interest the hearts of mankind if the rays of beauty do not irradiate at least some portion of the scene. But there is danger of being too uniformly placid and smooth. Writers on art have observed that roughness, in its different modes and degrees, is the ornament, the fringe of beauty, that which gives it life and spirit, and preserves it from baldness and insipidity. If the shaft of a column is smooth, the more ornamental part, the capital, is rough; the facing of the smoothest building has a frieze and cornice, rough and abruptly projecting; it is the same in vases and in everything that admits of ornament. Hence, Dryden, when describing the cup that contained the heart of Guiscard, calls it a "goblet rich with gems and rough with gold." The permanent attraction of an oration, like that of a temple or landscape, depends upon the happy union of warm and cool tints, of smooth parts and rough—picturesque and severely graceful, solemn and gay. The most striking effects are produced by bringing together features totally opposite to each other, but these must be skillfully arranged, and blended in various degrees, in order to produce that charm of combination which is manifest in the consummate works of art and nature. Beauty and force coalesce in true eloquence and glow with wholesome strength, like the masculine cheek of Minerva tinged with maidenly modesty.

Living Orators of America, Magoon.

AS Scott absorbed the crude minstrelsy of Scotland, and reproduced national songs and legends under a fairer, sweeter form, so Homer, grand old blind eclectic, gathered the fragmentary myths of heroic ages, and clothing them with the melody of wandering Greek rhapsodists, gave the world his wonderful epic—the first and last specimen of composite poetic architecture.

Augusta Evans, Macaria.

OUR determination to carry on this war for the Union is as deep as the sea, as firm as the mountains and calm as the heavens above us.

Beecher.

TO give pain is the tyranny—to make happy, the true empire of beauty.

Spectator.

THE most terrific thing in the world is sin. A man is never hurt until his soul is hurt, and the only thing that can hurt his soul is sin.

William Plumer, D.D.

GRATITUDE is the memory of the heart.

N. P. Will.

THE least error should humble, but we should never permit even the greatest to discourage us.

Bishop Potter.

————◆◆————

THE little molecule whose vibrations have given rise to the universe is the Logos of St. John's Gospel!

Prof. De Morgan.

————◆◆————

THE bullion we obtain at the college or seminary, in the way of a system of thought or theology, has to be coined for circulation and use. We must popularize what we know in order to reach the masses.

S. J. Wilson, D.D.

————◆◆————

IMMENSITY is made up of atoms.

Leibnitz.

————◆◆————

HE stands at an acute angle with the rest of the world.

Holmes.

————◆◆————

THE sterner powers called into play when our hopes have been blasted and our expectations disappointed are like the allies summoned to the rescue of a nation in driving out the enemy, they find a settlement for themselves.

Bulwer.

————◆◆————

PROVERBS are the cream of a nation's thought.

Anon.

————◆◆————

A LIVING statesman has not ill summed up life when he wrote: "Youth is a blunder, manhood a struggle, old age a regret."

Independent.

————◆◆————

THINGS were worse at Arcola.

Napoleon.

OUR National Convention is above all imitation, as above all authority; it is accountable but to itself, and can be judged but by posterity. Gentleman, you all remember the remark of that Roman, who, to save his country from a dreadful conspiracy, had overstepped the powers conferred on him by the laws: Swear, said a captious demagogue of that day, that you have observed the *laws.* I swear, replied this great man, that I have saved the *republic!* Gentleman, I swear that though you have broken the *laws,* you have saved the *commonwealth!*

Mirabeau.

———◦◦◦———

IT is by cannon-balls that the Convention must be made known to our enemies.

Danton.

———◦◦◦———

A NATION in a state of revolution is like the brass which simmers and sublimates itself in the crucible. The statue of Liberty is not yet cast, but the metal is boiling!

Danton.

———◦◦◦———

WHEN a people passes from a monarchical to a republican form of government, it is carried beyond the end by the projectile force it has given itself, and *vice versâ.*

Danton.

———◦◦◦———

GO say to the First Consul that I die with the regret of having done too little for posterity.

Dessaix.

———◦◦◦———

WE advanced to Waterloo as the Greeks did to Thermopylae—all of us without fear, and most of us without hope.

General Foy.

"IF I tremble, it is from cold," exclaimed the mathematician Bailly when led to the scaffold.

———◦◦———

LOVE is a plant of strange growth—now lifting its head feebly in rich, sunny spots, where every fostering influence is employed, and now springing vigorous from barren, rocky cliffs, clinging in icy crevices, defying adverse elements, sending its fibrous roots deeper and deeper in uncongenial soil, bending before the fierce breath of storms only to erect itself more firmly, spreading its delicate petals over the edge of eternal snow—self-sustaining, invincible, immortal.   Augusta Evans.

———◦◦———

LOVE has a thousand modes and forms, all of which may be consistent with reality and truth.   It may come like the burst of morning light, kindling the whole soul into new life and radiance; it may grow inaudibly and unknown, until its roots are found to be through and through the heart, entwined with its every fibre; it is unreal and false only when it is a name for some form of selfishness.
                                                        Peter Bayne.

———◦◦———

NATURE is fine in love; and, where 'tis fine,
    It sends some precious instance of itself
After the thing it loves.   Shakespeare.

———◦◦———

BASE men, being in love, have then a nobility in their natures more than is native to them.
                                                        Shakespeare.

———◦◦———

MAN'S love is of man's life a thing apart:
    'Tis woman's whole existence.
                                        Byron.

A MAN of sense may love like a madman, but never like a fool.

La Rochefoucault.

———◦◦◦———

LOVERS break not hours,
Unless it be to come before their time;
So much they spur their expedition.

Shakespeare.

———◦◦◦———

THERE'S beggary in the love that can be reckoned.

Shakespeare.

———◦◦◦———

WHEN love begins to sicken and decay,
It useth an enforced ceremony.

Shakespeare.

———◦◦◦———

IN jealousy there is more self-love than love.

La Rochefoucault.

———◦◦◦———

O LOVE! no 'habitant of earth thou art—
An unseen seraph, we believe in thee;
A faith whose martyrs are the broken heart.

Byron.

———◦◦◦———

THE molecule of oxygen roams lonely through the vast universe yearning for its mate, and finding no rest till, of a sudden, it meets the molecule of hydrogen in a quiet nook; when lo! a rush, an embrace, and then no more either oxygen or hydrogen, but a diamond drop of dew sparkling on the white bosom of the lily.

Gail Hamilton.

———◦◦◦———

IT was not song that taught me love,
But it was love that taught me song.

L. E. L.

LOVE, amid the other graces in this world, is like a cathedral tower, which begins on the earth, and at first is surrounded by the other parts of the structure. But at length, rising above buttressed walls, and arch, and parapet, and pinnacle, it shoots spire-like many a foot right into the air—so high that the huge cross on its summit glows like a spark in the morning light, and shines like a star in the evening sky, when the rest of the pile is enveloped in darkness. So love, here, is surrounded by the other graces, and divides the honors with them; but they will have felt the wrap of night and of darkness, where *it* will shine luminous against the sky of eternity. Beecher.

SAY never, ye loved *once.*
  God is too near above, the grave below,
And all our moments go
Too quickly past our souls, for saying so.
The mysteries of life and death avenge
Affections light of range:
There comes no change to justify that change.
Elizabeth B. Browning.

LOVE is not love
Which alters when it alteration finds,
Or bends with the remover, to remove.
Oh no! It is an ever-fixéd mark,
That looks on tempests and is never shaken.
Shakespeare

LOVE weepeth always—weepeth for the past,
  For woes that are, for woes that may betide:
Why should not hard ambition weep at last,
  Envy and hatred, avarice and pride?
Tennyson

O MYSTERY of Love, whose simplest signs
  Are hieroglyphics of another tongue
Love only can interpret, from a babe's
First smile of joyance at its mother's voice,
To the warm, ruddy glow of frostless age;
A web of heavenly warp and earthly woof;
Affections twined and intertwined; gold threads
Woven, unwoven and again rewove;
Links riveted, and loosened, and relinked,
Imperishable all—what shall I say?
How speak of thee in language worthy thee?
My spirit is willing, but my flesh is weak.
I see thee through a glass but darkly—beams
From the great Fontal Orb of love, which shone
Ere the foundations of the heavens were laid,
Self-luminous, self-centred, self-contain'd
In its own increate immensity.
Perfect, incomprehensible Triune;
But which in fullness of the age of ages
Brake effluent forth, the exuberance of life
Creative, till the universe of things
Rose underneath the hand of God, instinct
With his own nature, sinless, undefiled;
And when, foreseen, but not the less abhorr'd,
Evil arose from good, and cast its pall,
The pall of death, over the birth of life,
Which, not one ray of glory quench'd or dimm'd,
Ceased not to shine, immutably the same,
Through clouds of judgment and quick flames of wrath
On worlds perplexed with tempest.
> "Yesterday, To-day and For Ever."—Bickersteth

———◦◇◦———

PURE love ought to burn like oxygen in oxygen.
> John Foster.

LOVE is first inspired by magnetism that has a locked door. It is what women withhold in the coloring of a thought or the tone of a voice, the glance of an eye or the pressure of a hand, which ties the bandage over the first sentiment, and turns it into a Cupid.

N. P. Willis.

——◦◦◦——

IF I leave all for thee, wilt thou exchange
And be all to me? Shall I never miss
Home-talk and blessing and the common kiss
That comes to each in turn, nor count it strange
When I look up, to drop on a new range
Of walls and floors—another home than this?
Nay, wilt thou fill that place by me which is
Filled by dead eyes too tender to know change?
That's hardest. If to conquer love, has tried
To conquer grief, tries more, as all things prove,
For grief, indeed, is love and grief besides,
Alas I have grieved so, I am hard to love,
Yet love me, wilt thou? Open thine heart wide
And fold within the wet wings of thy dove!

Mrs. Browning, Sonnet from the Portuguese

——◦◦◦——

SHE scarce can tell if she had loved or not;
She of her heart no register has kept;
She knows but this, that once too blest her lot
Appeared for earth, and that ere long she wept.

Upon life's daily task without pretence
She moves, and many love her, all revere;
She will be full of joy when summoned hence,
Yet not unhappy while lingering here.

If once her breast the storms of anguish tore,
   On that pure lake no weeds or scum they cast:
Time has taken from her much, but given her more,
   And of her gifts the best will be the last.

Her heart is as a spot of hallowed ground,
   Filled with old tombs and stones to the past,
Such as near villages remote is found,
   Or rain-washed chancel, in some woodland waste.

It once was pierced each day with some new stone,
   And thronged with weeping women and sad men,
But now it lies with grass and flowers o'ergrown,
   And o'er it pipes the thrush and builds the wren.

Aubrey de Vere.

———◦◦◦———

L IKE an island in a river
   Art thou, my love, to me,
And I journey by thee ever,
   With a gentle ecstasy.

Bailey's Festus

———◦◦◦———

A S we generally hate those whom we have injured more
than we do those who injure us, so a lady feels more
indifferent toward those gentlemen whom she has rejected
than toward those who have rejected her.

N. P. Willis

———◦◦◦———

L IBERTY will not descend to a people: a people must
raise themselves to liberty. It is a blessing to be
earned before it can be enjoyed.

Tilton.

———◦◦◦———

P ERCEIVING that money can now do anything, men
are prepared to do everything for money.

Orpheus C. Kerr.

THESE longing eyes may never more behold thee,
   These yearning arms may never more enfold thee;
To my sad heart I never more may press thee,
But day and night I never cease to bless thee.

I do not envy those who may be near thee,
Who have that joy supreme, who see thee, hear thee·
I bless them also, knowing they too love thee,
And that they prize no earthly thing above thee.

I do not even hope again to meet thee,
I never dare to think how I should greet thee;
Low in the dust should I fall before thee,
And, kneeling there, for pardon should implore thee.

Alas! 'twould be a sin to kneel before thee—
A sin to let thee know I *still* adore thee,
I kneel and pray that Heaven may bless and guide thee;
Love of my life! to Heaven's care I confide thee.

                          Blackwood's Magazine.

———◦◦———

AH me! for aught that ever I could read,
   Could ever hear by tale or history,
The course of true love never did run smooth;
But either it was different in blood,
Or else misgraffed in respect to years,
Or else it stood upon the choice of friends,
Or, if there were a sympathy in choice,
War, death, or sickness did lay siege to it,
Making it momentary as a sound,
Swift as a shadow, short as any dream;
Brief as the lightning in the collied night,
That, in a spleen, unfolds both heaven and earth,
And ere a man hath power to say, Behold!
The jaws of darkness do devour it up;
So quick bright things come to confusion.

                          Midsummer Night's Dream.

A WOMAN'S love is essentially lonely and spiritual in its nature. It is the heathenism of the heart. She herself has created the glory and beauty with which the idol of her heart stands invested.   L. E. L.

————◦◦————

YOU, O man! who with your honey words and your tender looks steal away a young girl's heart, for thoughtless or selfish vanity, do you know what it is you do? Do you know what it is to turn the precious fountain of woman's first love into a very Marah, whose bitterness may pervade her whole life's current, crushing her, if humble, beneath the torture of self-contempt, or, if proud, making her cold, heartless, revengeful, quick to wound others as she herself has been wounded? And if she marry, what is her fate? She has lost that instinctive worship of what is noble in man, which causes a woman gladly to follow out the righteous altar-vow, and in "honoring" and "obeying" her husband to create the sunshine of her home; and this is caused by your deed! Is not such deed a sin? Ay, almost second to that deadly one which ruins life and fame, body and soul! Yet man does both toward woman, and goes smiling amidst the world, which smiles at him again.   The Ogfevies.

————◦◦————

THE process by which the image of God is thus imprinted on the soul and wrought into it is not like that which produces a photograph, struck off in a moment, impressed on perishable materials and laid in fading colors, but like that by which a great sculptor, slowly and by an infinite succession of touches, calls out of the solid marble a form of faultless grace and beauty—the tedious work of years indeed, but worth all the labor, for it is to be immortal.
                    Theological Ec'ectic.

MARRIAGE is not a union merely between two crea tures—it is a union between two spirits; and the intention of that bond is to perfect the nature of both, by supplementing their deficiencies with the force of contrast, giving to each sex those excellences in which it is naturally deficient; to the one, strength of character and firmness of moral will; to the other, sympathy, meekness, tenderness; and just so solemn and just so glorious as these ends are for which the union was contemplated and intended, just so terrible are the consequences if it be perverted and abused; for there is no earthly relationship which has so much power to ennoble and to exalt. There are two rocks, in this world of ours, on which the soul must either anchor or be wrecked—the one is God, and the other is the sex opposite.

F. W. Robertson.

————◆◆————

SHE was to make a brilliant match, whatever that may mean. One thing, however, it does not mean; to make a brilliant match is not another form of expression for marrying the man or woman you love. A brilliant match has become an arrangement not a feeling. It is the conjunction of Jupiter with his moons and Venus, the evening star. Mars may wax red with rage and weeping, and Pallas hide her face in the friendly night, but the brilliant match must be made. With all his moons Jupiter must endow his bride, and the sweet evening star never know what a life she has lost.

Harper's Magazine.

————◆◆————

WATCHED rose buds open slowly.

Proverb.

————◆◆————

THE dying never weep.

Proverb.

MODERN preaching has become a professional solemnity on the one hand, and a respectful non-attention on the other.

Dr. Hamilton of London.

———◦◦———

IF I had a thousand hearts, I would give them all to Jesus.

Rev. Frank Collier.

———◦◦———

IT was not the mere bodily death that Christ conquered: that death had no sting. It was the spiritual death which he conquered, so that at last it should be swallowed up—mark the word, not in life, but in victory. As the dead body shall be raised to life, so also the defeated soul to victory, if only it has been fighting on its Master's side—has made no covenant with death. Blind from the prison-house, maimed from the battle or mad from the tomb, these souls shall surely sit, astonished, at His feet who giveth his people peace and rest.

Ruskin.

———◦◦———

WE have an anticipation of the resurrection—of the liberation of humanity to its true ideal in statuary and painting—arts which would be without any true import if the dogma of the resurrection of the body had no reality, and if they could not be looked upon as a presage of a higher reality, which they shadow forth only in picture or in form.

Bishop Martensen

———◦◦———

ARE there not lofty moments when the soul
 Leaps to the front of being, casting off
The robes and clumsy instruments of sense,
And, pastured in its immortality,
Reveals its independence of the clod
In which it dwells?

Holland's Katharine

ARTISTS are nearest God.   Into their souls
He breathes his life, and from their hands it comes
In fair, articulate forms to bless the world.

Holland's Katharine.

WAR passes the power of all chemical solvents, break
ing up the old cohesions and allowing the atoms of
society to take a new order.

Emerson.

IT is a rule in games of chance that "the cards beat all
the players," and revolutions disconcert and outwit all
the insurgents.

Emerson.

LUXURY is the first, second and third cause of the ruin
of republics.   It is the vampyre which soothes us into
a fatal slumber while it sucks the life-blood of our veins.
It is coming upon us.   Already may we hear the roaring
of the surge; already do we begin to circle round the vortex
which is soon to engulf us.   Yet we see no danger.   In
vain does experience offer us the experience of past ages for
our direction; in vain does the genius of History spread her
chart, and point out the ruins to which we are advancing;
in vain do the ghosts of departed governments, lingering
rounds the rocks on which they perished, warn us of our
approaching fate.   In spite of past experience, we flatter
ourselves that the same causes which have proved fatal to
all other governments will lose their pernicious tendency
when exerted on our own.

Edward Payson.

CONFOUND the solar system!   It is too far off, don't give
enough of light, is bothered with comets and equinoxes.

S'dney Smith.

IF Adam fell in the days of innocency,
How could you expect Falstaff to stand
In the days of villainy?

Shakespeare

———◦◦———

THAT on the fountain of my heart a seal
Is set to keep its waters pure and bright
For thee.

Shelby

———◦◦———

WHO swerves from innocence, who makes divorce
Of that serene companion, a good name,
Recovers not his loss; but walks with shame,
With doubt, with fear, and haply with remorse.

Wordsworth.

———◦◦———

IF there is anything better than to be loved, it is loving.

Anon.

———◦◦———

BEFORE I will do it, I will stay here until the moss
grows over my eyes.

John Bunyan.

———◦◦———

THEN was I in a strait, and did not see
What was the best thing to be done by me.

John Bunyan.

———◦◦———

PLATE sin with gold, and the strong lance of
Justice hurtless breaks—
Arm it in rags, a pigmy's straw doth pierce it.

Shakespeare.

———◦◦———

EVERY man who rises in any profession must tread a
path more or less bedewed by the tears of those he
passes on his way.

Bayne.

WE hear much now about circumstances making us what we are and destroying our responsibility; but however much the external circumstances in which we are placed, the temptations to which we are exposed, the desires of our own nature, may work upon us, all these influences have a limit, which they do not pass, and that is the limit laid upon them by the freedom of the will, which is essential to human nature—to our personality.

Luthardt.

———◇———

LANGUAGE is the close-fitting dress of thought.

Trench.

———◇———

A FORCE as of madness in the hands of reason has done all that was ever done in the world.

Carlyle.

———◇———

THE human heart refuses to believe in a universe without a purpose.

Kant.

———◇———

WE can find nothing more in a study than we bring to the study of it.

Prof. Fraser.

———◇———

EXPRESSION is the mystery of beauty.

Bulwer.

———◇———

BE calm in arguing, for fierceness makes
　Error a fault and truth discourtesy.
Why should I feel another man's mistakes
More than his sickness or his poverty?
In love I should, but anger is not love,
Nor wisdom neither; therefore gently move.

George Herbert

I CARE but little for the dogmas of any particular church, for they are often but superficial prejudices, which men of all denominations throw aside in intercourse with their Christian brethren, joining in love and work for Christ, and in the obeying of his commandments, which are simple and easily comprehended.

Miss L. L. F.

———◦◦———

THEY sin who tell us love can die.

Southey.

———◦◦———

IT is a perilous undertaking to substitute *doctrines* for *duties*.

McKenzie.

———◦◦———

MEN who work among iron and brass, go to work for God.

K. A. Burnell to the Citizens of Pittsburg.

———◦◦———

TO have a virtuous heart, is to have a heart that favors virtue and is friendly to it, and not one perfectly cold and indifferent about it.

Edwards on the Will.

———◦◦———

IF the laws of motion and gravitation laid down by Sir Isaac Newton hold universally, there is not one atom, nor the least assignable part of an atom, but what has influence, every moment, throughout the whole material universe, to cause every part to be otherwise than it would be if it were not for that particular corporeal existence; and however the effect is insensible for the present, yet it may, in length of time, become great and important.

Edwards on the Will.

———◦◦———

WE ought to take up the name Jesus and pass it like a cry of fire through the streets.

M. W. Jacobus, D.D.

LET us not despair of saving men addicted to strong drink. Drink is strong, but Christ is stronger than strong drink!

D. L. Moody.

———◇◇———

THERE are men who tread all the way to hell on the blood of Jesus.

Rev. Strong of Cleveland.

———◇◇———

THE world bears the same relation to the universe as a grain of sand does to a mountain. It is only the death of Christ that has given it such an exalted position.

Bishop Martensen.

———◇◇———

IT is much harder to make a spiritual impression on a family you visit and to convince them you are a child of God, with a heart overflowing with sympathy and penitence and love, than it is to write brilliant sermons.

K. A. Burnell to Students of West. Theol. Sem.

———◇◇———

THE best of men and the most earnest workers will make enough of mistakes to keep them humble. Thank God for mistakes and take courage. Don't give up on account of mistakes.

D. L. Moody.

———◇◇———

MEN'S weaknesses and faults are known from their enemies, their virtues and abilities from their friends, their customs and lives from their servants.

Anon.

———◇◇———

THE preservation of the ministry in the face and in the midst of so many trials, difficulties and discouragements, in the midst of grief, perplexity, hardship and sorrow, is one of the most convincing proofs of the divinity of the Christian religion.

Rev. Dr Dickson of Baltimore

WHAT is meant by a "knowledge of the world" is simply an acquaintance with the infirmities of men.

Dickens.

———◦◦———

FOR all may have,
If they dare choose, a glorious life or grave.

George Herbert.

———◦◦———

ACCORDING to the Catholics, the apostolate is continued in the episcopate, through tradition; and the episcopate is centralized in the primacy. They contend more for the guarantees of Christianity than for Christianity itself.

Bishop Martensen.

———◦◦———

JUPITER made a lottery in heaven, to which mortals as well as gods were allowed to have tickets. The prize was *wisdom*, and Minerva got it. The mortals murmured, and accused the gods of foul play. Jupiter, to wipe off this aspersion, declared another lottery for mortals singly and exclusive of the gods. The prize was *folly*. They got it and shared it among themselves. All were satisfied. The loss of wisdom was neither regretted nor remembered—folly supplied its place, and those who had the largest share of it thought themselves the wisest.

Monsieur de la Motte.

———◦◦———

TO learn to speak off-hand in public, speak in your own room, privately, ten minutes every day, on some subject, to yourself. Don't experiment in public. It is an awful infliction.

Dr. Newman Hall.

———◦◦———

WE must for ever bow before the eternal mystery of God, and there praise and adore!

Saisset—Modern Pantheism.

DESCARTES speaks of a God whose omnipotence is so absolute as not only to make *beings*, but *truths*, at his will. No! exclaims Malebranche, the will of God is regulated by his goodness and wisdom. Here is Newton, who represents God as spread over duration and space, limiting his so-called fecundity to scattering across the infinite plains of immensity some atoms, whose frail economy is every instant threatened with dissolution. Leibnitz protests against this, and maintains that God is outside time and space, and that without falling into time, he fills spaces and ages with the fulgurations of his infinite power. Spinosa rejects all this, and says all things are of one substance: God is everything and everything is God. Then, says Kant, as two things only abide in the sciences, the facts of visible nature and the laws of thought, and as all metaphysical theories are changing and unsatisfactory, let us for ever suppress *things*, *being*, the *object*, and let us reduce science to the one, the human mind, the subject. To eliminate the objective for ever as absolutely inaccessible, and to resolve all into the subjective, this is the end, and here are the great lines of Kant's endeavors. His system is a system of mental abstractions—categories—which are but poorly confirmed by the facts of consciousness.

Saisset—Modern Pantheism.

———•◦•———

GOD becomes incarnate in man, but how is this taught to the Christian? Is it afforded to his reason to understand, or to his faith to adore? The Word made flesh is, we are told, a mystery—the great mystery. It is, in fact, the expressive mystery, for God made man, is the Eternal fallen into time, the Absolute become relative, the Infinite, finite. This is the common foundation of all religion, and the eternal despair of all philosophy.

Saisset—Modern Pantheism.

INTELLIGENCE is displayed in the whole universe. It is manifested among inferior beings by the laws which direct them unknown to themselves. It begins to work in the plants like a dim glimmer of life. It has the sentiment of itself in the beast. In man, finally, *it knows itself*, it possesses itself—it shines and is resplendent. But even in man it acknowledges itself subject to the law of development and change, to ignorance, to error, to endeavor, and is consequently incapable of existing or subsisting by itself. There is then above nature and man a first principle of intelligence, and this principle must be intelligent, otherwise there would be less in the cause than in the effect, which would be inadmissible. All that is positive and real in the effect can only come from its cause. Properly, there belong to the effect only limits and relatives. Now there is nothing more real, more positive or more clear than intelligence. God is, therefore, absolute intelligence, perfect thought, truth in itself.

Saisset—Modern Pantheism.

IT is two thousand years since Heraclitus said with graceful melancholy: "We cannot bathe twice in the same stream: everything becomes—nothing remains." Soon after came Pyrrho, who completed thus the formula of Heraclitus: "There is nothing that is more false than true, more beautiful than ugly, more good than bad"—all is relative. But no; all is not relative, all is not given up to change. There is one truth that remains, and that living truth is God.

Saisset—Modern Pantheism.

I REFLECT within myself and say: "Why and whence comes it that I must always think of God? I exist, I live—existence and life are dear to me. I find around me a thousand objects which please and interest. What need

I more to fill my soul? and why do I seek something beyond? Why? Because I feel but too well that I am imperfect and set in the midst of imperfection. When I consider my being, I see it pass away like a rapid stream. My ideas, my sensations, my desires, all change every hour, and, in the same way around me, there is no being that is not passing from motion to repose, from progress to decay, from life to death. Amid these vicissitudes, like a wave borne on by other waves, I roll in the immense torrent that bears all things to the unknown shore. This change, this perpetual change, is the universal law in my condition. I find myself confined in a corner of space and time, and with all my restless efforts I can only lay hold of the few objects that are within my grasp. With all my thinking, I can only seize a few truths. Whilst I am endeavoring, across the waves of time, to gather the broken fragments of my life and to develop imperfectly some of my powers, God, the self-sufficing and all-perfect One, concentrated in an immutable present, employs the absolute plentitude of his existence in its eternal expansion. This idea of the *Perfect Being* charms me. How vast, how sublime it is! but is it not too far from me? On the contrary, it is as near as possible. Plunged in the whirl of passing things, I may for an instant be seduced by their charms. I may, falling in love with myself, be sometimes dazzled and intoxicated with a feeling of my own strength, but it is because I only look at the surface of things. As soon as I return to myself, as soon as I examine the depths of my nature, I am terrified at the weakness, the inconsistency, the incurable fragility of my being, and I feel that it would vanish away if it were not supported by the true Being.

Saisset—Modern Pantheism.

———◇◇◇———

GRIEF most grieving is most blest.

Anon

WHEN Pantheism calls the Omnipotent Creator of heaven and earth a limited being, it forgets that the limitation in question, so far as it deserves the name, is self-limitation, and that self-limitation is inseparable from a perfect nature. The existence of created beings distinct from God is not such a limit as to clash with the idea of a Perfect Being.

Martensen.

THE Spinozists and Hegelians excel in bringing out the difficulties of a God distinct from the world, but it is a sufficient reply to say, that the all-perfect Being, God, limits his own power by calling into existence out of the depths of his own eternal life a world of created beings, to whom he gives, in a derivative manner, to have life in themselves.

Martensen.

THE philosophic mind is ever compelled to seek a reason for the realities of the world.

Martensen.

I BELIEVE in the resurrection of the memory, as well as of the body.

Dr. A. A. Hodge.

THE nothing of which God creates the world are the eternal possibilities of his will, which are the sources of all the actualities of the world. But as God can only have power over the possibilities of his being, so far as he is open and manifest to himself, and as these eternal possibilities are only known to him in the Son, the proposition that God creates the world only of nothing is inseparable from the other proposition, that he creates the world through the Son.

Martensen.

WE must go *head*-foremost toward the world, but *heart* foremost toward God.

J. W. Scott, D.D.

————◇————

'TIS well to have a theory, and
   Sit in the centre of it.

Holland's Katharina.

————◇————

THE goodness of God is seen even in the rude winds whistling a tune not unpleasant, and the tossing seas yielding a kind of solemn and grave melody.

Barrows.

————◇————

WE live in the consequences of past action.

Dr. A. A. Hodge.

————◇————

GEOLOGY gives us a key to the patience of God.

Holland.

————◇————

HOW would you like to have it said of you, when you get to heaven: This one was saved easily. He did not suffer much. He spent nothing for Jesus.

Dr. A. A. Hodge.

————◇————

WOMAN has been faithful in a few things. Now God is going to make her ruler over many things.

Susan B. Anthony.

————◇————

TO have the deep poetic heart
   Is more than all poetic fame.

Anon.

————◇————

SHAKESPEARE describes the bees as,
   "Those singing masons, building roofs of gold."

————◇————

THE world *does* move.

Galileo.

LIBERTY is tranquil because she is invincible, and invincible because she is contagious. Whoever attacks, gains her. The army sent against her rebounds upon the despot. That is why she is left in peace.

Victor Hugo.

———◇◆◇———

TRUTH, crushed to earth, shall rise again:
The eternal years of God are hers;
But Error, wounded, writhes with pain,
And dies amid his worshipers.

Bryant.

———◇◆◇———

SLANDER meets no regard from noble minds;
Only the base believe what the base only utter.

Anon.

———◇◆◇———

PROTESTANTISM is Christianity renouncing human authority, and asserting the supremacy of our Lord and Saviour Jesus Christ. It is Christianity reasserting its simplicity and purity—divesting itself of the burdens and corruptions imposed upon it by man. It is Christianity declaring the firm and paramount authority of the Word of God above the dictates of man, either individual or combined. It is Christianity indivisible, immutable, throwing off, discarding, denouncing the traditions and commandments of men, which are foreign to its own nature, though parting with nothing unsuited to its own integrity, but rejecting everything not enjoined by the sanctions of Christ himself in his unalterable word.

Rev. Dr. Adams of N. Y.

———◇◆◇———

THERE are greater things to be done in the future than in the past.

Rev. Dr. Adams of N. Y.

THERE is nothing so easy, nor in the long run so successful, as a simple, straightforward adherence to principle.   Measures and expediencies constantly go out of date. While their day lasts they are to be brought to the test of principles.   When the exigency that suggested them is past, they fall away like leaves in autumn; but the trees remain for ages, putting forth fresh foliage, each after its kind, with every returning season.   We can never restore greenness to withered leaves, but we can protect the tree whose **vitalizing sap** will in time send out a new crop.

N. Y. World.

----—◦◦◦—----

CREEDS are now the *masters*, not the *servants* of thought.

Essays and Reviews.

----—◦◦◦—----

MINDS of moderate calibre ordinarily condemn everything which is beyond their range.

La Rochefoucault.

----—◦◦◦—----

IN proportion as nations get more corrupt, more disgrace will attach to poverty and more respect to wealth.

Colton.

----—◦◦◦—----

OH beware of jealousy;
It is the green-eyed monster, which doth mock
The meat it feeds on.   Shakespeare.

----—◦◦◦—----

TO honor God, to benefit mankind,
   To serve with lofty gifts the lowly needs
Of the poor race for which the God-man died,
And do it all for love—oh this is great!
And he who does this will achieve a name
Not only great but good.

Holland's Katharira.

IF time supposes change, and if change supposes change-able beings, creatures whose successive conditions give birth to the present, the past and the future, it follows that when thought does away with creatures, it destroys time with the same blow. Therefore, to imagine a certain time which has preceded the world—that is to say, which has existed before the collection of creatures—is a contra-dictory idea; and to ask what God was doing before the creation of the world is a meaningless question, since the voids before the world suppose a time anterior to the world, that is to say, a time independent of every creature and of all change, which means a void time, a time in which there is neither present, past nor future, which is a palpable contradiction. In like manner, to say that the world and time are coeternal with God is to make use of unintelligi-ble language, for between the world and time, which, by their nature, change and pass, and God, who is an immu-table being, there is a radical opposition. Therefore, we must say with Plato, that the world and time were created together by the Eternal Architect. God precedes the world, not by a priority of time, for that would make him analo-gous to time by a priority of nature and of essence.

Saisset.

IT is when God's glory is reflected back to him, not merely from a kingdom of ideas, but from a kingdom of actual spirits, a kingdom of souls, all united together under Christ, and all witnesses, not merely of the eternal power and god-head of God, but also of his saving grace, and then only, that the divine blessedness becomes in the full sense perfect. It then for the first time becomes perfect, in so far as it is the will of God not merely to rest in his eternal majesty, for in this the Triune God was able to rest independently of the world before the foundations of the world were laid :

but to rest and be blessed in the completed work of grace and love, in the glorious liberty of the children of God—a good which will not be reached until, in the words of the Apostle Paul, "God shall be all in all." Then first, in the new economy, in the new heavens and the new earth, will the glory of the Triune God be perfectly revealed—the glory which is reflected from his perfect communication of love to the creature.   Martensen.

———◦◇◦———

WHAT is truth? What is truth? Why, God and his glorious attributes, Christ and his finished work, the Holy Spirit with his sanctifying and comforting power, the divinity and indestructibility of the revealed word of God, the aim and achievements of Christianity, the peril of the ungodly and the eternal safety of every believer in Christ, however humble! This is truth, which can never be shaken nor overthrown.   Pittsburg Evening Chronicle.

———◦◇◦———

THAT is the theology best suited to the age which is put forth by living men of the age, drinking of the living Word for themselves by the power of the living Spirit.
                                                    McCosh.

———◦◇◦———

ALL things are artificial, for nature is the art of God.
                                              Sir Thomas Browne.

———◦◇◦———

GIANTS in the closet are often but pigmies in the world.
                                                    Plumer.

———◦◇◦———

IF a man has any brains at all, let him hold on to his calling and drift with the current of existence, and in the grand sweep of things his turn will come at last.
                                              Walter McCune, Esq.

DEEP in our hidden heart
Festers the dull remembrance of a change,
But no emotion.

Anon.

———◇———

THE "Grecian Bend" is not so beautiful for woman as
the bend over the wash-tub, the spindle, the cradle, and
the bend at the altar of prayer.

Western Paper.

———◇———

To be womanly is the greatest charm of woman.

Gladstone

———◇———

Most of us would rather dress good than be good.

Pittsburg Evening Mail.

———◇———

WHAT scholar has not passages in his favorite authors
which he understands better than all the commentators.

Prof. March, Lafayette College.

———◇———

OUR government is a representative democracy. We call
it a government of the people—it is really a government of the majority. In our day, tyranny of the majority
is worse than the tyranny of one man or a few men, because it has no restraint.

Prof. March, Lafayette College.

———◇———

It is not the poet alone who is born.

Prof. March, Lafayette College.

———◇———

ALL imagination, properly so called, proclaims the activity of the æsthetic emotions.

Prof. March, Lafayette College.

AN eminent educator has enforced his doctrine of "power-culture" by saying that Napoleon might have summoned all the force of his mighty mind and struck out at a blow a new system of mental philosophy! But such blows are never struck. Truth is not conquered; it is read. It comes to earnest, humble seekers.

Prof. March, Lafayette College.

———◦◦◦———

THE scholar in these times should believe all he can.

Prof. March, Lafayette College.

———◦◦◦———

SHAKESPEARE's fools are the "smartest" men in his plays.

Prof. March, Lafayette College.

———◦◦◦———

THE great thinker is seldom a disputant. He answers other men's arguments by stating the truth as he sees it.

Prof. March, Lafayette College

———◦◦◦———

WHEN we have been years out of college, we find that it is not the struggles of the recitation-room or the society-hall, perhaps, that make the epochs of our lives; but the summer evenings on the chapel steps, the simmering of thought and heart at the hearth of a friend, from which sprang the thoughts which made us free of the realms of beauty and truth.

Prof. March, Lafayette College.

———◦◦◦———

NOR should it be forgotten how far the greatness of New England is due to the quickening of her common mind by the truths of theology. A Westminster Catechism is a battery that gives a rousing shock.

Prof. March, Lafayette College.

THE feeling of a direct responsibility of the individual to God is almost wholly a creation of Protestantism.

John Stuart Mill.

———◆———

MR. HERBERT SPENCER is one of the small number of persons the character of whose knowledge is admittedly solid yet encyclopædical.

John Stuart Mill.

———◆———

TO say that men's intellectual beliefs do not determine their conduct, is like saying that the ship is moved by the stream and not by the steersman. The stream indeed is the motive-power; the steersman, left to himself, could not advance the vessel a single inch; yet it is the steersman's will and the steersman's knowledge which decide in what direction it shall move and whither it shall go.

John Stuart Mill.

———◆———

IT was ever the fashion of Cromwell's pikemen to rejoice greatly when they beheld the enemy.

Macaulay.

———◆———

POPE CELESTINE III., A.D. 1191, kicked the Emperor Henry VI.'s crown off his head while kneeling, to show his prerogative of making and unmaking kings.

Hayward's Book of all Religions.

———◆———

BUT for your own sakes, brethren—for God's sake—let your thought rise. Bid it, force it to rise. Think of the Face of Jesus, of your future home in heaven, of the loved ones who have gone before you. Think of all that has ever cheered, quickened, braced you. In such thoughts, to such thoughts, Jesus will assuredly and increasingly reveal himself. H. P. Liddon to the Students of Oxford.

THE distinctive character of truly evangelical religion is, that men are not to be led to do by being told to do, but that the secret springs within man must be moved, and that the will to do must precede all Christian doing. This strikes a fatal blow at the roots of all the modern preaching that insists upon doing without supplying the motives to do.

Caution and Advice by a Dean of the Church of England.

———◦◦◦———

FRANCE is now able to vindicate her status in the destinies of the world.

Louis Napoleon.

———◦◦◦———

WHEN Science keeps within its proper bounds, when it is content to explore the material universe and learn its beautiful laws of order and harmony, when it is content to discover the hidden things of physical nature and with its inventions contribute to the happiness of man, then it is a blessing; but when it invades the domain of morals, it runs the risk of being pursued and driven back by the lawful rulers there.

Rev. J. B. Grier.

———◦◦◦———

A "ROUGH" on a throne!

London Spectator on Andrew Johnson.

———◦◦◦———

WHEN anything happens in this world, we say it is providential, meaning that it is intended for our chastisement and discipline. We forget that events happen often for our punishment as well as for our correction. The ills of life are not all medicinal. There is such a thing as retributive justice even in this life, and the sorrows of the ungodly are often meant to be punitive. They are sent as the rewards of their wickedness.

Anon.

SINCE the Reformation, there have been four different tendencies in the Church, corresponding to the four different stages in the progress of astronomy. The *Papal* tendency corresponds to the *Mythological* stage; the *Zuinglian*, making the Bible central, to the *Ptolemaic;* the *Lutheran*, making justification by faith central, to the *Copernican;* the *Calvinistic* corresponds with the *theory of La Place*, in looking beyond Christ and the Bible to the Eternal Purpose of God, making that the central sun of the spiritual kingdom.
Dr. Stuart Robinson.

BEYOND the stars that shine in golden glory,
    Beyond the calm, sweet moon,
Up the bright ladder saints have trod before thee,
    Soul! thou must venture soon.
Anon.

ANCIENT learning may be distinguished into three periods: Its commencement, or the age of poets; its maturity, or the age of philosophers; and its decline, or the age of critics. In the poetical age, commentators were very few, but might have, in some respects, been useful. In its philosophical, their assistance must necessarily become obnoxious; yet, as if the nearer we approached perfection the more we stood in need of their directions, in this period they began to grow numerous. But when polite learning was no more, then it was those literary lawgivers made the most formidable appearance.
Goldsmith.

MEN believe that their reason governs their words, but it often happens that words have power to react on reason.
Bacon

THE material universe is so great that the highest intelli
gence in heaven can never fully grasp or know it
Through all eternity, should its limits ever be found, the
mind would be shocked.   John Foster.

OUR ideas are transformed sensations.
                                          Condillac.

LANGUAGE is the sensible portraiture or image of the
mental process.   Bacon.

THE proper motives to religion are the proper proofs of it.
                                          Bishop Butler.

SUSPICIONS which may be unjust need not be stated.
                                          Abraham Lincoln.

THE occasion is piled high with difficulty, and we must
rise high with the occasion.   Abraham Lincoln.

I PREFER solids to solutions.
                                          Emerson.

LANGUAGE is simply a medium for concealing thought.
                                          Talleyrand.

A HIGH heart is a sacrifice to Heaven.
                                          Anon.

HAVE you ever thought of it? The memory of an eye is
the most deathless of memories, because there, if anywhere, you catch a glimpse of the visible soul as it sits by
the window.   Ike Marvel

WEALTH in our country must long be, and properly is, a great measure of force; and by force I mean cha- racter, talent, activity and mental leverage. It is the forerunner, too, of those comforts and that indulgence which give time and room for cultivation; it is the grand furnace- warmer of those nursery-beds from which sprout up the tropical crop of refined luxuries. But in Heaven's name let us know it for what it is, and not for what it is not; most of all, let us avoid that particular fallacy which sees in wealth the essence, and not the provocative, of refine- ment.

Ike Marvel's Lorgnette.

THE stroke that blasts life's hope blasts also its smile.

Ike Marvel.

AND yet I know, past all doubting truly,
    A knowledge greater than grief can dim:
I know, as he loved, he will love me duly,
    Yea better, e'en better, than I love him.

And as I walked by the vast calm river,
    The awful river so dread to see,
I say, Thy breadth and thy depth for ever
    Are bridged by his thoughts that cross to me.

Jean Ingelow

WITH her two lips, that one the other pressed
    So poutingly with such a tranquil air;
With her two eyes, that on my own would rest
    So dream-like, she denied my silent prayer,
Fronted unuttered words, and said then nay,
And smiled down love, till I had naught to say.

Jean Ingelow

AND still I changed; I was a boy no more,
  My heart was large enough to hold my kind;
And all the world, as hath beer oft before
  With youth, I sought, but I could never find
Work hard enough to quiet my self-strife,
And use the strength of action-crowning life.

Jean Ingelow

TRUE love, like Greek fire, is inextinguishable.

Ike Marvel.

AND I, being parted from her loveliness,
  Looked at the picture of her in my mind!
I lived alone, I walked with soul oppressed,
  And ever sighed for her, and sighed for rest.

Jean Ingelow

THEN I had risen to struggle with my heart,
  And said, "O heart! the world is fresh and fair,
And I am young; but this thy restless smart
  Changes to bitterness the morning air;
I will, I must, these weary fetters break—
I will be free—if only for her sake."

Jean Ingelow.

THE symbols of the invisible are the loveliest of what is
visible.

Byron.

HERE all our countless actions touch the strings
  That send a thrill throughout infinity,
On earth our erring fingers strike the keys
That shall resound in endless cadences
Of harmony or discord evermore.

Thomas E. Taylor.

HERE'S health to all that we love,
　Here health to all that love us,
Here's health to all those that love them
That love those that love them
That love us.
Archbishop Dennison.

———◇◆◇———

OH! man may bear with suffering; his heart
　Is a strong thing, and godlike in the grasp
Of pain that wrings mortality; but tear
One chord affection clings to, part one tie
That binds him unto woman's delicate love,
And his great spirit yieldeth like a reed.
N. P Willis.

———◇◆◇———

IT is the supernatural in man which reveals to him the
　God whom Nature conceals.
Jacobi.

———◇◆◇———

THERE is no misery like that of a divided heart and a
　spotted Christian robe.
Dr. A. A. Hodge.

———◇◆◇———

A CHRISTIAN'S robes will become soiled if he wears
　them too flowingly.
Archbishop Leighton.

———◇◆◇———

THE conscience of man can never maintain its supremacy
　over the passions unless its decisions are enforced by a
belief in the existence of such a Deity as the Scriptures
reveal—an Omnipotent Being of almighty power, boundless
goodness, immaculate purity and inflexible justice. Nothing less than this will hold in check the violence of human
passion, and repress the all-grasping tendency of human
selfishness.
Wayland.

THE tail of a comet is simply the reflection of the sun's light by the nebulous substance of the body of the comet. It is always from the sun and diverges as it lengthens. Scientific American.

———•◇•———

BE not amazed at life. 'Tis still
    The mode of God with his elect,
Their hopes exactly to fulfill
    In times and ways they least expect.
Alford.

———•◇•———

THERE is always sunset and sunrise somewhere.
    The sun goes round the world preceded
And followed by a heaven of glory.
Anon.

———•◇•———

THE great sin of this age is a love of materialism in almost every shape, but especially of material display and physical, animal pleasure. Woman is at the bottom of it. Men will do anything to secure money for her—to keep her better dressed and in a prouder position than her neighbor. Round Table.

———•◇•———

THE New Testament is only the beginning of books, not a finished and sealed document, according to popular notions of finality, but the beginning of a literature punctuated and paragraphed by tears and laughter, by battle and pestilence, and all the changes of a tumultuous yet progressive civilization. Ecce Deus.

———•◇•———

IN many things, a comprehensive survey of a whole subject is the shortest way of getting at a precise knowledge of a particular division of it. Princeton Review.

THE small mud-huts of bigotry will be submerged by the mighty cataclysm of human progress, but the Church, founded upon a rock, will remain above the floods.

Ecce Deus.

———◦◦———

ENGINEERS say that locomotives are always low-spirited and indisposed to work in damp, foggy weather.   In this respect they are very human.

Pittsburg Chronicle.

———◦◦———

LEAVE God to order all thy ways,
  And hope in Him whate'er betide;
Thou'lt find Him in the evil days
  An all-sufficient Strength and Guide.
Who trusts in God's unchanging love
Builds on a rock that naught can move.

George Newman

———◦◦———

THE Bible, its history, philosophy and poetry, stands a mighty lighthouse on the shores of time, flashing its beams far out over the dark ocean of eternity, setting

> "The clouds on fire with redness,
>   Leaving on the level waters
>   One long track of trail and splendor,
>   Down whose stream, as down a river,"

the ransomed spirit will glide until, disappearing

> "Far in the purple distance,"

it will be lifted high

> "Into the land of the hereafter."

H. Bucher Swope, Esq.

— ——◦◦———

UNITARIANISM is the diverging focus of all the non-sense of the country.

Thomas H Benton

THERE are some ladies who are proud to be the monthly roses of fashion, changing with the seasons; others boast that they are the evergreens of gentility, living superior to all the changes and fluctuations of manners and fashions.

Frank Leslie's Magazine.

——◇——

IN religion, as in every other profession, *practicing* is the great thing. We practice law, practice medicine, and ministers must practice what they preach—Christians must practice their religion.

Jacobus.

——◇——

THERE is a serious and resolute egotism that makes a man interesting to his friends and formidable to his opponents.

Whipple.

——◇——

AS unseen reservoirs and conduits supply cities with water and light, so does the unseen Christ, often through invisible agencies, supply his people with all needed grace.

Rev. S. F. Scovel, Pittsburg.

——◇——

IT is idle to attempt to legislate in advance of public opinion.

N. Y. Herald.

——◇——

AN advertising people are always a thrifty people.

N. Y. Herald

——◇——

AS the grains of gold are hid amid the baser earth, as the grains of wheat are hid amid the chaff, so the true people of God are hid among those who make an eternal profession of his name.

Rev. Dr. Murray of Elizabeth, N. J.

THE atrocious crime of being a young man, which the honorable gentleman has, with such spirit and decency, charged upon me, I shall neither attempt to palliate nor deny, but content myself with hoping that I may be one of those whose follies cease with their youth, and not of that number who are ignorant in spite of experience.

Pitt's reply to Walpole.

WHEN the people of Chicago want fresh water they push their pipes out, beyond the brink of the lake, into the pure, clear current, tossed and convulsed by storm and tempest. So must we get at the heart of the people if we would know what is best for the government. It is the breath of the people that purifies the blood of our nation.

Fred. Douglass.

THE Constitution of the United States was framed in the face of monarchy and slavery. No wonder, then, it contains in it much that should not be there.

Fred. Douglass.

COULD the stocks and chains—the fetters and blood and agony—of slavery be placed in a heap in front of the American pulpit, it would be a more powerful argument in favor of the Gospel of the Son of God than hundreds of volumes of law and constitutions.

Fred. Douglass.

WHEN Theodore Parker said, looking at the stars, "All the spaces between my mind and the mind of God are full of truths waiting to be crystallized into law for the government of the masses," he expressed the voice of the nineteenth century more perfectly than anything else could.

Fred. Douglass.

A GOVERNMENT founded on Impartial Liberty, where all have a voice and a vote irrespective of color or of sex,—what is there to hinder such a government from standing firm?   Fred. Douglass.

———•◦•———

IN the natural exercise of their liberties, most of the churches of Protestantism freely incorporate into their worship whatever of sacred song successive generations may produce, which its spiritual instincts recognize as a worthy expression of its worship and ever varying life. The canon of revealed truth is closed—that which God has given to man as a sufficient instruction for every life; but not the canon of worshiping song—that which successive lives give to God. Who may presume to write "finis" upon any human form of prayer or collection of song? When Ambrose has brought his contributions to worship-song, is Gregory to be forbidden? When Gregory has completed his Hymnarium, is Luther to be interdicted? When Luther has filled the churches of the Reformation with sacred song, is Gerhardt to be declared contraband? When Sternhold and Hopkins have presented their versions of the psalms, is Watts to be delivered over to the "uncovenanted mercies?" When Watts has completed his wonderful canon of psalms and hymns, are the contributions of Wesley and Cowper, Montgomery and Keble, to be put into an apocrypha? Who will presume to discriminate their inspiration? The ever-varying and ever-developing spiritual life of each generation will necessarily adapt and create its own hymnody, and the presumption is, that the inspiration of the later Christian ages will be more precious than that of the earlier. The ever-enriching thought—the ever-enlarging experience—the ever-depending sanctity of the Church, will produce a richer, nobler song. He only

reveres the past who accepts all its fruitage, who recognizes the spirit of Ambrose in the latest sacred poet and the
spirit of Gregory in the latest sacred musician. The alter-
native of a present that knows no past is surely not a past
that allows no present. Rev. H. Allen of London.

IF there were no other argument for a future life, sin
would furnish one never to be refuted; for it tells of a
cause standing over between the Judge and ourselves, for
the hearing and decision of which a time must certainly
come. Isaac Taylor.

FAITH is not a belief that we are *saved*, but that we are
loved. Dr. Kirk of Boston.

WHATEVER is, is right, excepting man's own sinful self.
Dr. A. A. Hodge.

QUEEN VICTORIA said she "had a lump in her throat"
as she heard Norman McLeod of Scotland preach.

THE hammer of geology has long been ringing on the
shields of Christian warriors, and the telescopes of
astronomy, in searching the heavens for new stars, have
scorned to catch a ray from the Star of Bethlehem.
Harper's Monthly.

BE a bold, brave, true, honest man. If you know a thing
is right, do it. If you have a solemn conviction, dare
to utter it in the fear of God, regardless of the wrath of
man. Gough.

THREE-FOURTHS of the popular novels of the day enfeeble the intellect, impoverish the imagination, vulgarize the taste and style, give false or distorted views of life and human nature, and, which is worst of all, waste that precious time which should be given to solid mental improvement.

Greyson Letters.

———◇———

TO judge of God's proceedings toward anybody on earth besides ourselves, so long as the window in each man's breast remains shut, is just as wise as to criticise the sentence of a judge without knowing anything of the law or the evidence, or to pronounce the prescription of a physician without knowing either his science or the symptoms of the patient. Each man must judge for himself, and in that case it seems each man gives a sentence for God, for almost every man will admit that God has been better to him than he deserves.

Greyson Letters.

———◇———

THERE are passages of Scripture that glow with the poetry of heaven and immortality.

Greyson Letters.

———◇———

A CHRISTIAN is like a locomotive. A fire must be kindled in the heart of the thing before it will go.

M. W. Jacobus, D.D

———◇———

WHEN Cæsar felt the mortal wound he folded his garments round him, that he might fall with dignity.

Zwingle

———◇———

EPICURIANISM is human nature drunk, Cynicism is human nature mad, and Stoicism is human nature in despair.

Dr. S. J. Wilson.

TAKE the earth and grind it into the smallest sand and scatter it throughout space, and there will not be a grain for each star.

Agassiz.

———◇———

NAPOLEON had a friend who was sent to the madhouse, and on being asked by the surgeon what was the cause of his malady, whether it was loss of riches, honor or reputation, he replied: "None of these; my father was an infidel, and I have been influenced by his views; but for two long years, waking or sleeping, the word eternity has been sounding in my ears till it has driven me mad.

D. L. Moody.

———◇———

A WEALTHY man in the West, a railroad king, became deranged, was taken to the asylum, and when reaching there he threw himself in a chair and exclaimed, "Sixty years, millions of money, and in the mad-house."

D. L. Moody.

———◇———

OH, if the spirits of the departed could return and take my place, would they not with united voice call you to prepare to meet your God? Ye men with conscience! ye restless souls, burdened with guilt! ye frail, short-lived mortals! ye near neighbors of the spirit-land! ye borderers upon heaven or hell, oh loose your hearts from earth!

Spurgeon.

———o———

THE sad consequence of defection in principle is corruption in practice.

Dickens.

———o———

MANY of the psalms begin mournfully and end triumphantly, to show us the prevailing power of devotion and to convince us of the certain return of prayer.

Bishop Horne.

13

THE excellence of religion is proved by the fact that many pretend to possess it. The odorous balsam is imitated, because it is so precious and fragrant, and necessarily there are many spurious kinds, but no man takes trouble to imitate common oil. *Chrysostom.*

———◇———

THERE is nothing, no nothing, innocent or good that dies and is forgotten. An infant—a prattling child, dying in its cradle—will live again in the better thoughts of those who loved it, and play its part through them, in the redeeming actions of the world, though its body be burnt to ashes and drowned in the deepest sea. There is not an angel added to the host of heaven but does its blessed work on earth in those that loved it here. Forgotten! oh, if the good deeds of human creatures could be traced to their source, how beautifully would even death appear! for how much charity, mercy and purified affection, would be seen to have their growth in dusty graves! *Dickens.*

———◇———

AS the conversion of a sinner produces joy in heaven, so the fall of a believer disgraces the Gospel of Christ, opens the mouths of the adversaries, and, if such a thing could be, would produce joy in hell. *Bishop Horne.*

———◇———

TASTE and smell are chemical, touch is mechanical, hearing and seeing are ethereal, the ear is emotive and the eye intellectual. *Tyndall.*

———◇———

A MAN'S ideal, like his horizon, is constantly receding from him as he advances toward it. *Shedd.*

WE want *originality* and *authority* in our preaching, and
we can only get them by being deeply imbued with
the Scriptures. We must master their meaning and structure and must drink deep of their inspiration. Thus, to be
effective in this age of the world, when mind is so active
and men's taste is so cultivated, our style must have the
three great properties of plainness, force and beauty.

Shedd.

THE highest effect of eloquence requires an eloquent
speaker and an eloquent hearer.

Shedd.

WHENEVER the preacher asserts that God loves the
righteous, let him assert it with energy and warmth.
Let him make his hearers see and know that the great God
is personal in his emotion, that he pours out upon those
who are in filial sympathy with him and his law the infinite
wealth of his pure and stainless affection, and whenever he
asserts that God hates sin and is angry with the sinner, let
nim assert it without any abatement or qualification.

Shedd.

THE introduction of a discourse should be a rifle-shot at
the theme.

Rev. W. M. Paxton, D.D.

INFINITY is the type of Divine Incomprehensibility;
unity is the type of Divine Comprehensiveness; repose
is the type of Divine Permanence; symmetry is the type
of Divine Justice; purity is the type of Divine Energy;
moderation is the type of Divine Government and Law;
and beauty is the type cf Divine Holiness.

Ruskin.

THIS, from some opium experiences of mine, I can believe; I have, indeed, seen the same thing asserted twice in modern books, and accompanied by a remark which I am convinced is true, namely: that the dread book of account, which the Scriptures speak of is, in fact, the mind itself of each individual. Of this, at least, I feel assured—that there is no such thing as forgetting possible to the mind; a thousand accidents may and will interpose a veil between our present consciousness and the secret inscriptions on the mind. Accidents of the same sort will also rend away this veil; but alike, whether veiled or unveiled, the inscription remains for ever; just as the stars seem to withdraw before the common light of day, whereas, in fact, we all know that it is the light which is drawn over them as a veil, and that they are waiting to be revealed, when the obscuring daylight shall have withdrawn.

Thomas De Quincy.

THERE are as many comets in the heavens as there are fishes in the sea.

Kepler.

SUCH is the artless fear of guilt that it spills itself in fearing to be spilt.

Shakespeare.

ONE may smile and smile and be a villain.

Shakespeare.

THERE are many steps between the brow and foot of the hill, some of which command a charming prospect and all a new horizon.

Gail Hamilton.

HE who scrubs the head of an ass wastes his soap.

My Novel.—Bulwer.

BUT were I Brutus, and Brutus Antony, there were an Antony would ruffle up your spirits, and put a tongue in every wound of Cæsar, that should move the stones of Rome to rise and mutiny.

Shakespeare.

WE have no right to feel badly because other people do not like us.

Rev. A. K. H. Boyd.

OH! sweet, fond dream of human love!
  A rose-cloud, dimly seen above,
Melting in heaven's blue depths away.

Whittier.

YOUNG men, what are you going to do in the great future?

K. A. Burnell.

I MUST see the graves cleaving, the sea teeming, and swarms unsuspected, crowds unnumbered, yea, multitudes of thronging nations, rising from both. I must see the world in flames, must stand at the dissolution of all earthly things and be an attendant upon the burial of Nature. I must see the vast expanse of sky wrapt up like a scroll, and the Incarnate God issuing forth from light inaccessible and full of glory, with ten thousand times ten thousand angels, to judge both men and devils. I must see the curtain of Time drop, see all eternity disclosed to view, and enter upon a state of being that will never, never have an end!

Hervey's Meditations.

LOVE for one human being ought to endear all the world to us.

Miss L. L. F.

WILL the coming man ever come?

N. Y. Evening Mail.

IT is not necessary for me to have a telegram from Paris or San Francisco to know how my fellow-men feel when any great event happens. My knowledge of the human heart tells me how they feel.   Beecher.

———◇◇———

PITTSBURG, at night, looks like hell with the lid off!   Parton.

———◇◇———

WE can refute assertions, but who can refute silence?   Dickens.

———◇◇———

THERE will be a resurrection of reputations as well as of bodies.   Vincent on Milton

———◇◇———

THE word constitution in that connection ought to have burst his pen like vitriol and reddened the page with shame.   The N. Y. World on a Letter of Secretary Stanton's.

———◇◇———

THE crown can thunder for itself!   Queen Elizabeth.

———◇◇———

WEEPING the tearless weeping of hell.   Martensen.

———◇◇———

THE tendency or direction of the soul at death is not outward but inward, a going into itself, a going back, not a going forth; and instead of the modern notion that the soul wings its way to the stars, which is sometimes understood in a literal sense, as if the soul were borne to another world, the idea is far more correct that it draws itself back into the innermost and mystical chambers of existence which underlie the outward.   Martensen.

REPENTANCE is not only grief on account of this or that particular act; it is a fundamental grief—a deep-seated sorrow on account of the discrepancy and division between the outward acts of the will and that ideal which is presented to the conscience in the new Adam—the typical man. Martensen.

WITH all this rant and cant about reunion there is a substantial unity between all Evangelical denominations—a unity of doctrine, worship and government. The tribes of Israel, when they took the line of march for the Promised Land, did not go up in one union-mob, but each tribe under its own flag and its own leader. So let the chosen tribes of the spiritual Israel who are journeying to the Better Land march each tribe under its own chosen leaders and with its own distinctive banner, for high over all the tribes and all the banners is the banner stained with blood, and the Captain who leads the whole host is the Incarnate Son of God, and to all the tribes the same heavenly manna is given and the same cloudy pillar guides them all. Ecce Deus-Homo.

TOM CORWIN was going to denounce Theodore Parker for saying some harsh things about him. He went to hear him preach, and when he came away he remarked: "That will do; any man who can talk that way about Jesus Christ it matters not what he says about poor sinful Tom Corwin. N. Y. World.

REVERE thyself, and yet thyself despise,
His nature no man can o'er-rate; and none
Can underrate his merit. Young

A COQUETTE is one who tries on hearts like shoes and throws them away with as little ceremony as mis-fits i' morocco.

N. P. Wills.

———◦◦———

Doing as Rome does, is occupying one's self.

London Punch.

———◦◦———

ARE we not formed, as notes of music are,
For one another, though dissimilar?

Anon.

———◦◦———

RHYTHM in prose, should be cultivated not only for the sake of embellishment, but also for the sake of perspicuity.

Bulwer.

———◦◦———

THERE is a river in the ocean. In the severest droughts it never fails and in the mightiest floods it never overflows. Its banks and its bottoms are of cold water, while its current is of warm. The gulf of Mexico is its fountain. and its mouth is the Arctic seas. It is the Gulf Stream. There is in the world no other such majestic flow of waters. Its current is more rapid than the Mississippi or the Amazon and its volume more than a thousand times greater.

M. F. Maury.

———◦◦———

THE vibrations which produce the impression of red light are slower, and the ethereal waves which they generate are longer, than those which produce the impression of violet; while the other colors are excited by waves of an intermediate length. Light travels through space at the rate of one hundred and ninety-two thousand miles per second. Reducing this to inches, we get 12,165,120,000! Now it is found that thirty-nine thousand waves of red light placed end to end would make up an inch! Multiply the number of inches in one hundred and ninety-two thousand miles by thirty-nine thousand, and we obtain the number of waves of red light in one hundred and ninety-two thousand miles—474,439,680,000,000! All these waves enter the eye in a single second! ᐧTo produce the impression of red in the brain, the retina of the eye must be hit at this almost inconceivable rate! To produce the impression of violet a still greater number of impulses are necessary. The number of shocks required to produce this color amounts to 699,000,000,000,000! The other colors of the spectrum rise gradually in pitch from red to violet.

Tyndall.

———◦◦◦———

WATER goes on contracting till it reaches the temperature of 39° Fahr., at which point the contraction ceases. This is the point of maximum density of water. From this downward to its freezing point it expands contrary to the general law, and when it is converted into ice the expansion is large and sudden.

Tyndall.

———◦◦◦———

FOR many years it has been one of my constant regrets that no schoolmaster of mine had a knowledge of natural history, so far at least as to have taught me the grasses that grow by the wayside and the little winged and wingless neighbors that are continually meeting me with a salutation which I cannot answer, as things are. Why didn't somebody teach me the constellations, too, and make me at home in the starry heavens, which are always overhead, and which I don't half know to this day?

Car yle.

———◦◦◦———

MANY a college-student has mastered a *disqualifying* culture.

Youmans.

WHO can blame me if I cherish the belief that the world is still young—that there are great possibilities in store for it?

Tyndall.

———◇———

SCIENCE limits the function of the instructor by showing that mental operations are corporeally conditioned, that large regions of our nature are beyond direct control, and that mental attainment depends in a great degree upon inherited capacity and organic growth. It limits it by showing that ancestral influences come down upon us as we enter the world like the hand of Fate; that we are born well or born badly, and that whoever is ushered into existence at the bottom of the scale can never rise to the top, because the weight of the universe is upon him.

Youmans.

———◇———

GREAT griefs are the medicines for our lesser sorrows.

Shakespeare.

———◇———

THERE are three kinds of people in the world, the wills, the won'ts and the can'ts. The first accomplish everything; the second oppose everything; the third fail in everything.

Eclectic Magazine.

———◇———

WOMAN, like gold, is a legal tender the world over, no matter what image or superscription is stamped on it by the national mint.

Beecher.

———◇———

I PROPOSE to move immediately upon your works.

Gen. Grant at Fort Donelson.

———◇———

THE strongest position a soldier should desire to occupy is one from which he can most easily advance against the enemy.

Gen. Pope

ARMED forces are raised and supported simply to sustain the civil authorities, and are to be held in strict subordination thereto in all respects. Gen. McClellan.

———◈———

THE remedy for political errors, if any are committed, is to be found only in the action of the people at the polls. Gen. McClellan.

———◈———

WITH malice toward none, with charity for all, with firmness in the right, as God gives us to see the right, let us strive to finish the work we have begun. Lincoln.

———◈———

WHOEVER hesitates to utter that which he thinks the highest truth, lest it should be too much in advance of the time, may reassure himself by looking at his acts from an impersonal point of view. Let him duly realize the fact that opinion is the agency through which character adapts external arrangements to itself—that his opinion rightly forms part of this agency—is a unit of force, constituting, with other such units, the general power which works out social changes, and he will perceive that he may properly give full utterance to his innermost conviction, leaving it to produce what effect it may. It is not for nothing that he has in him these sympathies with some principles and repugnance to others. He, with all his capacities, and aspirations, and beliefs, is not an accident, but a product of the time. He must remember that while he is a descendant of the past he is a parent of the future. and that his thoughts are as children born to him, which he may not carelessly let die. Not as adventitious therefore will the wise man regard the faith which is in him. The highest truth he sees he will fearlessly utter. Know-

ing that, let what may come of it, he is thus playing his right part in the world—knowing that if he can effect the change he aims at—well; if not—well also; though not *so* well.
Herbert Spencer.

———◆◇◆———

WE must conform, to a certain extent, to the conventionalities of society, for they are the ripened results of a varied and long experience.
Dr. A. A. Hodge.

———◆◇◆———

ASK you where the place of religious might is? Not the place of religious privileges—not where prayers are daily and sacraments monthly—not where sermons are so abundant as to pall upon the pampered taste, but on the hill-side with the Covenanter; in the wilderness with John the Baptist; in our own dependencies, where the liturgy is rarely heard and Christian friends meet at the end of months; there, amidst manifold disadvantages, when the soul is thrown upon itself, a few kindred spirits and God, grow up those heroes of faith, like the centurion, whose firm conviction wins admiration even from the Son of God himself.
F. W. Robertson.

———◆◇◆———

WHILE our sins should make us fear to approach Christ they should make us fear to keep away from Christ.
Rev. Dr. Swope.

———◆◇◆———

SELF-RIGHTEOUSNESS may save from degradation but it will prevent saintliness.
Robertson.

———◆◇◆———

METHOD in study, with a proper division of time, will give us time for leisure and recreation.
Rev. Dr. Nevin.

THE fundamental doctrine of a true philosophy, according to M. Comte, and the character by which he defines positive philosophy, is the following: We have no knowledge of anything but phenomena, and our knowledge of phenomena is relative, not absolute. We know not the essence, nor the real mode of production, of any fact, but only its relations to other facts in the way of succession or of similitude. These relations are constant; that is, always the same in the same circumstances. The constant resemblances which link phenomena together, and the constant sequences which unite them as antecedent and consequent, are termed their laws. The laws of phenomena are all we know respecting them. Their essential nature and their ultimate causes, either efficient or final, are unknown and irresistible to us. John Stuart Mill.

THE attention of the intellect is a natural prayer by which we obtain the enlightenment of the reason.
Malebranche.

IN aspiring to reach the lofty height of Christ's virtue we shall resemble pilgrims climbing up different sides of the same mountain, who draw nearer at every step not only to the summit, but also to one another.
J. G. Hoyt.

A MAN'S antecedents are constantly coming up.
Rev. Dr. Crowell of Phila.

THERE are few signs in a soul's state more alarming than that of religious indifference; that is, the spirit of thinking all religions equally true, the real meaning of which is, that all religions are equally false.
F. W. Robs tson

MANY persons have the negro question on the brain, but not much brain on the negro question.

George D. Prentice.

———◦◦◦———

IT is not what men eat but what they digest that makes them strong; not what we gain but what we save that makes us rich; not what men read but what they remember that makes them learned; and not what we profess but what we practise that makes us Christians. These are great but common truths, often forgotten by the glutton, the spendthrift, the book-worm and the hypocrite.

Bacon.

———◦◦◦———

I HAVE had many foes, but none like thee.

Byron

———◦◦◦———

I KNOW not what I could have been, but feel I am not what I should be.

Byron.

———◦◦◦———

WHEN traveling I must remember that though corporations have no soul, yet I have one, and I must therefore pay all bills on cars and at hotels without murmuring.

Anon.

———◦◦◦———

THE maelstrom attracts more notice than the quiet fountain; a comet draws more attention than the steady star; but it is better to be fountain than maelstrom, and star than comet, following out the sphere and orbit of quiet usefulness in which God places us.

Rev. John Ha   D.D.

———◦◦◦———

THEY rarely die and never resign.

Jefferson on Office-holders.

IDEAS often reach the people just as they are leaving the schools, and often, on the other hand, the schools go on spinning their tough threads long after the people have lost all their interest.   Guesses at Truth.

———◦◦———

I COULD hardly feel much confidence in a man who had never been imposed upon.   Guesses at Truth.

———◦◦———

FORMS, like barrels, are of great use, though sometimes empty.   Guesses at Truth.

———◦◦———

THE taste for ever refines in the study of women.

N. P. Willis.

———◦◦———

I CANNOT lose a world for thee,
But would not lose thee for the world.

Anon

———◦◦———

HE did not notice that I never spoke to her in the same key of voice to which the conversation of others was attuned.   He saw not that while she turned to him with a smile or a preparation to listen, she heard my voice as if her attention had been arrested by distant music, with no change in her features except a look more earnest.   She would have called him to look with her at a glowing sunset or to point out a new-comer in the road from the village; but if the moon had gone suddenly into a cloud and saddened the face of the landscape, or if the wind had sounded mournfully through the trees, as she looked out upon the night, she would have spoken of that first to me!

N. P. Willis.

POLITICAL economists tell us that self-love is the bond of society. Strange, then, must be the construction of what is called society, when it is cemented by the strongest and most powerful of all solvents.

Guesses at Truth.

———•◇•———

IT will afford sweeter happiness in the hour of death to have wiped away one tear from the cheek of sorrow than to have ruled an empire, to have conquered millions or enslaved the world.

Ecce Deus.

———•◇•———

HE was not all unhappy. His resolve
Upbore him, and firm faith, and evermore
Prayer from a living source within the will,
And beating up through all the bitter world,
Like fountains of sweet water in the sea,
Kept him a living soul.

Enoch Arden.

———•◇•———

WHAT is ministerial success?—crowded churches, full aisles, attentive congregations, the approval of the religious world, much impression produced. Elijah thought so; and when he found out his mistake, and discovered that the applause on Carmel subsided into hideous stillness, his heart wellnigh broke with disappointment. Ministerial success lies in altered lives and obedient, humbled hearts; unseen work recognized in the Judgment-day.

F. W. Robertson.

———•◇•———

I LIKE that wit whose fittest symbol is the playful pinch which a father gives to the cheek of his roguish boy or the pretended bite which a mother prints upon the tempting, snowy shoulder of her babe.

Ike Marvel.

THE little that I have seen in the world, and known of the history of mankind, teaches me to look upon their errors in sorrow, not in anger. When I take the history of one poor heart that has sinned and suffered, and represent to myself the struggles and temptations it passed through, the brief pulsations of joy, the tears of regret, the feebleness of purpose, the scorn of the world that has little charity, the desolation of the soul's sanctuary and threatening voices within, health gone, happiness gone, I would fain leave the erring soul of my fellow-man with Him from whose hands it came.

Chalmers.

——◦◦——

EXPRESSION is second only to acquisition.

Prof. Kidd.

——◦◦——

O NATURE! glorious mirror of Divinity; what constant students were we of thy myriad forms and mysteries all through the years of our childhood.

Bulwer

——◦◦——

YESTERDAY is as to-morrow in the for ever.

Anon.

——◦◦——

THERE are some causes so sacred as to carry with them an irresistible appeal to every honest heart, and he needs but little power of eloquence who defends the honor of his country.

Washington Irving.

——◦◦——

THERE is an atmosphere in the letters of those we love which we alone—we who love—can feel.

Marion Harland.

——◦◦——

WE cast our ballots as we shot our bullets.

Republican Motto.

14

IN all our decisions and actions it would be well for us to remember the suggestive inscription that was written on the gates of Busyrane. As the traveler entered that ancient city, he read on the first gate, "Be bold;" and on the second gate, "Be bold, be bold and evermore be bold;" and then he paused, as he read on the third gate, "Be not too bold!" A man's strength should be like the momentum of a falling planet and his discretion like the return of its due and perfect curve.

Emerson.

———◦◦———

WE gather shells from youth to age,
    And then we leave them like a child.

Anon.

———◦◦———

OUR enemies speak of us as they *hear;* we judge of ourselves as we *feel.*

Hannah More.

———◦◦———

ENVY has no interval. Ambition never cools. Pride never sleeps. The principle at least is always active.

Hannah More.

———◦◦———

CAIUS MARIUS, while in poverty and exile, caused, by his intrepid look, the dagger to drop from the hand of his executioner.

Hannah More.

———◦◦———

I PITY the man who has not judgment enough to know who are his friends and who are his enemies.

Rev. Ed. Lewis.

———◦◦———

MANY persons I once thought great dwindle into very small dimensions on a short acquaintance.

Rob Roy McNulty.

ONE cannot live upon criticism. It is truth which is the food of the mind, and the duty of criticism is to establish truth.

Luthardt.

————✦————

WILLIAM H. EVARTS, in his impeachment speech, compared an oath to a lightning-rod, absorbing and conducting from the dark clouds of passion their angry and dangerous elements. He also spoke about the tremendous difficulty of a paper constitution placing adequate buttresses of defence between the co-ordinate branches of our government. He also spoke of truth as being the gravitation principle of the universe, by which it is supported and in which it coheres.

————✦————

THERE is never jealousy where there is not strong regard.

Washington Irving.

————✦————

THE human mind is like an inebriate on horseback— prop it on one side and it falls on the other.

Luther

————✦————

WHAT would be the state of the highways of life, if we did not drive our thought-sprinklers through them, with valve open, sometimes?

Holmes.

————✦————

JERKY minds say bright things on all possible subjects, but their zigzags rock you to death.

Holmes.

————✦————

THERE are important cases in which the difference between half a heart and a whole one makes just the difference between signal defeat and splendid victory.

Rev. A. K. H. Boyd.

THE pulpit is now crowded with goodish nobodies—men who have no power—no unction—no mission. They strain their brains to write common-places and wear themselves out repeating the rant of their sect and the cant of their schools.

Holland.

————◦◦————

I WOULD rather have zeal without knowledge than knowledge without zeal.

D. L. Moody.

————◦◦————

THE sports of children satisfy the child.

Goldsmith.

———— ◦◦◦ ————

CONVERSATION should always be a selection.

Sir William Hamilton.

————◦◦————

EACH is bound to all.

Herbert Spencer.

————◦◦————

SCIENCE owes its development to students attending to intimations overlooked by the generality.

Bishop Butler.

————◦◦————

HE is but a weak man who cannot twist and weave the threads of his feeling, however firm, however tangled, however strained or however strong, into the great cable of Purpose, by which he lies moored to a life of action.

Ike Marvel.

————◦◦————

BE serious!

Grotius.

————◦◦————

A DYING man can do nothing easy.

Benjamin Franklin.

EVERY day's experience shows how much more actively education goes on out of the school-room than in it.

Anon.

———•◦•———

THE soul of liberty is the love of Law.

Anon.

———•◦•———

ALWAYS be as solicitous to shun applause as assiduous to deserve it.

Chesterfield.

———•◦•———

THE might and truth of hearts are never shown but in loving those whom we ought not to love or cannot have.

Bailey's Festus.

———•◦•———

ONE heart-throb sometimes earneth heaven—one tear.

Bailey's Festus.

———•◦•———

LOVE is the art of hearts and heart of arts. Conjunctive looks and interjectional sighs are its vocabulary's greater half.

Bailey's Festus.

———•◦•———

HER cheek had the pale, pearly pink of the seashell, the world's sweetest tint, as though she lived, one half might deem, on roses sopped in silver dew.

Bailey's Festus.

———•◦•———

THE day hath gone to God
Straight, like an infant's spirit, or a mocked
And mourning messenger of grace to man.

Bailey's Festus.

———•◦•———

PLEASURE is the reflex of unimpeded energy.

Sir W. Hamilton

WHAT would I not give for the lantern of Diogenes to read the heart of Danton and learn if he be the friend or the enemy of the Republic.
Robespierre.

———◦◦◦———

IF God did not exist, it would behoove man to invent him.
Robespierre.

———◦◦◦———

I HAD rather be guillotined than a guillotiner.
Danton

———◦◦◦———

LIGHT, more light, still!
Goethe.

———◦◦◦———

THE landscape, like a veil over beauty's breast, heightens the charms it half conceals.
Washington Irving.

———◦◦◦———

A FLIRT is like a dipper attached to a hydrant; every one is at liberty to drink from it, but no one desires to carry it away.
N. P. Willis.

———◦◦◦———

ART is to conceal art.
Latin Poet

———◦◦◦———

KITES rise against, not with, the wind.
Anon.

———◦◦◦———

INSTINCT is prior to experience and independent of instruction.
Paley.

———◦◦◦———

THE brightest rainbows ever play
Above the fountains of our tears.
Mackey

OF all sad words of tongue or pen,
The saddest are these: " It might have been."

Whittier

———◦◦———

LIKE moonlight on a troubled sea,
Brightening the storms it cannot calm.

Anon

———◦◦———

NOTHING so soon mortifies as to spend one's scorn in vain.

John Foster.

———◦◦———

MEN can now believe everything but the Bible.

Napoleon.

———◦◦———

PROVIDENCE is always on the side of the strongest
battalions.

Napoleon.

———◦◦———

IT is a principle of war, that when you can use the thunderbolt you must prefer it to the cannon. Earnestness
is the thunderbolt.

Napoleon.

———◦◦———

SUCH has been the crushing effect of public sentiment
that women feel almost like apologizing for being on
the earth at all!

The Revolution.

———◦◦———

WHEN you hear a man always prating about the Constitution, spot him as a traitor.

President Johnson.

———◦◦———

IF any man pulls down the American flag, shoot him on
the spot.

Gen. Dix.

———◦◦———

THE Christian Commission is not only *sanitary* but *saving*

George H. Stuart.

THE greatness of London conquered my misery, and I determined to conquer London by my greatness.

Disraeli.

———◦◦◦———

THERE is a past which is gone for ever.   But there is a future which is still our own.

F. W. Robertson.

———◦◦◦———

SLAVE to no sect, who takes no private road,
But looks through Nature up to Nature's God.

Pope.

———◦◦◦———

THE only disadvantage of an honest heart is credulity.

Sir Philip Sydney.

———◦◦◦———

IT is only those who are despicable who fear being despised

La Rochefoucault

———◦◦◦———

'TIS late before
The brave despair.

Thompson.

———◦◦◦———

THEY say best men are moulded out of faults;
And, for the most, become much more the better
For being a little bad.

Shakespeare.

———◦◦◦———

REAL goodness does not attach itself merely to this life— it points to another world.   Political or professional reputation cannot last for ever, but a conscience void of offence before God and man is an inheritance for eternity.

Daniel Webster.

———◦◦◦———

WE are near waking when we dream that we dream.

Novalis.

LOVE thyself last; cherish those hearts that hate thee.
Corruption wins not more than honesty;
Still in thy right hand carry gentle peace,
To silence envious tongues.   Be just, and fear not;
Let all the ends thou aimest at be thy Country's,
Thy God's and Truth's; then, if thou fallest, O Cromwell
Thou fallest a blessed martyr.   Shakespeare.

———◦◦———

I VENERATE the man whose heart is warm,
Whose hands are pure, whose doctrine and whose life
Coincident, exhibit lucid proof
That he is honest in the sacred cause.
                                              Cowper.

———◦◦———

DECISION OF CHARACTER—REQUISITES.

1. CONFIDENCE in our own judgment.
2. A strenuous will.
3. Burning, but disciplined feeling.
4. Courage.
5. Reliance upon God.

CONDUCIVES OR INCENTIVES.

1. Opposition.
2. Desertion.
3. Failure—will bring experience.
4. Success.

CAUTIONS.

1. There must be sound, vigorous thought.
2. You must have the approbation of conscience.
                                      John Foster

———◦◦———

OF all the dispositions and habits which lead to political
prosperity, religion and morality are indispensable
supports.   Washington.

POPULAR FALLACIES.

1. THE confounding of profound learning with practical uselessness.

2. The confounding of wealth with material riches. Wealth is a subjective term, relating primarily to the quality of the man; while riches is an objective term, and refers exclusively to the external world, to farms and flocks, ships and merchandise.

3. The confounding of law with legislative enactments.

4. The confounding of reverence with servility.

5. The confounding of a religious life with a theological creed.

6. The confounding of joy with happiness. Joy depends upon character—happiness upon condition. Happiness is outward—that which happens; joy is literally a leap—a spring within.   Anon.

PRACTICAL SUGGESTIONS.

1. TAKE care of your bodily health.

2. Acquire the habit of being beforehand with whatever you undertake. Plan and division of time will give leisure for recreation.

3. Men mistake in not holding on to the calling or profession which they choose.

4. Have some fresh, intellectual acquisition always on hand.

5. Do not limit your studies to your own specialty nor your intercourse to your own set or caste.

6. Cultivate the art of conversation.

7. Cultivate good manners. Be not servile but reverential.

8. Be a Christian—the highest form of a gentleman.

Mistakes of Educated Men.

SEIZE the moment of excited curiosity on any subject, to solve your doubts; for if you let it pass, the desire **may** never return, and you may remain in ignorance.

Wirt.

———◦◦◦———

IF a cause be good, the most violent attack of its enemies will not injure it so much as an injudicious defence of it by its friends.

Colton.

———◦◦◦———

CRITICS are sentinels in the grand army of letters, stationed at the corners of newspapers and reviews, to challenge every new author.

Longfellow.

———◦◦◦———

THE ancients believed that the seat of the memory was in the tip of the ear; hence their custom of touching it in order to remind another of a thing.

Prof. Anthon.

———◦◦◦———

OH what a tangled web we weave
When first we practice to deceive!

Scott.

———◦◦◦———

I CONQUER provinces, but Josephine wins hearts.

Napoleon.

———◦◦◦———

NOVELTIES please less than they impress.

Dickens

———◦◦◦———

A WISE physician, skilled our wounds to heal,
Is more than armies to the public weal.

Anon

———◦◦◦———

To do is to succeed.

Schiller

EVERY man has some peculiar train of thought which he falls back upon when alone. This, to a great degree, moulds the man.   Dugald Stewart.

———◦◦———

THERE is nothing so sad as happiness to the sight of the unhappy.   Anon.

———◦◦———

THE sun which ripens the corn and fills the succulent herb with nutriment also pencils with beauty the violet and the rose.   J. C. Abbott.

———◦◦———

HISTORY proves that although woman, swayed by lofty impulses, approaches the angels, yet when yielding to a master passion, she is capable of a refinement of wickedness which men never attain.   Macaulay.

———◦◦———

THEN black despair,
The shadow of a starless night, was thrown
Over the world in which I moved alone.
                    Shelby.

———◦◦———

NO pent-up Utica contracts our powers,
But the whole boundless continent is ours.
                    J. M. Sewall.

———◦◦———

A GILDED frame makes a good picture in the eyes of nearly all the world.   Anon.

———◦◦———

I HAVE thought
Too long and darkly, till my brain became,
In its own eddy, boiling and o'erwrought,
A whirling gulf of fantasy and flame.
                    Byron.

ONE self-approving hour whole years outweighs
Of stupid starers and of loud huzzas.

Pope.

———◇———

THEY walk with speed who walk alone.

Proverb.

———◇———

THE smaller the *calibre* of mind, the greater the *bore* of
a perpetually open mouth.

Holmes.

———◇———

BEAUTY is excluded from the Temple of *Wisdom* only
from an apprehension that the torch of love might obscure the sweet but feeble lustre of truth.

Anon.

———◇———

GOOD temper, like a sunny day, sheds a brightness over
everything. It is the sweetener of toil and the soother
of disquietude.

Washington Irving.

———◇———

THE geologist is like a gnat mounted on an elephant, and
laying down theories as to the whole internal structure
of the vast animal from the phenomena of the hide.

Bishop Watson.

———◇———

YOU might as well try to tell the amount of money in a
safe by feeling the knobs, as to tell what is in a man's
head by feeling his bumps.

Holmes.

———◇———

THERE are men who can think no deeper than a fact.

Voltaire.

———◇———

MEN, in their innovations, should follow the example of
Time, which innovateth greatly, but quietly and by
degrees scarce to be perceived.

Bacon.

IT used to be that *anything for slavery* was constitutional, but now *anything for human rights* is constitutional.

Charles Sumner.

———◦◦◦———

IT is a mistake to suppose that history ever repeats itself.

Rev. J. B. Grier.

———◦◦◦———

THE highest minds live in thought with the great dead far more than with the living, and, next to the dead, with those ideal human beings yet to come, whom they are never destined to see.

M. Comte.

———◦◦◦———

ALL education and all moral discipline should have but one object, to make *altruism* predominant over *egotism.*

M. Comte.

———◦◦◦———

RIDICULE is the test of truth.

Lord Shaftesbury.

———◦◦◦———

A PROFOUND conviction raises a man above the feeling of ridicule.

John Stuart Mill.

———◦◦◦———

TO be just to any opinion, it ought to be considered not exclusively from an opponent's point of view, but from that of the mind which propounds it.

John Stuart Mill.

———◦◦◦———

SAVING faith is the flight of a penitent sinner to the mercy of God in Christ.

Mestrezat.

———◦◦◦———

NOT yet dead,
But in old marbles ever beautiful.

Keat's Endymion.

MAN *is* the hero of the eternal epic composed by the Divine intelligence.

Schelling.

THE Jew is the pilgrim of commerce, trading with every nation and blending with none.

Conybeare.

WHEN we are happy, autumn brings no melancholy to our hearts; but the mournful sound of the wind, the fading leaves and the hazy beauty of the landscape are fraught with sadness to one already anxious and dejected.

Irving.

TEARS, idle tears, I know not what they mean.
  Tears from the depth of some divine despair
Rise in the heart, and gather to the eyes
In looking on the happy autumn fields,
And thinking of the days that are no more.

Tennyson.

A GARBLED quotation may be the most effectual perversion of an author's meaning, and a partial representation of an incident in a man's life may be the most malignant of all calumnies.

McCosh.

IF, then, this temple so blessed, to the roof of which men look for a protection, coextensive with the Continent, a shelter and a model to infant republics that need it—if this temple is tottering on its base, what, I ask, can be a higher or nobler duty for the Senate to perform than to rush to its pillars and uphold them, or be crushed in the attempt?

Jefferson Davis.

HOW often have the judgments of God visibly alighted upon the daring opposers of his will, while others have escaped—just as the lightnings strike the bold cliff and the lofty tower which rise proudly to heaven, while the plains and the lowly cottages are unmolested.

McCosh.

———•◇•———

WITHOUT the Bible man would be in the midst of a sandy desert, surrounded on all sides by a dark and impenetrable horizon.

Daniel Webster.

———•◇•———

IF to love my country, to revere the Constitution, to cherish the Union; if to abhor the madness and hate the treason which would lift up a sacrilegious hand against either; if to read that in the past, to behold it in the present, to foresee it in the future of this land, which is of more value to us and to the world, for ages to come than all the multiplied millions who have inhabited Africa from the creation to this day, if this is to be pro-slavery, then in every nerve, fibre, vein, bone, tendon, joint and ligament, from the topmost hair of the head to the last extremity of the foot, I am all over and altogether a pro-slavery man.

C. L. Vallandigham.

———•◇•———

OF all the Presidents who have ruled over this nation, I think General Jackson has the deepest hold on the popular heart. That enduring fame, that wealth of love which attaches to his memory, does not arise from his great military services. It does not spring from his veto of the United States bank nor from any one act of his administration, but from a glorious principle which underlaid all the acts of his public life, and is embodied in those emphatic words: "The Federal Union; it must and shall be preserved."

Hon. William Montgomery.

IN social phenomena the elementary facts are feelings and actions, and the laws of these are the laws of human nature, social facts being the results of acts and situations. But as society proceeds in its development, its phenomena are determined, more and more, not by the simple tendencies of universal human nature, but by the accumulated influence of past generations over the present.

Auguste Comte.

———◦◦◦———

FROM this time any political thinker who fancies himself able to dispense with a connected view of the great facts of history, as a chain of causes and effects, must be regarded as below the level of the ages; while the vulgar mode of using history, by looking in it for parallel cases, as if any cases were parallel or as if a single instance or even many instances not compared and analyzed could reveal a law, will be more than ever and irrevocably discredited.

John Stuart Mill.

———◦◦◦———

THE Sovereignty of the People, that metaphysical axiom which in France and the rest of the Continent has so long been the theoretic basis of radical and democratic politics, Comté regards as of a purely negative character, signifying the right of the people to rid themselves by insurrection of a social order that has become oppressive; but when erected into a positive principle of government, which condemns indefinitely all superiors to an arbitrary dependence upon the multitudes of their inferiors, he considers it as a sort of transportation to people of the Divine right so much reproached to kings.

John Stuart Mill.

———◦◦◦———

HE who isn't contented with what he has wouldn't be contented with what he would like to have.

"On the Heights."—Auerbach.

15

STRENGTH of character is not mere strength of feeling —it is the resolute restraint of strong feeling. It is unyielding resistance to whatever would disconcert us from without or unsettle us from within.

Dickens.

———◦◦◦———

THINGS are in a shape to push.

Gen. Sheridan to Gen. Grant.

PUSH things!

Gen. Grant to Gen. Sheridan.

———◦◦◦———

MAN is all the higher in the scale of civilization the oftener he changes his clothes in material, cut and color. It is only man who is ever clothing himself anew, ever differently.

"On the Heights."—Auerbach.

———◦◦◦———

WHAT gathering flowers in a wood is to children, that shopping in large towns is to women. To wander from shop to shop, to compare, to choose, to appropriate— it is like gathering flowers.

"On the Heights."—Auerbach.

———◦◦◦———

WE receive with our life the mind of centuries; and he who in truth becomes a human being is the whole humanity in himself.

"On the Heights."—Auerbach.

———◦◦◦———

FRIENDSHIP which flows from the heart cannot be frozen by adversity, as the water that flows from the spring does not congeal in winter.

Cooper.

DON'T talk about it; one feels the best things without speaking of them.

"On the Heights."—Auerbach.

THE eternal clockwork of the skies.

Edward Everett.

WAR is dread when battle-shock and fierce affray
Perpetuate a tyrant's name,
But, guarding Freedom's holy fane,
Confided to her valiant keeping,
The sword from scabbard leaping,
Flashes a heavenly light.

Frank Birch.

I HAVE thought of war until my very dreams were mimic-battles.

Jeremy Taylor.

WORDS, at the touch of the poet, blossom into poetry.

Holmes.

LOVE is never lost. If not reciprocated it will flow back and soften and purify the heart.

Irving.

AMBITION is the spur that makes man struggle with destiny. It is heaven's own incentive to make purpose great and achievement greater.

Donald Mitchell.

UNLESS the Southern States submit to the rightful issues of the war, I would keep them out of the Union till the heavens melt with fervent heat.

Gen. Butler.

THE present government was not the government of my choice. I did not vote for it, nor for any part of it, but it is the government of my country; it is the only organ by which I can exert the force of the country to protect its integrity, and as long as I believe that government to be honestly administered I will throw a mantle over any mistake that I may think it has made, and support it heartily with hand and purse, so help me God.

Gen. Butler.

———◆◆◆———

LIBERTY! eternal spirit of the chainless mind.

Byron.

———◆◆◆———

NATIONS in war have ever moved slowly.

Gen. Butler.

———◆◆◆———

FOR Freedom's battle once begun,
　　Bequeathed by bleeding sire to son,
Though baffled oft is ever won.

Byron.

———◆◆◆———

IT is said that as the traveler enters the Bosphorus, the Turkish capital bursts on his view like a vision of gorgeous beauty. Its myriads of swelling domes and graceful minarets, its magnificent surroundings of dark verdure, of blue waters, of serene sky, render it a scene of surpassing loveliness. But let the stranger approach the city—the charm is dispelled; it is nothing but ill-paved, dirty, narrow-streeted Constantinople. See what a magic effect distance, dancing waves and flashing sunlight produce! Thus do we young men stand on the threshold of the unmapped future—a future freighted with our individual destinies; and peering with straining vision into its vague, shadowy depths, under the ardor of youthful enthusiasm, we would fain believe it a succession of pleasant pictures; but experience cries out with warning voice that these distant prospects are nothing but illusions; that the future, like the city of the Bosphorus, on a nearer approach may shrivel from magnificence into positive littleness, that even its realities are gilded.

Frank Birch.

THE features and the phenomena of nature are a kind of foreshadowed and distributive incarnation.

Rev. Dr. J. Edwards.

PERSEVERANCE is a Roman virtue
That wins each godlike act, and plucks success
E'en from the spear-proof crest of rugged danger.

Owen Meredith.

IF I take care of my character, my reputation will take care of itself.

D. L. Moody.

HAS it never occurred to us, when surrounded by sorrows, that they may be sent to us only for our instruction, as we darken the eyes of birds when we wish them to sing?

Jean Paul Richter.

THOSE with whom we can apparently become well-acquainted in a few moments are generally the most difficult to rightly know and to understand.

Hawthorne.

NOTHING ever happens but once in this world. What I do now I do once and for ever. It is over—it is gone, with all its eternity of solemn meaning.

Carlyle.

I WILL look straight out—see things—not try to evade
   them.

Fact shall be fact for me, and the truth the truth for ever.

Anon.

———◦◦———

BUT for the steady foresense of a free and larger existence, think you that man could consent to be circum-
scribed here into action?   But for the assurance within of
a limitless ocean divine, o'er whose great tranquil depths,
unconscious, the wind-tossed surface breaks into ripples of
trouble that come and change and endure not; but that in
this, of a truth, we have our being, and know it, think you
we men could submit to live and move as we do here?

Bulwer.

———◦◦———

MAN is a living waterfall; so is a nation—preserving its
   identity, its appearance, but constantly changing and
losing its individual particles.

Draper.

———◦◦———

SAID a woman to Dr. Johnson: "How did you happen
   to make such a mistake in defining that word?"   "Ignorance, madam, pure ignorance," was the reply.

Boswell.

———◦◦———

CHOOSE that which is best and custom will make it most
   agreeable.

Dr. J. W. Scott.

———◦◦———

THE idea of philosophy is Truth; the idea of religion is
   Life.

Peter Bayne.

———◦◦———

THERE is but one thing in this universe that will over-
   master the spirit of man—the sight of God Almighty
laying hold of his thunderbolts.

Peter Bayne.

AMONG all the vices which it is necessary to subdue in order to build up the human character, there is none to be compared, in strength or in virulence, with that of impurity. It can outlive and kill a thousand virtues; it can corrupt the most generous heart; it can madden the sternest intellect; it can debase the loftiest imagination. But besides being so poisonous in character, it is, above all others, the most difficult to conquer.

Essays and Reviews.

———◆◆———

WHEN the carcase of a nation lies dead, tainting the solar system, there will not want lightning to kindle its funeral pyre.

Peter Bayne.

———◆◆———

AS a true view of the heinousness of sin lies at the bottom of all true theology, so each man's conviction of sin will lie at the bottom and will determine his own religious experience.

Voices of the Soul.—Reid.

———◆◆———

THE struggle and warfare between the flesh and the spirit, felt and described by Paul, is the normal state of the Christian, but it is a state of victory. There is a worse state than this—a state of insensibility and apathy—an unconsciousness of sin, when the man is steeped in guilt and is sinking into an awful hell.

Dr. A. A. Hodge.

———◆◆———

SIN contracts our views of things and narrows the circle in which our feelings move. But grace expands, liberalizes, vitalizes our views, emotions and purposes.

Prof. S. J. Wilson.

———◆◆———

I WOULD rather be right than be President.

Henry Clay

OH child of many prayers, oh child of baptism and covenants, oh child of the Sabbath-school and the early church, if you are going on from glory to glory, how joyful is your lot! but if you are going on from insensibility to insensibility, if you sin more and feel less, if you are becoming harder and harder, if moral waste is more and more manifest in you, if death already begins to show itself in the supernal and superior part of your nature, if conscience ceases any more to speak, and hope is gone, and faith is lost, and wreck and ruin have come upon the crystalline sphere of your being, then woe is you, woe is you!

Beecher.

— · —

THE opera is an experiment bold even to the verge of absurdity. It is a musical drama. Inheritor of every material objection which lies against the drama, it further taxes common sense to witness a whole career, or, at least, an appreciable fraction of a career, of man executed in music. To think of buying and selling and journeying, of toiling and scolding and complaining, with love and hate, conspiracy and crime and shame, all addressed in pantomime of sound to the ear! It changes our whole estimate of the celestial art of music. It transforms St. Cecilia to the veriest Cinderella. Music is a fine art, but music at the opera is music overloaded, out of place, degraded beyond recognition.

Dr. J. Edwards, President of Washington and Jefferson College

— · —

FEELING is the exponent of condition.

Dr. J. Edwards

— · —

THE exhibition of vice makes men vicious.

Dr. J. Edwards

ON the whole, these are much sadder ages than the early ones; not sadder in a noble and deep way, but in a dim, wearied way—the way of ennui, and jaded intellect, and uncomfortableness of soul and body. Not that we are without festivity, but festivity more or less forced, mistaken, embittered, incomplete, not of the heart. And the profoundest reason of this darkness of heart is, I believe, our want of faith.　　　　　　　　　　　　　**Ruskin.**

———◦◦———

IT is urged, on behalf of the drama, that it employs living representatives to embody the poet's conception, that not a single point merely may be represented, but whole scenes; characters may be unfolded in due order and measure; incidents may be reproduced with their proper antecedents and results; in short, that it is the most flexile of all arts, and that painting, sculpture, architecture and music fairly devote themselves to heighten its effects. There is a show of truth in these pretensions. It may be conceded that such are the attractions of the drama, and it may be conceived that with such facilities it may fully portray a phase in human character or illustrate a chapter in human history, which is also a chapter of providence—a record of God's government in the world. But in all human experience and observation throughout the now lengthened history of the drama, it is found that what it gains in surface it loses in substance—its multiplied machinery is at the expense of its power, its increased attractions are subversive of its spirituality. When civilization is young, when art is feeble, when the sources of knowledge are few and the facilities for its diffusion do not exist—in a land without the pulpit, the press, the common school, the railroad and the telegraph, the drama may be a convenience and a power to put the public in possession of a poet's best thoughts and a

patriot's soundest maxims and noblest resolves; and it is
not impossible that even yet, in this land and in these times,
the capability of the drama in illustration may occasionally
render it serviceable to the young.   But if it retain the
possibility of being a school of history, it is not and cannot
be a school of character.   This it has never been, nor can
be.   It has no principles, no conscience, no authority.   Its
agents have only in rarest instances, never as a class,
commanded the respect of the wise and good, the industrious
and the peaceable.   Besides, goodness is usually too tranquil, virtue too uniform, in its career, to furnish the points
of a play.   On a careful and extended survey of the whole
case we conclude that the means of information among us
render the theatre unnecessary; the pressure and tension of
business leave no time for it; economy forbids its useless
cost; prudence discountenances its exposure of health; purity
stands aghast at its notoriously low and vile associations;
civilization has outgrown and now disdains its puerilities;
religion has superseded its best endeavors by its light, its
law, its glorious model, its grace and its glory.   Let not,
then, the impudent claim be made that the drama receive
the consideration and the patronage which are fairly the
meed of the fine arts.   Let not the Thespian succeed to win
public regard by his boldness and his deceitful pretensions,
while his whole profession debauches at once our tastes and
our morals.   Rev. J. Edwards, D.D.

COWARDICE asks, Is it safe?   Expediency asks, Is it
politic?   Vanity asks, Is it popular? but Conscience
asks, Is it right?   Punshon.

MALICE has a keen scent for blemishes.
                                               Punshon.

THE waves of the ocean spring up, we know not where or why. They come careering past us, the very emblems of resistless power. They subside and are lost among the succeeding waves. In like manner, on the vast sea of human life, individuals, then empires, mysteriously emerge. They raise their ephemeral forms conspicuously high, overwhelming whatever stands in the way of their march. They also subside and are lost, but the unfathomable abyss of humanity still remains, and God's eternal purpose moves on toward the accomplishment of the determined end.

Draper.

IT seems to be a part of the plan of divine Providence that every marked advance in national as in individual life must begin amidst the throes of tumultuous and conflicting emotion. Thus it has been with the present struggle in our own land. Already under the blood-stained grass of a hundred battle-fields lie the seeds of a new growth, waiting to sprout into a greenness that shall crown the land with freedom and brotherhood and peace.

Galusha A. Grow.

AS the tree is fertilized by its own broken branches and fallen leaves and grows out of its own decay, so men and nations are bettered and improved by trial, and refined out of broken hopes and blighted expectations.

F. W. Robertson

PEOPLE living inland know but little about the ocean, only what comes to them in the rain and tempests. So we Christians are now living inland, far away from the ocean of God's infinite love, getting only droppings of grace and joy and truth. By and by we will be upon the ocean.

Dr. A. A. Hodge.

BETTER fall covered and scarred with the wounds of glory than to surrender through expediency what is right, or to yield for the sake of expediency to what is wrong.

Joseph Holt.

———◦◦◦———

THE wind strikes the cascade, and for a moment interrupts the flow of its waters, dashing it into spray and tossing it into foam, but below the continuity is regained, and it flows on and on, a thing of beauty and splendor. So the blasts of envy and slander may for a moment interrupt the current of your fame; but stand firm and put your trust in God, and the stream of your life will flow on and on, sparkling with the brilliancy of its goodness, and unstemmed by the malice of your enemies.

Punshon.

———◦◦◦———

AN incident occurred at the National Convention assembled in the great city of New York which was at once an omen and a warning. The grand hall where the convention met was full of patriotic men. Upon its walls were poised two shields of the whole thirty-seven States, and around every shield was the American flag. Upon the platform stood two bronze statues of noble soldiers, one leaning upon a great bronze sword. The convention had been in session for several days. Ballot after ballot had taken place. First one was up, then another, and presently a gallant general, whose name has never anywhere been mentioned but with respect—I mean Hancock. No man knew whether on the next ballot he was or was not to be chosen. Everything was uncertain, when, suddenly, the great bronze sword in the statue's hand snapped asunder at the hilt. It was not touched by a mortal hand. No human agency broke it. Some mysterious, invisible and irresistible power snapped it at the hilt, and the word went forth that the country was to have hereafter a statesman and not a soldier for its leader. My friends, the people throughout the nation are being stirred, not by any human agency, not by any word of public speakers in public assemblages, but there is a power as mysterious as unseen, as irresistible as that which broke the sword, which is moving on the masses of the people, and which will elevate to the chair of State one whom we honor as an excellent citizen, a Christian gentleman and a noble statesman.

Hon. John T. Hoffman.

THE first characteristic of life everywhere is change, growth, adaptation to modifying circumstances and events. The point which marks the end of change in a body or a mind, in a society or a party, is the end of its life. That this change shall be true growth—that every moment shall be in the line of a development and manifestation of the principles it embodies and which justify its existence—is the responsibility of those who control and direct it.

New York Evening Post.

A GREAT deal of talent is lost to the world for the want of a little courage. Every day sends to their graves a number of obscure men who have only remained in obscurity because their timidity has prevented them from making the first effort, and who, if they could only have been induced to begin, would in all probability have gone great lengths in the career of fame. The fact is, that in order to do anything in this world worth doing, we must not stand shivering on the bank thinking of the cold and danger, but jump in and scramble through as well as we can. It will not do to be perpetually calculating risk and adjusting chance. It all did very well before the flood, when a man could consult his friends upon an intended publication for a hundred and fifty years, and then live to see its success for six or seven centuries afterward; but at present a man waits, and doubts, and hesitates, and consults his brother, and his uncle, and his first cousin, and his particular friends, till one day he finds that he is sixty-five years of age, that he has lost so much time in consulting first cousins and particular friends that he has no more time left to follow their advice. There is so little time for over-squeamishness at present the opportunity slips away; the very period of life at which a man chooses to venture, if ever, is so confined that it is no bad rule to preach up the necessity, in such instances, of a little violence done to the feelings, and of efforts made in defiance of strict and sober calculation.　　　　　　　　　　　　　Sydney Smith.

———◦◦◦———

EVERY man's life is a plan of God.

Bushnell.

———◦◦◦———

LOGIC is a close and compendious eloquence.

Magoon.

———◦◦◦———

HAD I read as much as others I might have been as ignorant.

Hobbes

———◦◦◦———

THERE are no trifles in the moral universe of God.

Punshon.

———◦◦◦———

ALL things hold their march
As if by one great will;
Moves one moves all—
Hark to the footfall!
On, on for ever!

Miss Martineau.

THE lines of our life stretch farther than we think. We lay our plans for the future, and they prove to be tracks that never end. All our paths go out into the unseen world. As you look across the street the line of your vision is terminated by some building. You can see nothing beyond. If that building were away you could see other buildings and streets, and if these too were gone, the line of your vision would shoot off beyond the stars till it had reached the utmost verge of the great universe. So the hopes of this earthly life—its plans and schemes and busy contrivings—are all endless lines that reach into an endless eternity. Within the little circle of yourself, the plans you make for to-morrow, the wishes and hopes you entertain for the coming months and years, you may not see or realize how far your favorite purposes stretch off into the distance. Do you ever think how they touch on the margin of an endless future? Do you never see how all earthly things are embosomed in an always present eternity? We walk every day in the embrace of futurity. The issue of every purpose is there; the end of every plan is there; the result of every deed is there; no path will end this side.

Congregationalist.

———◦◦◦———

MAN is the creature of a day, a helpless immortal, finite, complicate, wonderful. He is the child of thought and passion, yet there is something more earnest than this same thought and passion, something more characteristic of that dim destiny to which he is born, which may be written in that fearful word—for ever! He is but a pebble on Time's shore, and the battling waves chafing against him polish him and make him a jewel fit to be set in heaven. His life from the cradle to the grave is a tale that is soon told and soon forgotten. Yet the moment this frail creature is imbued with life, there is given into his charge an ever-living soul. He is entrusted with a work—a deep, earnest life-work. His duty is to perform it with a firm, faithful and prayerful heart. How nobly it can be done, but what a sad, miserable, shameful record he can send above, if he choose! Each unuttered thought, each heart-feeling floats upward, a fearful condemner or happy justifier. It is a fearful yet glorious responsibility, elevating man next to his God. For us, this life-work is just begun. All these years gone serve but to teach how few of the great and glorious truths we have learned. Locked up in these immortal minds of ours is a countless store of wealth, waiting only for the hand of energy to be applied. God has entrusted to us the key: what if it requires almost an iron grasp to turn it! what if the first excavation hardly seems to repay our efforts! Let us slacken not, relax not, and the end will surely be attained. Let us remember that not a chord we touch but vibrates through eternity, not a sound we utter but reports at the throne of God. Glancing back into the past, what an infinitesimal part of this work is accomplished, compared with what lies before! Standing as we do now in the vestibule of Time's great temple, and looking forward, we catch faint glimpses of the interior resplendent with radiance. Through long vistas of dazzling brightness, Fame, Genius and Happiness stand side by side, each with fresh laurels to crown our young brows. There are high columns wreathed with glory, bearing the names of heroes gone before. The walls are hung with crowns, glorious in their brilliancy, sparkling with gems of untold worth: those crowns are clasped with a magic seal. The watchwords, God and Glory, in our hearts, and truth engraven on our brows, will admit us there. In the distance we discern the mines of science, glittering with gems; it is for us to explore and wreathe a diadem which shall but grow brighter and brighter as time rolls on. Such may be the picture imagination paints on the outspread canvas of the future, but reality's sombre colors may reveal little of the gay blendings of perspective vision. Yet, aided by the lamp of Divine Help, we can explore the deepest, darkest recesses of earth's mines and come forth uncontaminated by the vile dust, bearing only beautiful gems. The world's workshop is wide. Toiling hands and hearts and minds are wanted. We have these hands to work, these hearts to feel, these minds to think. Remember God but lends to us. He asks for his reward ripened sheaves and fruits. Shall we then appear before his throne, bearing naught but withered leaves? Let us "act, act in the living Present." No more intrepid flights of imagination, no more gorgeous realm-making. Through dreamland-life we shall soon wake to find the cords that bind our heart-doors broken. We launch our frail bark of womanhood on a stormy sea. Huge billows of political strife are raging—hissing, traitorous serpents lie coiled in every wave. But it is a time which will call forth all that is earnest in our nature—a time when labor will bring its own reward. If our paths lie through suffering, sorrow and care, let us work heroically, untiringly, remembering that many narrow footpaths patiently traveled lead into broad avenues in our onward march. When we have reached the end, it will cheer our hearts to look back and see we have *lived* by the way! And then, when this life-work is all accomplished, when the record is sealed and sent above, what is written therein will either send us to happiness or misery, to joy or anguish, life or death.

Miss Mary Bausman, now Mrs. Diehl of Phila.

———⋄⋄———

MAN is the glory, jest and riddle of the world.

Pope.

MANY, if not all, of those who attain eminence in life, keep constantly before them an ideal character, adorned with virtue and excellences, which they strive to make their own. The ambitious youth forms a conception of such an ideal. He attributes to it every valuable quality, invests it with every grace. Henceforth it becomes his model. Here is a combination of virtue to whose possession he may aspire, a perfection toward which he may approach. True, he may never attain it. Like the mariner guided by the polar star, he may never be able to reach that bright object which hovers over his pathway and directs his course; yet without it he would wander aimless and purposeless upon the great ocean of existence.

Bulwer.

HOW narrowly we miss the road
  That might our future life decide!
   So many paths are vainly tried,
So many but the right one trod.

Anon.

WE do not what we ought,
  What we ought not, we do,
And lean upon the thought
  That *chance* will bring us through.

Matthew Arnold.

SELF-VINDICATION never does a man any good, unless he has been assailed.

Gladstone.

IT is just when a man gets down the lowest, and things look the darkest around him, that light breaks in and hope begins to live again.

R. B I.

OUR youthful troubles and their sources are soon forgotten, but the objects of beauty which gladden the early life never cease to yield us delight. They become the stars of the firmament of youth, lighting up the pathway of the past, and when in later years, the night of sorrow gathers round the soul, memory, like the astronomer's tube, piercing the surrounding gloom, sweeps that distant sky, and reveals those stars still shining with undiminished lustre. The heart renews its youth, and the whole man is cheered and invigorated by the contemplation of those things of beauty that were the delight of happier days.

Henry A. Walker, Wheeling, Va.

———◦◇◦———

GOD help us! Of what avail are experience, foresight, prudence, wisdom in this world, when at every chance step the silliest trifle, the most commonplace meeting, a turn down the wrong street, the dropping of a glove, the introduction to an unnoticed stranger, an unguarded word or act, will fling down every precaution, and build for us a fate of which we never dream? Of what avail for us to erect our sand-castle where every chance blast of air may blow it into nothing, and drift another into form that we have no power to move? Life hinges upon seeming hazard, and at every turn wisdom is mocked by it, and energy swept aside by it as the battle-dykes are worn away and the granite walls beaten down by the fickle ocean waves, which, never two hours together alike, never two instants without restless motion, are yet as changeless as they are capricious, as omnipotent as they are fickle, as cruel as they are countless. Men and mariners may build their bulwarks, but unless God is their guide and shield, hazard and the sea will overthrow and wear away both alike at their will, their wild and unreined will, which no foresight can foresee, which no strength can bridle.

Ouida.

THERE is this difference in the love of women and of men—that in the former when once admitted, it engrosses all the sources of thought and excludes every object but itself; but in the latter it is shared with all the former reflections and feelings which the past yet bequeaths us, and can neither, however powerful be its nature, constitute the whole of our happiness or woe. The love of man, in his maturer years, is not so much a new emotion as a revival and concentration of all his departed affections to others. Who, when he turns to recall his first and fondest associations—when he throws off, one by one, the layers of earth and stone which have grown and hardened over the records of the past—who has not been surprised to discover how fresh and unimpaired those buried treasures rise again upon his heart? They have been laid up in the storehouse of time—they have not perished; their very concealment has preserved them: we remove the lava, and the world of a gone day is before us.   Bulwer.

———•◦•———

LOVE in John's heart is something like a divine complacency and satisfaction—a calm, unruffled lake, the reflected heaven slumbering on its bosom, and the hills of holiness watching around it. Paul's love is not like a divine complacency. It is much like what we would fancy a seraph's fervid fire. It cannot be still. It rests not day nor night. It cannot be hid. Blaze after blaze bursts forth, brighter and brighter still. John lies basking, so to speak, in the full sunshine of his Saviour's love, and so he seems as if he could fain lie still and enjoy it. "This is my rest, here will I dwell, for I have desired it." Paul, like the skylark roused from its lonely bed by the rising sun, spreads forth his willing wings; away he soars to heaven, and as he soars, he sings far above the world the praise of that Saviour, who hath called him out of darkness into his marvelous light. John's love was like his life—calm, still, either leaning on Jesus' bosom or seeing visions in the lonely, sea-girt Patmos. Paul's love was like his life, too—either journeying to Damascus, or shipwrecked in his way to Rome, or fighting with wild beasts at Ephesus, or daring to carry the gospel into the very palace of the Cæsars.

Rev. R. B. Nichol.

IF any one should give me a dish of sand and tell me there were particles of iron in it, I might look for them with my eyes, and search for them with my clumsy fingers, and be unable to detect them; but let me take a magnet and sweep through it, and how would it draw to itself the almost invisible particles by mere power of attraction! The unthankful heart, like my finger in the sand, discovers no mercies; but let the thankful heart sweep through the day, and as the magnet finds the iron, so it will find in every hour some heavenly blessings; only the iron in God's hand is gold.

O. W. Holmes.

WHEN we look through a red glass, the whole heavens appear bloody, but through pure, uncolored glass we receive the clear light that is so refreshing and comfortable to behold. So when sin unpardoned is between, and we look on God through that, we can perceive nothing but anger and enmity in his countenance; but make Christ the medium, and through him, as clear, transparent glass, the beams of God's favorable countenance shine upon the soul. The Father cannot look upon his well-beloved Son but graciously and pleasingly. God looks on us out of Christ, sees us rebels, and fit to be condemned. We look on God as being just and powerful to punish us; but when Christ is between, God looks on us in him justified, and we look on God in him pacified, and see the smiles of his favorable countenance. Take Christ out, all is terrible; interpose Christ, and all is full of peace.   Leighton.

———◆◆———

MANY, owing to their education and associations, their keen enjoyment of life, and their eager interest in it, and their buoyancy of soul, do in effect make a mock at sin, and treat it as a morbid fiction. That which underlies the whole Bible, as among its deepest foundations, that without which all God's inspirations and all the agencies of moral providence are either mockery or folly, that to which the laws of all nations and the history of all times bear emphatic witness, that which the consciousness of every thoughtful man attests as strongly as it attests his existence, is put aside as worthy of no consideration.   John Young, LL.D.

———◆◆———

O IMPENITENT sinner! abodes of sorrow await you where every past benefit will but be an instrument of torture, where memory and conscience will hold up the mirror of bygone privilege and promise, of abused mercy, of forsworn and perjured vows, only that remorse may strike upon the soul its more than scorpion sting, and where grace and hope can never alleviate the wailings that will reverberate through the dungeons of outer darkness for ever and for ever.   Mr. Parsons of York.

———◆◆———

JUSTICE sheathed his sword, and Mercy went smiling round the throne of God, singing such a song of praise as the arches of heaven never echoed to before—the song of the redeemed of the Lord.   Rev J. B. Patterson

MAN sins! the trembling culprit stands self-condemned, heaven-condemned before his Judge. The blow of Almighty Justice is raised—the terrible blow that must smite the wretched sinner down to an everlasting hell is just ready to descend, when lo! Love, Divine Love, springs forward: "Father Almighty, forbear; on me let the stroke of thy vengeance fall; smite the Shepherd!" The fiery blade is seized, and its burning point turned in upon the bosom of the innocent victim. Love bleeds, the languid head droops exhausted, Mercy rises from the tomb a lovely form, a new attribute, heretofore unknown in the universe of God. Angelic messengers now for the first time, beholding in its fullness the glory of God, escort the heaven-generated but earth-born stranger to the realms of day. The song of salvation swells from myriads of golden harps, and all heaven is filled with the echo of the Beloved name.

George Junkin, D.D.

WE can sing away our cares easier than we can reason them away. The birds are the earliest to sing in the morning; the birds are more without care than anything else I know of. Sing in the evening. Singing is the last thing that robins do. When they have done their daily work, when they have flown their last flight, and picked up their last morsel of food, and cleansed their bills on a napkin of a bough, then on a top twig they sing one song of praise. I know they sleep sweeter for it. They dream music, for sometimes in the night they break forth in singing, and stop suddenly after the first note, startled by their own voice. Oh that we might sing evening and morning, and let song touch song all the way through! Oh that we could put songs under our burdens! Oh that we could extract the sense of sorrow by song! Then these things would not poison so much. Sing in the house—teach your children to sing. When troubles come, go at them with songs. When griefs arise, sing them down. Lift the voice of praise against cares. Praise God by singing; that will lift you above trials of every sort. Attempt it. They sing in heaven, and among God's people on earth song is the appropriate language of Christian feeling.

Beecher.

THE devil cannot stand music.

Luther.

THE man that hath no music in himself,
  Nor is not moved by concord of sweet sounds,
Is fit for treasons, stratagems, and spoils.
* * * * * * *
Let no such man be trusted.

Shakespeare

WHAT is commonly called musical criticism is a misnomer. If we have heard a piece of music before— if it be pleasantly associated in our history—if it recall fond scenes of the past, which we would fain renew—we love it. We are indulgent listeners, whatever be the voice, the instrument, the style, and are grateful for the occasion of being so agreeably affected. There are those dear to our hearts who have passed away from earth. The grave has closed over them. The buds which last they gathered have crumbled into dust. Flowers which they planted have ceased to bloom. The precious lock of hair which we have so long treasured with jealous care seems somehow sadly wanting in its power to recall the dear face it once shaded. Our very memory of their features, voice and bearing, we are conscious, is gradually giving place to a mere ideal of their worth and loveliness. But there was an air, a piano-piece, a song, a psalm-tune, which they were wont to sing, or to play, or to admire, and with which they are now sweetly, inseparably associated. There is nothing like music to embalm and to reproduce the past. And thus we love the music, not for its own sake, but for theirs who now live for us in its strains. We praise its every repetition. We are indignant when some fastidious musical editor pronounces it ungrammatical, and we count it a token of degeneracy when our favorite, so hallowed, is at last superseded by some later composition. In the case of music which is new to us, though the elements of our judgment are different, its practical value is no better, but substantially the same as before, in both cases the merits of the tune being measured by the amount of emotion it has stirred within us. All this is purely personal, and, in truth, not far from selfish. Such judgments are worthless, being often unsound in fact and always unsafe in principle.

Dr. J. Edwards.

THE music of art is but the imitation of the music of nature; there are voices of grief in the winds, joy in the songs of spring and melody in the rippling stream. These æolian strains God employs to educate the finer feelings; and man, conspiring to the same result, adds these artificial charms, which elevate the sentiment, quicken the imagination, touch the heart, transport the soul and draw the finite closer to the Infinite.

William H. Robertson.

IT were an error to suppose that an artist has only to follow and copy nature. The truth is, this is impracticable. Nature, as the very word implies, is ever in a state of transition, and can never be seen all at once. What can be comprehended at a single glance will be partial, and so far untrue. To revert to the case of the portrait painter, in whose branch of art, if anywhere, the ideal is to be ignored and nature strictly followed, the sitter comes at intervals of days, and often of weeks and months, and is closeted with the artist in his studio for hours together. The sittings are not always at the same hour of the day, nor with the same conditions of light and shade, or of health and spirits, or of temper and expression. The painting is sketched through all the variations of these, and is finally completed in such a way as to give a kind of resultant of all the observations taken; and those observations are largely æsthetic—readings of character and of the play of feature as its exponent.

Dr. J. Edwards.

PORTRAIT painting is painting from recollection and from a conception of character, with the object before us to assist the memory and understanding.

Hazlitt.

ART is a glorious boon to man. It prompts to a most intimate acquaintance with the soul, and to a most delicate and careful analysis of its operations. It is the enduring record of man's purest conceptions in terms universally and for ever intelligible. It improves taste, refines manners and adorns scholarship. It promotes a genial sympathy between men of different and distant generations. It establishes new and precious communion between man and nature. As the quick, warm logic of the heart, it oft outstrips the inductions of science and stands waiting to bless its achievements. Its voice, seemingly of revery or of introspection, is ofttimes the hymn of prophecy —the parable of the unseen. As the handmaid of religion, the ally of a pure faith, how it rises in dignity and power and glory! Delivered by the knowledge of God and of grace from mere man-worship, it recognizes the presence, the skill and the purpose of the great Creator. To sancti-fied art, nature is the grand theatre of redemption. Crea-tion has its boundaries, its elements, its laws, such as to set forth most suitably and effectively the cross of mercy.

Dr. J. Edwards.

THE gallery of art runs back through the ages of the world's life, and has gathered and treasured the finest conceptions of the finite mind. Within the golden gates of this Minervian temple the canvas and the stone are full of vitality and intense with expression. Along its polished walls are hung the matchless invention of Raphael, the glowing colors of Titian, the grandeur of Angelo, the sweet-ness of Guido and the richness of Rubens. Along its lengthened corridors, its fretted arches and towering domes, architecture has inscribed her very name, and lent her love-liness for its pillar and canopy; while in the gorgeous aisles the sculptured marble stands radiant with grace and beauty. Ages have lent their souls to these, and thousands of hearts have rejoiced over these masteries of genius, and taken courage and hope from the achievements of others. Classic writing, too, the great type of æsthetic perfection, breathes out its pathetic accents, instinct with vitality, clear-ness, variety and durability. Like a crystal sea, it reflects the images of the outward and stamps them on the inward. Its golden lyre thrills beneath the poet's touch, who, with one bold sweep, can excite within us a world of images, of sentiment, of thought—can strike, from its consecrated strings, strains, those lofty strains, which meet responses from the inward recesses of the soul. And yet there resides in the midst of us a spirit of utilitarian reform which mocks at the glories of art and scorns the noblest efforts of the race—a headlong empiricism which takes up the puling cry of "Expediency! expediency!" and repudiates every system of science whose influence is not directly manifest in the building of warehouses or the construction of railways —a reckless materialism which discards all ornament, seeks for immediate and tangible results, dotes on physical agencies, and rests the success of the present, the hopes of the future, the destiny of the world on "practical utility." But if this be all that is necessary, why did God form the snow in crystals, the leaves of the forest of every shape and hue—the rose for beauty, the human countenance instinct with intelligence? Why did he bespangle the heavens and send the sun down to such a gorgeous setting, or rain on rocks and wilderness? Why hide diamonds in the earth and pearls in the bottom of the sea? Such reformers forget the parallelism of the outward and the inward, and that God in his works teaches man in his. Strip the earth of its ornaments; rob the countenance of its beauty; blot from the brow of heaven its rainbow and its nebulæ; and what a cheerless waste! what a dismal abode of eternal mist and cloud and gloom were the habitation of man! Like this would be the mind stripped of its legitimate ornament and the harmonious action of its faculties. Æsthetics, then, as the science of the beautiful, the educator of what is to us aspiring, noble, benevolently beautiful and holy, must wield a most important influence upon the culture of society. This it will do by tending to promote a symmetrical mental discipline.

William H. Robertson.

————

WE know æsthetic studies are not the regenerators of society. We claim them not as the primary means of moral development, but as the channels through which man's moral feelings may gain vitality and strength. Classic writing has often been the organ of religious truth—

"the picture of silver" in which the golden apples of the gospel have been set and preserved from age to age. Eloquence in the council-chamber partly controls the national mind; in the pulpit, thrills and moves the heart. Poetry, as embodied in the hymn of praise, becomes an instrument of power—a vein which feeds and vitalizes even devotional feeling. And music, as it rises from the family altar or echoes from the sanctuary, addresses the highest and holiest emotions of the soul. The human mind, æsthetically developed, is continually grasping at the ideal of perfection, and in the agonizing pursuit of its realization catches the harmony of God's work, and learns to look upon the entire universe as one great cosmos linked together by one invisible chain—the outward to the inward, the material to the spiritual, the finite to the infinite. Thus from the perfection of the canvas and the stone the mind may catch the divine outline, the faint ideal of a perfect life, and from the requirements of the classic page it may move beyond the mere physical, beyond the visible and tangible, along the chain that links the material with the spiritual, and learn to look upon the Bible as the only true model of classic writing, the only standard of moral perfection. Nor are we permitted to pause here, but, aided by revelation, we are borne onward along the golden chain until we may see in our ideal of the future the hideous deformity of vice and sin supplanted by the beauteous form of virtue and holiness until we see the old heavens passing away and the Perfect Man, the spotless Nazarene, seated in the midst of a new heaven, clothed in the robes of his millennial glory, and waving the sceptre of righteousness over a regenerated world. Thus æsthetics begins with a perfect form, moves along the everlasting chain to the idea of a perfect life, then to that of a perfect man, and finds its last and true end in the Son of God.

Rev. J. M. Smith.

COMMON things are quite as much neglected and despised in the education of the rich as of the poor. It is wonderful how little a young gentleman may know when he has taken his university degree, especially if he has been industrious and has stuck to his studies. He may really spend a long time in looking for somebody more ignorant than himself. If he talks with the driver of the stage-coach that lands him at his father's door, he finds he knows nothing of horses. If he falls into conversation with a gardener, he knows nothing of plants or flowers. If he walks in the fields, he does not know the difference between barley, rye and wheat; between rape and turnips; between lucerne and sainfoin; between natural and artificial grass. If he goes into a carpenter's yard, he does not know one wood from another. If he comes across an attorney, he has no idea of the difference between common and statute law, and is wholly in the dark as to those securities of personal and political liberty on which we pride ourselves. If he talks with a county magistrate, he finds his only idea of the office is, that the gentleman is a sort of English sheikh, as the mayor of the neighboring borough is a sort of cadi. If he strolls into a workshop or place of manufacture, it is always to find his level, and that a level far below the present company. If he dines out, and as a youth of proved talents, and perhaps university honors, is expected to be literary, his literature is confined to a few popular novels—the novels of the last century, or even of the last generation, history and poetry, having been almost studiously omitted in his education. The girl who has never stirred from home, and whose education has been economized, not to say neglected, in order to send her own brother to college, knows vastly more of those things than he does. The same exposure awaits him wherever he goes, and whenever he has the audacity to open his mouth. At sea he is a landlubber, in the country a cockney, in town a greenhorn, in science an ignoramus, in business a simpleton, in pleasure a milksop—everywhere out of his element, everywhere at sea, in the clouds, adrift, or by whatever word utter ignorance and incapacity are to be described. In society and in the work of life he finds himself beaten by the youth whom he despised at college as frivolous or abhorred as profligate. He is ordained and takes charge of a parish only to be laughed at by the farmers, the tradespeople, and even the old women, for he can hardly talk of religion without betraying a want of common sense. **London Times.**

THE impossibility of equality among men, the good which arises from this inequality, the compensating circumstances in different states and fortunes, the honorableness of every man who is worthily filling his appointed place in society, however humble, the proper relations of poor and rich, governor and governed, the nature of wealth and mode of circulation, the difference between productive and unproductive labor, the relation of the products of the mind and the hand, the true value of works of the higher order, and the possible amount of their production, the meaning of "civilization," its advantages and dangers, the meaning of the term "Refinement," the possibilities of possessing refinement in a low station, and of losing it in a high one, and above all, the significance of almost every act of a man's daily life in its ultimate operations upon himself and others,—all this might be, and ought to be, taught to every boy in the nation so completely that it should be just as impossible to introduce an absurd or licentious doctrine among adult population as a new version of the multiplication table. **Ruskin.**

THERE never yet was a generation of men, savage or civilized, who, taken as a body, so woefully fulfilled the words, "having no hope, and without God in the world," as the present civilized European race. A red Indian or Otaheitan savage has more sense of a Divine existence round him, of government over him, than the plurality of refined Londoners and Parisians. And those of us who may in some sense be said to believe are divided up into classes and sects. Hence nearly all our powerful men in this age of the world are unbelievers; the best of them in doubt and misery, the worst in reckless despair, the plurality in plodding hesitation—doing, as well as they can, what practical work lies ready to their hands. Most of our scientific men are in the last class. Our popular authors either set themselves against all religious forms, pleading only for simple truth and benevolence, as Thackeray and Dickens; or give themselves up to bitter and fruitless statement of facts, as De Balzac; or surface-painting, as Scott; or careless blasphemy, sad or smiling, as Byron, Beranger. Our earnest poets and deepest thinkers are doubtful and indignant, as Tennyson and Carlyle—one or two, anchored, indeed, but anxious or weeping—Wordsworth and Mrs. Browning.

Ruskin.

———◦◦———

HONOR is not a matter of any man's calling merely, but rather of his own actions in it.

Dwight.

———◦◦———

LOVE depends on the *loving*, and not on the *loved!*

Bulwer.

———◦◦———

A GUILTY conscience is like a whirlpool, drawing in all to itself which would otherwise pass by.

Victor Hugo

IDEAS are the wellsprings of all the joy and sorrow of our mortal life.

Augusta Evans.

A MAN is what his heart is—his faith and hopes and purposes. These are himself, both the foundation and the superstructure of his entire personality. As he thinketh in his heart, so is he.

Dwight.

LOVE me as well as you can.

Johnson to Boswell.

THE man with whom prayer is a habit will soon acquire the language of prayer; and if a minister has not this language of prayer, this vocabulary of the Christian closet a congregation will do well to reject him. They who never attend drill will appear badly on review.

Hugh Miller.

THERE are no footprints backward!

Hampden's Motto.

O PUSILLANIMOUS heart! be comforted,
And like a cheerful traveler, take the road,
Singing beside the hedge.

Anon.

CARTHAGINIAN women used to give their black locks to string their country's bows and to furnish cordage for its shipping.

Augusta Evans.

I AM not a little sunburnt by the glare of life, but weather-beaten by its storms.

Stephen A. Douglas.

17

No stream from its source
Flows seaward, how lonely soever its course,
But what some land is gladdened.   No star ever rose
And set without influence somewhere.   Who knows
What earth needs from earth's lowest creature? No life
Can be pure in its purpose and strong in its strife,
And all life not be purer and stronger thereby.

Mrs. Browning.

———◦◦◦———

REMORSE! remorse!

John Randolph.

———◦◦◦———

THE stars heat the earth sufficiently to melt a belt of ice seventy-five feet thick in a single year.

Eclectic Magazine.

———◦◦◦———

A WOMAN'S heart, like the moon, is always changing, but there is always a man in it.

London Punch.

———◦◦◦———

MY worst enemies are more valuable to me than my best friends.

Luther.

———◦◦◦———

THERE are smiles and tears in that gathering band,
    Where the heart is pledged with the trembling hand.
What trying thoughts in the bosom swell
As the bride bids parents and home farewell!
Kneel down by the side of the tearful fair,
And strengthen the perilous hour with prayer.

Henry Ware, Jr.

———◦◦◦———

NONE without hope e'er loved the brightest fair;
    But Love can hope where Reason would despair.

Lord Lyttleton

WHAT is good-looking but looking good?

Horace Smith.

———◦❖◦———

GRACE GREENWOOD says common things in an uncommon way.

Pittsburg Commercial.

———◦❖◦———

HERE comes the ever-welcome ugly face of a beautiful soul!

Anon.

———◦❖◦———

THE world is out of tune, and our hearts are out of tune;
and the more our souls vibrate to the music of heaven,
the more must they feel the discords of earth.

Schoenberg-Cotta Family.

———◦❖◦———

HEAVEN must be very near us, else how can the angels
be so near to us and yet so near to God?

Schonberg-Cotta Family.

———◦❖◦———

I ADMIRE the coarse arts full as much as the fine arts.

Anon.

———◦❖◦———

FROM torch reversed the flame
Still streameth, rising straight;
So struggleth up the brave man
Stricken down by fate.

Anon.

———◦❖◦———

THE sweetest wine, if left exposed to feed on its own
sweetness, turns to sourest vinegar; so the best affections,
if turned back to prey upon themselves, are changed to the
bitterest hatred.

Bulwer.

———◦❖◦———

HIS steps were taken with the deliberateness of **Destiny.**

Holland on Lincoln.

GOETHE says that Shakespeare's characters are like watches with dial-plates of transparent crystal—they show you the hour like others, and the inward mechanism also is all visible.

Carlyle.

———◇———

I HAVE conquered adversity, but it remains to be seen whether I can conquer prosperity.

Holden.

———◇———

COULD we see the secret lists of God's friends, we would find no blots or erasures there.

James' Anxious Inquirer.

———◇———

EVERY new book we read, every new man we meet, our hearts beat with expectation!

Miss Anna E. Dickinson.

———◇———

SANCTIFICATION will always be attended with pain. We must be crucified with Christ before we can reign with him.

Dr. A. A. Hodge.

———◇———

AS our natural life is a constant breathing, exhalation and inhalation, expiration and inspiration—dependent on the constant commerce between the vital blood and the oxygen of the air—so our spiritual life is a constant repenting of sin and going to Jesus; and the oftener we truly repent, the more intense will be our hatred of sin, and the oftener we go to Jesus, the more intimate will be our communion with him.

Dr. A. A. Hodge.

———◇———

A BED watered with tears for the sins of the land is rare to be found among us.

Rutherford.

IT gives one pain to think of a screw propeller stirring the blue depths of the sea of Galilee—of slackwatering, for the purpose of navigation, the Jordan's slender but hallowed stream, of spanning it with a wire suspension bridge at the spot where the tribes of Israel passed over to the conquest of their God-given inheritance, of joint-stock companies to search for petroleum on the shores of the Dead Sea, of McCormick's reaper scouring the fields where Ruth, the Moabitess, once gleaned, of the whirr of a modern threshing machine at the floor of Araunah the Jebusite, of an iron mill at Damascus, and a cotton factory at Bethlehem, of the shrill scream of the locomotive as it rushes along its iron track from Jerusalem to Jericho, of the Capernaum Gazette and the Nazareth Times, of a straggling line of telegraph poles from Joppa to Jabesh Gilead, of a macadamized turnpike through the valley of Jehoshaphat, and of lighting up with gas the dark and narrow streets of the sacred city.   Presbyterian Banner.

THE clergyman who lives in the city *may* have piety, but he *must* have taste.   Emerson.

WHAT you call barrenness and poverty is simplicity to me.   God could not be unkind to me if he tried.   I love best to have each thing in its season only, and enjoy doing without it at all other times.   It is the greatest of all advantages to enjoy no advantage at all.   I have never got over my surprise that I was born in the most estimable place in the world, and in the very nick of time, too.
                    Henry Thoreau as quoted by Emerson.

A NATION cannot afford to do a mean thing.
                    Charles Sumner

YOU may depend upon it that there are as good hearts to serve men in palaces as in cottages.

Robert Owen.

———◦◦◦———

SO I may express the hope that the state will steadily ad-vance, or it is a day without a night.

Emerson.

———◦◦◦———

WE cannot live on our past reputation, any more than our frames can be sustained on the food of which we have partaken days ago. In these times, when it is known that all things move—earth and sun, stars and constellations—we cannot stop or remain stationary, except at the risk of being thrown out of our sphere without the power of return-ing to it. In this new country we have to look to our children more than to our fathers, and "instead of the fathers shall be the children."

McCosh's Inaugural at Princeton College.

———◦◦◦———

RELIGION is never fashionable. The way to eternal happiness is not the broad way superintended by Paris, but the narrow way watched by the Redeemer. It is fashionable to neglect the spirit. It is fashionable to make the body less than raiment and the soul less than the body; but in the judgment day the conduct of the life will not be tried by fashion-plates, nor by the rule of society, but by the truth of God, and we shall all be there.

From the Episcopal Methodist

———◦◦◦———

I CAN afford to wait.

Salmon P. Chase.

———◦◦◦———

TREASON must be made odious.

Andrew Johnson.

THE idea of the Supreme Being has this peculiarity: that as it admits of no substitute, so from the first moment it is formed it is capable of continued growth and development. It borrows splendor from all that is fair, subordinates to itself all that is great, and sits enthroned on the riches of the universe.

Robert Hall.

A STRANGER to our people would, from reading our journals, conclude that we were a nation of the most degraded character. All our leading and rising men he would learn to regard as mean, lowlived, immoral and irreligious. The chief officer of the government could hold no higher place in his judgment than a drunken perjurer, surrounded by a number of artful, wicked, thieving scoundrels as his auxiliaries, and bent on the destruction of the country, the betrayal of the most sacred rights and the subversion of the rights and well-being of the people. To read such things daily, to hear the meanest and most insulting epithets poured out on all sides, to listen to the coarsest and most indecent assaults on the morality of others, cannot but have a very evil influence, and, in time, make our language rich in all that degrades and barbarizes it. It is time that a stop be put to this: if a political party can gain its end only by having recourse to such foul means, then let the party fail, for a cause that needs such a support is a bad cause. Lying and misrepresentation have not now for the first time proved the fruitful source of misery to man. Falsehood can only thrive for a time, and will, in the end, recoil with disgrace on the liar.

Pittsburg Catholic.

WHAT we *say* here will soon be forgotten, but what they *did* here will ever live in the nation's memory.

Lincoln at Gettysburg

I SHALL have no policy to execute that will conflict with the will of the people.

Gen. Grant.

———◦◦◦———

GOD bless my country!

James Buchanan.

———◦◦◦———

EXTREMES meet when expediency renders it desirable.

Round Table.

———◦◦◦———

THE object of all true preaching is to tell men how to live and die happy.

Joseph Brooks of Boston.

———◦◦◦———

THE great reason why we have so little good preaching is that we have so little piety. To be eloquent one must be earnest; he must not only act as if he were in earnest, or try to be in earnest, but *be* in earnest, or he cannot be effective. We have loud and vehement, we have smooth and graceful, we have splendid and elaborate preaching, but very little that is in earnest. One man who so feels for the souls of his hearers as to be ready to weep over them will assuredly make himself felt. This is what makes him effective; he really feels what he says. This made Cookman eloquent. This especially was the charm of Summerfield, above all men I ever heard. We must aim, therefore, at high degrees of warmth in our religious exercises if we would produce an impression upon the public mind. Without an increase of our numbers, the very men we now have, if actuated with burning zeal for God, might work a mighty reformation in our country.

Dr. J. W. Alexander.

———◦◦◦———

A GOOD man's faults—if the sun be eclipsed for one hour, it attracts more attention than by its clear shining the whole year.

Christian at Work.

HAD the language of Revelation been scientifically accurate, it would have defeated the object for which the Scriptures were given; for it must have anticipated scientific discovery, and therefore have been unintelligible to those ignorant of such discoveries.   Hitchcock.

————◇————

A CORDIAL, warm shake of the hand takes my heart.
N. P. Willis.

————◇————

I WISH it was customary to publish the causes of marriage as it is of deaths.   Ike Marve..

————◇————

ART thou happy or unhappy? What wilt thou, what seekest thou in life? According to these rules, I botanize among human souls and classify them.
Jean Paul Richter.

————◇————

THERE is generally something that requires *hiding* at the bottom of a mystery.   Hawthorne.

————◇————

IF it has pleased God to save men by the foolishness of preaching, it has not been by choosing fools to be preachers.   Gail Hamilton.

————◇————

AS faith rests upon reason, so does all lofty religious energy and joy upon high, strong thought.
Dwight.

————◇————

MEN are born with two eyes, but with one tongue, in order that they should see twice as much as they say.
Colton.

GENIUS is of the soul, talent of the understanding, genius is warm, talent is passionless. Without genius there is no intuition, no inspiration; without talent, no execution. Genius is interior, talent exterior; hence genius is productive, talent accumulative. Genius invents, talent accomplishes. Genius gives the substance; talent works it up under the eye, or rather under the feeling, of genius. Genius is emotional, talent intellectual; hence genius is creative, and talent instrumental. Genius has insight, talent only outsight. Genius is always calm, reserved, self-centred; talent is often bustling, officious, confident. Genius gives the impulse and aim as well as the illumination; talent the means and implements. Genius, in short, is the central, finer essence of the mind, the self-lighted fire, the intuitional gift. Talent gathers and shapes and applies what genius forges. Genius is often entirely right, and is never wholly wrong; talent is never wholly right. Genius avails itself of all the capabilities of talent, appropriates to itself what suits and helps it. Talent can appropriate to itself nothing, for it has not the inward heat that can fuse all material and assimilate all food to convert it into blood; this only genius can do. Goethe was a man of genius, and at the same time of immense and varied talents; and no contemporary profited so much as he did by all the knowledges, discoveries and accumulations made by others. For full success the two, genius and talent, should coexist in one mind in balanced proportions, as they did in Goethe's, so that they can play smoothly together in effective combination. The work of the world, even the higher ranges, being done by talent, talent, backed by industry, is sure to achieve outward success. Commonplace is the smooth road on which are borne the freights that supply the daily needs of life; but genius, as the originator of all appliances and aids and motions and improvements, is the parent of what is to-day common—of all that talent has turned to practical account.

Genius involves a more than usual susceptibility to divine promptings, a delicacy in spiritual speculation, a quick obedience to the invisible helmsman; and these high superiorities imply fineness and fullness of organization. The man of genius is subject, says Joubert, to "transport, or rather rapture, of mind." In this exalted state he has glimpses of truth, beauties, principles, laws, that are new revelations, and bring additions to human power. Goethe might have been thinking of Kepler when he said, "Genius is that power of man which by thought and action gives laws and rules;" and Coleridge of Milton, when he wrote, "The ultimate end of genius is ideal;" and Hegel may have had Michael Angelo in his mind when, in one of his chapters on the plastic arts, he affirms that "talent cannot do its part fully without the animation, the besouling, of genius."

Round Table.

———◦◦———

HAD I miscarried, I had been a villain;
  For men judge actions always by events;
But when we manage by a just foresight,
Success is prudence, and possession right.

Higgons

———◦◦———

IT is success that colors all in life;
  Success makes fools admired, makes villains honest;
All the proud virtue of this vaunting world
Fawns on success and power, however acquired.

Thomson.

———◦◦———

A STATISTICIAN says a man stands sixteen chances to be killed by lightning to one of being worth a million of money.

Pittsburg Evening Mail.

HE that has never known adversity is but half acquainted with others or with himself. Constant success shows us but one side of the world, for, as it surrounds us with friends who will tell us only our merits, so it silences those enemies from whom alone we can learn our defects.

Colton.

THE great man down, you mark his favorite flies;
The poor advanced makes friends of enemies,
And hitherto doth love on fortune tend;
For who not needs shall never lack a friend;
And who in want a fellow-friend doth try
Directly sees in him an enemy.

Shakespeare.

MEN are judged not by their *intentions*, but by the results of their *actions*.

Chesterfield.

YOU may either win your peace or buy it; win it, by resistance to evil; buy it, by compromise with evil. You may buy your peace with silenced consciences; you may buy it with broken vows—buy it with lying words— buy it with base connivances—buy it with the blood of the slain, and the cry of the captive, and the silence of lost souls over hemispheres of the earth, while you sit smiling at your serene hearths, lisping comfortable prayers morning and evening, and so mutter continually to yourselves, "Peace, peace," when there is no peace; but only captivity and death for you as well as for those you leave unsaved; and yours darker than theirs.

Ruskin.

ALL minds quote.

Emerson.

YOUR great man always at last comes to see something the public don't see. This something he will assuredly persist in asserting, whether with tongue or pencil, to be as *he* sees it, not as *they* see it; and all the world in a heap on the other side will not get him to say otherwise. Then, if the world objects to the saying, he may happen to get stoned or burnt for it, but that does not in the least matter to him; if the world has no particular objection to the saying, he may get leave to utter it to himself till he dies, and be merely taken for an idiot; that also does not matter to him. Mutter he will, according to what he perceives to be fact, and not at all according to the roaring of the walls of Red Sea on the right hand or left of him.

Ruskin.

———⋄———

STUDENT. How does the book begin, go on and end?
FESTUS. It has a plan, but no plot. Life hath none.

Bailey.

———⋄———

THALAGRAM—A sea-despatch.

N. Y. Herald.

———⋄———

IT is good discretion not to make too much of any man at the first, because one cannot hold out that proportion.

Lord Bacon

———⋄———

THE worst is not
So long as we can say, This is the worst.

Shakespeare.

———⋄———

THE world is the book of women. Whatever knowledge they may possess is more commonly acquired by observation than by reading.

Rousseau.

WHAT makes us like new acquaintances is not so much any weariness of our old ones, or the pleasure of change, as disgust at not being sufficiently admired by those who know us too well, and the hope of being more so by those who do not know so much of us.

La Rochefoucault.

———◆◇◆———

WHAT causes the majority of women to be so little touched by friendship is, that it is insipid when they have once tasted of love.

La Rochefoucault.

———◆◇◆———

HER voice was ever soft,
Gentle and low; an excellent thing in woman.

Shakespeare.

———◆◇◆———

DEATH tarries not in its approach to the unfortunate and the abandoned.

Miss Annie E. Dickinson.

———◆◇◆———

I CHALLENGE any man to show me anything better, anything more suited to man and his wants, than the Gospel of Christ. It is better than philosophy. Philosophy can only disclose, only describe and classify. It cannot heal —it cannot cure. It is like a physician who knows the disease, but has no remedy; while the Gospel of Christ not only lays bare the malady, but prescribes an infallible and universal cure. It is better than education. Education can only call out and develop what is in fallen man; but the Gospel recreates man's heart and nature, and then lifts him up to the fullness of the stature of Christ. Education stops at the surface; the Gospel, which is the power of God unto salvation, penetrates to the centre of man's necessities. It is better than morality. Morality is conformity to law. When perfect it is a star rolling on in its God-appointed orbit. But man has broken law—the star has swerved from its orbit. Morality cannot bring it back and keep it in its course. The Gospel can. It brings man back to God—makes him at one with God—gives man a new start and keeps him safe in his heavenward course. The Gospel is better than philanthropy. Philanthropy is the love of man as man and for man. Christianity is the love of man for God and the love of God in man. The one would better man's condition here; the other would not only save man now, but would lift him to where he belongs—to heaven and to God.

Rev. F. A. Noble of Pittsburg.

GOD has put something noble and good into every heart which his hand has created.

Mark Twain

DEATHBED repentance is burning the candle of life in the service of the devil, then blowing the snuff in the face of Heaven.

Lorenzo Dow

THE generous heart
Should scorn a pleasure which gives others pain.

Thomson.

ONE touch of nature makes the whole world kin.

Shakespeare.

HEALTH is the soul that animates all the enjoyments of life

Sir W. Temple.

SELF-LOVE is not so vile a sin
As self-neglecting.

Shakespeare.

WHO can arrest a calumnious tongue, or who can stop the consequences of a calumnious misrepresentation? You may refute it, you may trace it to its source and expose its author; you may sift every atom, explain, annihilate it, and yet, like Greek fire, it remains unquenched and unquenchable; or, like weeds, which, when extirpated in one place, sprout forth vigorously in another spot. Half truths are often more calumnious than whole falsehoods. Not a word may be uttered, but a half-suppressed innuendo, a dropped lip, an arched eyebrow, a shrugged shoulder, a significant look, an incredulous expression of countenance, nay, even an emphatic silence, may do the fiendish work; and when the light and trifling thing which has done the mischief has fluttered off, the venom is left behind to work and rankle and fester, to inflame hearts, to fever human experience, and to poison human society at the fountain-springs of life.　　　　　　　F. W. Robertson.

GOOD and bad men are each less so than they seem.
S. F. Coleridge.

COMPENSATION is the law of existence the world over.
Emerson.

EVERY one has his day, from which he dates.
Old Proverb.

THIS world is a world of discipline, and the discipline that is no discipline is the worst of discipline.
Henry Vincent.

THE story of human life, with its lights and shadows, its strength and weakness, will be an interesting story so long as the human race shall endure.
Henry Vincent.

THE world is what we make it. Forward then, forward, in the power of faith, forward in the power of truth, forward in the power of friendship, forward in the power of freedom, forward in the power of hope, forward in the power of God.

Henry Vincent.

———

WHEN I reflect on what I have seen, what I have heard, and what I have done, I can hardly persuade myself that all that frivolous hurry and bustle of pleasure in the world had any reality; but I look upon all that is passed as one of those romantic dreams which opium commonly occasions, and I do by no means desire to repeat the nauseous dose.

Chesterfield.

———

COL. KANE tells us that one day, as he was sailing in the Arctic Ocean, he suddenly discovered two immense icebergs nearing each other from opposite directions, and threatening to crush his frail ship to pieces. For a time he could see no means of escape, and was expecting every moment to be dashed to pieces and engulfed in a watery grave, when, to his inexpressible relief, a third iceberg, drawn in by the current, came sailing past them between the mountains of snow and ice that were rapidly approaching. Quick as thought, the grappling irons were fixed upon it, and the ship was rescued from danger just in time to escape the awful shock of the crashing masses of ice. So, my impenitent hearer, as the sins and sorrows and dangers of life confront you and threaten to sink you down to hell, believe on the Lord Jesus Christ, lay hold of eternal life, flee for refuge to the hope set before you in the gospel, and your soul will be safe—you will be for ever delivered from the perils that are seeking to destroy you.

Anon.

18

THE Emperor of Russia once employed an engineer to survey a route for a railroad between St. Petersburg and Moscow. The engineer did so, and presented to the emperor the plan of the road upon paper. The route as surveyed was very irregular and presented a zigzag, serpentine appearance. The emperor scanned it for a moment, then seizing a pencil drew a straight line from St. Petersburg to Moscow, and said to the engineer, "Build that!" So, if the authorities at Washington would draw a straight line from the Potomac to Richmond and command the general of our armies to lead forward his forces, the war for the Union would soon be victoriously ended.

Rev. Dr. Sloan of New York.

A SHIP on Lake Erie, bound for the Cleveland harbor, was overtaken by a storm, and as they neared the port the pilot could only see the upper light—the light from the lighthouse streaming to them through the storm and darkness. The lower lights were not burning—the pilot could not see how to steer into the harbor. It was impossible to sail back again upon the lake; the ship had to go forward, and for want of the lower lights on the shore, the vessel, now at the mercy of the huge roaring waves, was dashed to pieces on the rocks, and many of the crew perished before help could reach them. So now, my Christian friends, workers for the Son of God, keep the lower lights burning! pray and work for the salvation of perishing souls. God will keep the upper lights, the "Morning Star" and the "Sun of Righteousness," ever burning, shining bright and resplendent upon this dark world; but do you do your duty by keeping the lower lights of prayer and effort ever burning, so that none perish on account of your example and influence?

D. L. Moody

THINGS are passing; our friends are dropping off from us; strength is giving way; our relish for earth is going, and the world no longer wears to our hearts the radiance that once it wore. We have the same sky above us and the same scenes around us; but the freshness that our hearts extracted from everything in boyhood, and the glory that seemed to rest once on earth and life, have faded away for ever. Sad and gloomy truths to the man who is going down to the grave with his work undone—not sad to the Christian, but rousing, exciting, invigorating. If it be the eleventh hour, we have no time for folding of the hands; we will work the faster. Through the changefulness of life; through the solemn tolling of the bell of time which tells us that another, and another, and another are gone before us; through the noiseless rush of a world which is going down with gigantic footsteps into nothingness, let not the Christian slack his hand from work, for he that doeth the will of God may defy hell itself to quench his immortality.

F. W. Robertson

———◆◇◆———

I HAVE not loved the world, nor the world me.

Byron.

———◆◇◆———

LIFE lies before you, young man, all gleaming and flashing in the light of your early hopes, like a summer-sea; but bright though it seem in the silvery sheen of its far-off beauty, it is a place where many a sunken rock and many a treacherous quicksand have made shipwreck of immortal hopes; and calm though its polished surface may sleep, without a ripple or a shade, it shall yet be overhung to you by the darkness of the night and the wildness of the tempest. And oh! if in these lonely and perilous scenes of your voyage, you were left without a landmark or a beacon, how sad and fearful were your lot! But, blessed be

God! you are not. Far up on the Rock of Ages, there streams a light from the eternal Word—the light that David saw and rejoiced; the light that Paul saw and took courage; the light that has guided the ten thousand times ten thousand that have already reached the happy isles of the blest. There it stands, the pharos of this dark and stormy scene, with a flame that was kindled in heaven and that comes down to us reflected from many a glorious image of prophet, apostle and martyr.

Rev. T. V. Moore, Richmond, Va.

A TRUE Christian living in the world is like a ship sailing on the ocean. It is not the ship being in the water which will sink it, but the water getting into the ship. So, in like manner, the Christian is not ruined by living in the world, which he must needs do whilst he remains in the body, but by the world living in him. The world in the heart has ruined millions of immortal souls. How careful is the mariner to guard against leakage, lest the water entering into the vessel should, by imperceptible degrees, cause the vessel to sink; and ought not the Christian to watch and pray, lest Satan and the world should find some unguarded inlet to his heart?

N. Y. Observer.

THOUGH scoffers ask, Where is your gain?
　And mocking say your work is vain,
Such scoffers die, and are forgot:
Work done for God, it dieth not!

Press on! press on! nor doubt nor fear;
From age to age, this voice shall cheer—
Whate'er may die, and be forgot,
Work done for God, it dieth not.

Thomas Knox, Edinburgh

OH, if every one in this assembly could put his arms round one other one and save him from perdition, it would be worth a lifetime of exertion. If you can lie down upon the bed of death, and ask, Of what avail has been my living? and only one redeemed by your agency, only one shall stand before you, only one upon whom you can fix your dying eyes, and feel, God has given me that as a seal to my ministry, oh it were enough! It were enough for the redemption of one human soul—when we consider what man is—worth all God's material universe—is worth a lifetime of toil and self-denial to accomplish.

Gough.

SAY not the struggle naught availeth,
　The labor and the wounds are vain;
The enemy faints not nor faileth,
　And as things have been, things remain.

Though hopes were dupes, fears may be liars:
　It may be, in yon smoke concealed,
Your comrades chase e'en now the fliers,
　And but for you possess the field.

For though the tired wave, idly breaking,
　Seems here no tedious inch to gain,
Far back, through creek and inlet making,
　Comes silent, flooding in, the main.

And not through eastern windows only,
　When daylight comes, comes in the light;
In front the sun climbs slow—how slowly!—
　But westward, look, the land is bright!

Arthur Hugh Clough

THANK God! there's still a vanguard
  Fighting for the right!
Though the throng flock to rearward,
  Lifting ashen-white
Flags of truce to sin and error,
Clasping hands, mute with terror,
Thank God! there's still a vanguard
  Fighting for the right!

Through the wilderness advancing,
  Hewers of the way,
Forward far their spears are glancing,
  Flashing back the day.
'Back!" the leaders cry, who fear them;
'Back!" from all the army near them;
They, with steady tramp advancing,
  Cleave their certain way.

Slay them! from each drop that falleth
  Springs a hero armed,
Where the martyr's fire appalleth,
  So they pass unharmed.
Crushed beneath thy wheel, Oppression,
How their spirits hold possession,
How the cross-purged voice outcalleth,
  By the death-throes warmed!

Thank God! there's still a vanguard
  Fighting for the right;
Error's legions know their standard
  Floating in the light.
Where the league of sin rejoices,
Quick outring the rallying voices:
Thank God! there's still a vanguard
  Fighting for the right!

Mrs. H. E. G. Arey.

WE are living, we are dwelling
    In a grand and awful time,
In an age on ages telling:
    To be living is sublime.
Hark! the waking up of nations—
    Gog and Magog to the fray!
Hark! what soundeth? Is creation
    Groaning for its latter day?

Will you play, then, will you dally
    With your music and your wine?
Up! it is Jehovah's rally!
    God's own arm hath need of thine.
Hark the onset! will you fold your
    Faith-clad arms in lazy lock?
Up! oh up! thou drowsy soldier—
    Worlds are charging to the shock.

Worlds are charging—heaven beholding;
    Thou has but an hour to fight;
Now the blazoned cross unfolding,
    On, right onward, for the right;
On! let all the soul within you
    For the truth's sake go abroad:
Strike! let every nerve and sinew
    Tell on ages—tell for God.

Bishop Coxe.

IN this God's world, with its wild whirling eddies and mad-foam oceans, where men and nations perish as if without law and judgment for an unjust thing sternly delayed, dost thou think that there is therefore no justice? It is what the fool has said in his heart. It is what the wise in all times were wise because they desired and knew for ever not to be. I tell thee again, there is nothing else but justice; one strong thing I find here below—the just thing, the true thing. My friend, if thou hadst all the artillery of Woolwich marching at thy back in support of an unjust thing, and infinite bonfires visibly awaiting ahead of thee, to blaze centuries to come for thy victory on behalf of it, I would advise thee to call, Halt! to fling down thy baton and say: "In God's name, no!" What will thy success amount to? If the thing is unjust, thou hast not succeeded, though bonfires blazed from north to south, and bells rang, and editors wrote leading articles, and the just thing lay trampled out of sight to all mortal eyes—an abolished and annihilated thing.   **Thomas Carlyle.**

———•◦•———

BEYOND all doubt, the worst of our enemies are those which we carry about in our own hearts. Adam fell in paradise, Lucifer in heaven, while Lot continued righteous among the people of Sodom. Indifference to little sins and mistakes; the self-flattering voice of the heart, ever ready to sing its lullaby the moment conscience is aroused; the subtle question of the serpent, "Hath God indeed said?" —these are unquestionably the adversaries we have most to fear. There never was a fire but it began with smoke. I beseech thee, therefore, dear Master, to give me a sensitive conscience, that I may take alarm at even small sins. Oh, it is not merely great transgressions which bring a man to ruin. Little and imperceptible ones are perhaps even more deadly, according to the beautiful figure of Tauler, who says: "The stag, when attacked, tosses from him the great dogs and dashes them to pieces upon the trees, but the little ones seize him from below, and tear open his body."   **Tholuck.**

HOLINESS is power. It utilizes ability, fertilizes the soul and energizes the whole man. It is the fire and water in the engine, bringing out to their fullest capacity the strength of all the parts of the machinery, so that the greatest amount of spiritual power may be expended ir rolling back a revolted world to God. Holiness is God's power with man, and man's power with God. Thus they become co-workers. Every man who dwelleth in God, and God in him, in an accommodated sense is God's man, which makes him a positive power against all evil and for all good—to pluck careless souls from the incoming flood and storm of wrath, lifting them up into the sweet serenity and protection of the Rock of Ages. Without holiness, we are weaker than a bruised reed; with it, we are like an impregnable and well-garrisoned fort, which will stand un-harmed the hottest siege; at the same time, raining like a hailstorm red-hot balls from the magazine of the Gospel on an armed world against Christ

Rev. W. H. Wilson.

THE Christian must hold on to God through conflicts and agonies; he must fight while his blood runs down and glues his hand to his sword. So must he hold on when that hand is benumbed and stiff with cold; when strength and consciousness seem gone together, and only an instinct remains through which the soul is able to fling itself like a dead weight upon Christ.

Patience of Hope.

THE sinner stands face to face with God, dependent for eternal life upon his good pleasure, with every possible encouragement, and if he is lost it is his own fault, not God's. "How often would I, but ye would not!" This is the language of God to the lost soul. God has never thrust a sinner upon trial in the sheer strength of his freedom, and then left him alone. God has been more than just to the sinner; the cross of Christ has blocked his way to destruction more impassably than by a flaming sword, intercession in heaven has been made for him with uplifted hands; the Holy Spirit has striven with him to turn him back, by all the devices which infinite ingenuity could frame, at the bidding of infinite compassion: his history has been one long struggle against obstacles to the suicide of his soul. Silently, darkly, often with conscience and willful repugnance to holy restraint, yet as often with that adroit suspense of conscience with which a sinner may serenely, even joyously, fraternize with sin, he has sought out and discovered and selected and seized upon and made sure of his own way over and around and through these obstacles to the world of despair. *He* has done it—*he*, and no other. Such is every lost soul. Is it any marvel that a lost soul is speechless?

Austin Phelps.

———————

THERE can be no real conflict between Science and the Bible—between nature and the Scriptures—the two Books of the Great Author. Both are revelations made by him to man; the earlier telling of God-made harmonies coming up from the deep past, and rising to their height when man appeared; the later teaching man's relations to his Maker, and speaking of loftier harmonies in the eternal future.

Dana.

———————

FLOWERS are the smiles of God's goodness.

Wilberforce.

———————

AT a certain depth all bosoms communicate—all hearts are one.

Frederika Bremer.

I KNOW not if the dark or bright
   Shall be my lot—
If that wherein my hopes delight
   Be best or not.

It may be mine to drag for years
   Toil's heavy chain;
Or day and night my meat be tears
   On bed of pain.

Dear faces may surround my hearth
   With smile and glee,
Or I may dwell alone, and mirth
   Be strange to me.

My bark is wafted to the strand
   By breath divine,
And on the helm there rests a Hand,
   Other than mine.

One who has known to sail
   I have on board;
Above the raging of the gale
   I hear my Lord.

He holds me; when the billows smite
   I shall not fall,
If sharp, 'tis short; if long, 'tis light;
   He tempers all.

Safe to the land, safe to the land!
   The end is this;
And then with him go hand in hand
   Far into bliss.

Dean Alford

Give thy thoughts no tongue,
Nor any unproportion'd thought his act.
Be thou familiar, but by no means vulgar.
The friends thou hast, and their adoption tried,
Grapple them to thy soul with hooks of steel;
But do not dull thy palm with entertainment
Of each new-hatch'd, unfledg'd comrade.   Beware
Of entrance to a quarrel; but, being in,
Bear it that the opposer may beware of thee.
Give every man thine ear, but few thy voice;
Take each man's censure, but reserve thy judgment.
Costly thy habit as thy purse can buy,
But not expressed in fancy; rich, not gaudy,
For the apparel oft proclaims the man.
Neither a borrower nor a lender be,
For loan oft loses both itself and friend,
And borrowing dulls the edge of husbandry.
This above all—to thine ownself be true;
And it must follow, as the night the day,
Thou canst not then be false to any man.

Polonius to Laertes.—Shakespeare.

———◆◇◆———

I HAVE known a country society which withered away all to nothing under the dry rot of gossip only. Friendship, once as firm as granite, dissolved to jelly, and then ran away to water, only because of this; love, that promised a future as enduring as heaven and as stable as truth, evaporated into a morning mist that turned to a day's long tears, only because of this; a father and a son were set foot to foot with the fiery breath of anger, that would never cool again between them, only because of this; and a husband and his young wife, each straining at the hated leash, which at the beginning had been the golden bondage of a

God-blessed love, sat mournfully by the side of the grave where all their love and joy lay buried, and only because of this. I have seen faith transformed to mean doubt, hope give place to grim despair, and charity take on itself the features of black malevolence, all because of the spell-words of scandal and the magic mutterings of gossip. Great crimes work great wrongs, and the deeper tragedies of human life spring from its larger passions; but woeful and most melancholy are the uncatalogued tragedies that issue from gossip and detraction; most mournfully the shipwreck often made of noble natures and lovely lives by the bitter winds and dead salt-waters of slander, so easy to say—yet so hard to disprove—throwing on the innocent, and punishing them as guilty or unable to pluck out the stings they never see, and silence the words they never hear. Gossip and slander are the deadliest and the cruelest weapons man has for his brother's heart.

All the Year Round.

————◇————

ADVICE is like snow, the softer it falls the longer it dwells upon and the deeper it sinks into the mud.

Anon.

————◇————

No wise man ever wished to be younger.

Dean Swift.

————◇————

WE exchanged our experience, and all learned something.

Emerson.

————◇————

I HAVE lived to know that the secret of happiness is never to allow your energies to stagnate.

Adam Clarke.

————◇————

In difficult cases do nothing.

Edgeworth.

NOW the days are all gone over
  Of our singing, love by lover—
Days of summer-colored seas,
Days of many melodies.

Now the nights are all past over
Of our dreaming, where dreams hover
In a mist of fair false things—
Nights with quiet folded wings.

Now the kiss of child and mother,
Now the speech of sister and brother,
Are but with us as strange words,
Or old songs of last year's birds.

Now all good that comes and goes is
As the smell of last year's roses,
As the shining in our eyes
Of dead summer in past skies.

Swinburne.

IT has been the enviable lot of here and there a favored individual to do some one important thing so well that it shall never need to be done again. Paley's writings, for instance, on the evidences of Christianity, are for ever decisive.

Peter Bayne.

LEISURE is a beautiful garment, but it will not do for constant wear.

Anon.

NO man ever became great or good except through many and great mistakes.

Gladstone.

Asses and savans to the centre!

A French General.

AS a pleasure party were sitting upon the banks of a river, they saw a large serpent upon a rock and an eagle circling in the heavens above it. All at once the eagle dashed upon the serpent, and sinking its talons into it, soared into the air and was soon circling again in the heavens. But just as the eagle was about to fly away to its mountain home, it wavered and stopped and soon dropped to the earth, with collapsed and imprisoned pinion. The serpent had coiled round the eagle, and sinking into it its deadly fangs, triumphed even in the eagle's proud flight, and at last came off victor. And so it is with the world. When we think we are the victors, and are escaping the world's deadly contagion, and rising, as we proudly think, to heaven, suddenly we waver and fall, shorn of our beauty and our strength, soon to plunge, it may be, into hopeless ruin and death.

Rev. J. B. Patterson.

ADRIANA. Nay, said I not—
And if I said it not, I say it now:
I'll follow thee through sunshine and through storm;
I will be with thee in thy weal and woe.
In thy afflictions, should they fall upon thee;
In thy temptations, when bad men beset thee;
In all the perils which must now press round thee,
And should they crush thee, in the hour of death
Let but thy love be with me to the last.
ARTEVELDE. My love is with thee ever; that thou
        knowest.

Henry Taylor.

O SHALLOW and mean heart! dost thou conceive so little of *love* as not to know that it sacrifices all—*love itself*—for the happiness of the one it loves?

Anon.

FIGHTING the battle of Life!
  With a weary heart and head;
For in the midst of the strife,
  The banners of Joy are fled.

Fighting the whole day long,
  With a very tired hand—
With only my armor strong—
  The shelter in which I stand.

There is nothing left of *me:*
  If all *my* strength were shown,
So small the amount would be,
  Its presence could scarce be known.

Fighting alone to-night,
  With not even a stander-by,
To cheer me on in the fight,
  Or to hear me when I cry.

Only the Lord can hear,
  Only the Lord can see,
The struggle within how dark and **drear,**
  Though quiet the outside be.

Fighting alone to-night,
  With what a fainting heart!
Lord Jesus, in the fight,
  Oh stand not thou apart.

Anon

———◆◆◆———

ALL Europe must become either Cossack or republican.

Napoleon

———◆◆◆———

FOLLOW up advantages

Napoleon

A DECENT boldness ever meets with friends.

Pope.

———◦◦———

FIDELITY is seven-tenths of business success.

Parton

———◦◦———

MAKE the best of everything;
Think the best of everybody;
Hope the best for yourself,
Do as I have done—persevere.

George Stephenson.

———◦◦———

To be great is to be misunderstood.

Emerson.

———◦◦———

GREATNESS appeals to the future.

Emerson.

———◦◦———

GUILT is the very nerve of sorrow.

Bushnell.

———◦◦———

AN acorn cannot make much headway in a flower-pot.

G. F. Train.

———◦◦———

SARCASM is the natural language of the devil.

Carlyle.

———◦◦———

NOBODY who is afraid of laughing, and heartily too,
at his friend, can be said to have a true and thorough
love for him; and on the other hand, it would betray a
sorry want of faith to distrust a friend because he laughs
at you. Few men are much worth loving in whom there is
not something well worth laughing at.

Guesses at Truth.

19

WHERE is the fiery furnace hot enough to burn despair
into our souls, so long as we see walking with us the
form of one like unto the Son of God?

Huntingdon.

—◦◦—

TREAT reports with indifference, and others will soon
learn to disregard them.

Oulda.

—◦◦—

THERE is danger of mistaking wandering thought for
brilliant thought.   Discursiveness is not brilliancy.

Blair's Rhetoric.

— —◦◦—

I NEVER met a lady the memory of whose smile was
preferable to the actual presenc. of all other ladies.

Steele.

—◦◦—

IT is not in the storm, no. in the strife
    We feel benumb'd and wish to be no more;
    But in the after silence on the shore,
When all is lost, except a little life.

Byr.

—◦◦—

THEY never fail who die
In a great cause; the block may roak their gore,
Their heads may sodden in the sun; their limbs
Be strung to city-gates and castle-walls,
But still their spirit walks abroad.   Though years
Elapse, and others share as dark a doom,
They but augment the deep and sweeping thought.
Which o'erpower all others, and conduct
The world at last to freedom.

Byr.

—◦◦—

THE pity of it, Iago! the pity of it!

Shakespt

TRANSCENDENTALISM is a super-sensuous insight
into the penetralia of essences.

The Author of Reederyll.

———◦◦———

BY all means, use sometimes to be alone;
　　Salute thyself; see what thy soul doth wear;
Dare to look in thy chest; for 'tis thine own,
　　And tumble up and down what thou findest there.

George Herbert.

———◦◦———

NATURE gave him more to govern than most men, with
only the ordinary capacity of self-government.

Charlotte Brontë.

———◦◦———

MEN have feeling: this is perhaps the best way of con-
sidering them.

Richter

———◦◦———

LET us go down with bare arms into the lowest recesses
of our souls, and there wrestle with sin and despair.

Rev. Athanase Coquerel.

———◦◦———

IN the march of life don't heed the order of "right
about" when you know you are about right.

Holmes.

———◦◦———

HOW important it is that things should be all right before they harden into shape!

Rev. Dr. Thorne, Cleveland, O.

———◦◦———

HIS discourse was a happy result of logic, with the logic
left out.

Tilton on Beecher.

———◦◦———

PASSIONS are likened best to floods and streams. The
shallow murmur, but the deep are dumb.

Raleigh

TAKE away the self-conceited, and there will be elbow-room in the world.

Whichcate.

SELDOM hath my tongue pronounced that name,
  But the dear love, so deeply wounded there,
I in my heart, with silent faith sincere,
Devoutly cherish till we meet again.

Southey.

THE affections, like the conscience, are rather to be led than drawn, and 'tis to be feared that they who marry where they do not love will love where they do not marry.

Thomas Fuller.

SOME feelings are to mortals given
  With less of earth in them than heaven.

Walter Scott.

'TIS time this heart should be unmoved
  Since others it has ceased to move;
Yet, though I cannot be beloved,
    Still let me love.

Byron.

THE tendency of modern science is to place the world under the control of absolute, impersonal Law, instead of the control of an absolute, personal God. Modern skeptics aim to get rid of the supernatural, and to deify the so-called natural and material. That law and order are sufficient to account for the beauty and harmony of the physical universe is the serpent-falsehood coiled in the heart of modern infidelity.

Dr. M. W. Jacobus.

WHILE I reject all this modern spiritualism, I believe in the existence of spirits, which are ever near and around us. It is absurd to suppose that man is the only intelligent agent; and as men are good and bad, why may there not be good and evil spirits? And if evil spirits in this world tempt us, why may not these invisible evil spirits tempt us also?

Dr. M. W. Jacobus

I SEE coming up upon the earth a mist filled with all forms of fear; and, to my terror, I see as distinctly as though I were a prophet that the tendency is to Pantheism or Atheism, and that it means to literalize nature, to denude it of order and to give us bones and chemical elements, and nothing else. But, as gaunt hunger has no heart for any-thing but bread, so man's immortal soul can be satisfied with nothing else but God—with nothing else but God in Christ.

Beecher.

FOIBLES are not inconsistent with generous and great qualities, and we judge wrongly of human nature when we ridicule its littleness. The very circumstances which make the shallow misanthropical, incline the wise to be benevolent. Fools discover that frailty is not incompatible with great men; they wonder and despise; but the discerning find that greatness is not incompatible with frailty, and they admire and indulge.

Bulwer.

THERE are points from which we can command our life,
    When the soul sweeps the future like a glass;
And coming things, full-freighted with our fate,
Jut out dark on the offing of the mind.
Let them come! Many will go down in sight;
In the billows' joyous dash of death, go down.

Shelley.

VIRTUE has resources buried in itself which we know not of till the invading hour calls them from their retreats. Surrounded by hosts without, and when nature itself turns traitor, is its most deadly enemy within; it assumes a new and a superhuman power, which is greater than nature itself. Whatever be its creed, whatever be its sect, from whatever segment of the globe its orisons arise, virtue is God's empire, and from his throne of thrones he will defend it. Though cast into the distant earth and struggling on the dim arena of a human heart, all things above are spectators of its conflicts or enlisted in its cause. The angels have their charge over it—the banners of archangels are on its side, and from sphere to sphere, through the illimitable ether, and round the impenetrable darkness at the feet of God, its triumphs are hymned by harps which are strung to the glories of the Creator.

Bulwer.

———◦◦———

ON Fame's eternal camping-ground
  Their silent tents are spread;
And glory guards with solemn round
  The bivouac of the dead.

Anon

———◦◦———

SUCH graves as theirs are pilgrim shrines—
  Shrines to no code or creed confined—
The Delphian vales, the Palestines,
  The Meccas of the mind.

Anon

———◦◦———

THE heart, like a tendril, accustom'd to cling,
  Let it grow where it will, cannot flourish alone
But will lean to the nearest and loveliest thing
  It can twine with itself, and make closely its own

Moore

BECAUSE you flourish in worldly affairs,
Don't be haughty and put on airs,
    With insolent pride of station;
Don't be proud and turn up your nose
At poorer people in plainer clothes,
But learn, for the sake of your mind's repose,
That wealth's a bubble that comes and goes;
And that all Proud Flesh, wherever it grows
    Is subject to irritation.

J. G. Saxe.

MIGHTIEST of the mighty means
On which the arm of Progress leans—
Man's noblest mission to advance,
His woes assuage, his weal enhance,
His rights enforce, his wrongs redress—
Mightiest of the mighty, is the *press*.

Bowring

WHAT stronger breastplate than a heart untainted?
    Thrice is he armed that hath his quarrel just,
And he but naked, though lock'd up in steel,
Whose conscience with injustice is corrupted.

Shakespeare.

THE hand of the reaper
    Takes the ears that are hoary,
But the voice of the weeper
    Wails manhood in glory.

Scott.

MANY an immortal work that is a source of exquisite
    enjoyment to mankind has been written with the blood
of the author, at the expense of his happiness and of his
life.

E. P. Whipple.

HER eyes are homes of silent prayer.

Tennyson

———◦◦———

I HOLD it true, whate'er befall;
I feel it when I sorrow most;
'Tis better to have loved and lost
Than never to have loved at all.

Tennyson.

———◦◦———

MY heart and mind and self never in tune;
Sad for the most part; then in such a flow
Of spirits I seem now hero—now buffoon.

Leigh Hunt.

———◦◦———

THE calmer thought is not always the right thought, just
as the distant view is not always the truest view.

Hawthorne.

———◦◦———

YET still there whispers the small voice within,
Heard through gain's silence and o'er glory's din:
Whatever creed be taught or land be trod,
Man's conscience is the oracle of God!

Byron.

———◦◦———

JEALOUSY is the injured lover's hell.

Milton

———◦◦———

THE great of old!
The dead but sceptred sovereigns who still rule
Our spirits from their urns!

Byron.

———◦◦———

THE pleasures of the present we doubly taste
By looking back with pleasure on the past.

Dryden

OF too much beauty let us complain when we have had a spring day too delightful, a sun-beam too delicately spun, an autumn too abundant. The finest writers in the world have been the most luxuriant.

Gilfillan.

———◦◇◦———

STILL panting o'er a crowd to reign,
    More joy it gives to woman's breast
To make ten frigid coxcombs vain,
    Than one true, manly lover blest.

Pope.

———◦◇◦———

A GOOD and true woman is said to resemble a Cremona fiddle—age but increases its worth and sweetens its tone.

Holmes.

———◦◇◦———

THAT stern joy which warriors feel
    In foemen worthy of their steel.

Scott.

———◦◇◦———

THE man who fails in business, but continues to live in luxury, is a thief.

Spectator.

———◦◇◦———

THE broadest mirth unfeeling folly wears
    Is not so sweet as virtue's very tears.

Anon.

———◦◇◦———

PLEASURES are like poppies spread:
    We nip the flower—the bloom is fled;
Or like the snow-flake on the river—
A moment white, then gone for ever.

Burns.

———◦◇◦———

I AM pining for the anodyne of a tender look.

Bulwer.

THE gentle heart that thinks with pain,
  It scarce can lowliest task fulfill,
    And if it dared its life to scan,
Would ask but pathway low and still;
Often such gentle heart is brought
To act with power beyond its thought,
  For God, through ways they have not known,
  Will lead his own.

Anon.

———◆◇◆———

THERE is an evening twilight of the heart,
  When its wild passion-waves are lull'd to rest,
And the eye sees life's fairy scenes depart,
  As fades the day-beam in the rosy West.
'Tis with a nameless feeling of regret,
  We gaze upon them as they melt away,
And fondly would we bid them linger yet;
  But Hope is round us with her angel-lay,
Hailing afar some happier moonlight hour:
Dear are her whispers still, though lost their early power.

Halleck

———◆◇◆———

THE deepest emotions of this world remain unseen and unknown to all around, for the strength of character which gives power to feel, gives power also to hide, and there is a modesty in real sensibility which admits not of display.

Anon.

———◆◇◆———

WE love women a little for what we do know of them, and a great deal more for what we do not.

Ike Marvel.

———◆◇◆———

BREVITY may be the soul of wit, but it is very far from being the soul of truth.

Holmes.

GREAT fleas have little fleas
    Upon their backs to bite 'em,
And these again have lesser fleas,
    And so—ad infinitum.

                          Anon.

EVERY flower, even the fairest, has its shadow beneath
it as it swings in the sunlight.

                          Anon.

I AM not impressible, but I am impressionable.

                          Emerson

WHO then shall lightly say that Fame
    Is but an empty name?
When, but for these our mighty dead,
    All ages past a blank would be,
Sunk in oblivion's murky bed,
    A desert bare—a shipless sea.
They are the distant objects seen,
The lofty marks of what hath been,
Where memory of the mighty dead
    To earth-worn pilgrim's wistful eye,
The brightest rays of cheering shed
    That point to Immortality.

                          Anon.

OF all blessings, ladies are the soothinest!

                          Artemus Ward

NO! Failure's a part of the Infinite plan:
    Who finds that he can't, must give way to who can;
And as one and another drop out of the race,
Each stumbles at last to his suitable place.

                          Crangles.

WOULD I describe a preacher such as Paul,
　Were he on earth, would hear, approve and own,
Paul should himself direct me.   I would trace
His master-strokes and draw from his design.
I would express him simple, grave, sincere;
In doctrine uncorrupt, in language plain,
And plain in manner; decent, solemn, chaste
And natural in gesture; much impress'd
Himself, as conscious of his awful charge,
And anxious, mainly, that the flock he feeds
May feel it too; affectionate in look
And tender in address, as well becomes
A messenger of grace to guilty men.

Cowper.

———◦◦———

HOW great a creature must that be that, looking down upon himself from some high eminence in itself, some throne of truth and judgment which no devastation of order can reach, withers in relentless condemnation of itself, gnaws and chastises itself in the sense of what it is! Call it a ruin as it plainly is, there rises out of the desolated wreck of its former splendor that which indicates and measures the sublimity of the original temple. The conscience stands erect, resisting all the ravages of violence and decay, and by this we distinguish the temple of God, that was a soul divinely gifted, made to be the abode of his spirit, the vehicle of his power, the mirror of his glory. A creature of remorse is a divine creature of necessity, only it is the wreck of a divinity that was.

Bushnell

———◦◦———

HUMILITY is the base of every virtue,
　And they who dig the deepest build the safest.
God keeps all his pity for the proud.

Bailey's Festus.

OPINIONS, they still take a wider range :
Find if you can, in what you cannot change,
Manners with fortunes, humors turn with climes,
Tenets with books and principles with times.

Pope.

———◦◦———

LET every teacher go to the bottom of his subject and show its relations to God and religion. Let him exhibit to the mind of the student, in clear and comprehensive delineation, the great leading principles of religion, and indicate the relations, connections, articulations, dispositions and adjustments of these principles with all the various branches of universal knowledge.

Rev. Dr. G. McMaster.

———◦◦———

THERE are two unalterable prerequisites to man's being happy in the world to come. His sins must be pardoned and his nature must be changed. He must have a title to heaven and a fitness for heaven. These two ideas underlie the whole of Christ's work, and without the title to, and the fitness for, no man can enter the kingdom of God.

Ecce Deus-Homo.

———◦◦———

AMONG the rubbish which the world had heaped upon the Church, Luther felt round till he laid his hand upon the Rock of Ages.

Rev. Dr. John Todd.

———◦◦———

HUMILITY in religion, as in the world, is the avenue to glory.

Guesses at Truth

———◦◦———

DOCTRINE is the very edge of the two-edged sword.

Rev. Dr. McIlwaine, Ind. Pa.

PLINY speaks of certain animals that will fatten on smoke! How lucky 'twould be for many Pittsburgers and for sundry would-be statesmen if they could get men to do the same!

Anon.

———◆———

THE soul is never so hampered by its enthrallment within the body as when it loves.

Fowler.

———◆———

WE represent our fictions as though they were realities, while you preach your realities as though they were fictions.

The Actor to the Minister.

———◆———

CONSTITUENCIES control their representatives as the tail of a serpent does its head.

G. W. Curtis.

———◆———

THE foundations of our public morality must be laid deep in the public intelligence and virtue.

G. W. Curtis.

———◆———

PRUSSIA is great because her people are intelligent. They know the alphabet. The alphabet is conquering the world.

G. W. Curtis.

———◆———

GET leave to work.
In this world 'tis the best you get at all;
For God, in cursing, gives us better gifts
Than man in benediction. God says, "Sweat
For foreheads;" men say, "crowns," and so we are crowned,
Ay, gashed by some tormenting circle of steel
Which snaps with a secret spring. Get work, get work,
Be sure 'tis better than what you work to get.

Mrs. Browning.

CORRUPT legislators are the offspring and index of a corrupt public opinion.

G. W. Curtis.

———◦◦———

A SORROW'S crown of sorrow
Is remembering happier things.

Dante.

———◦◦———

. . . . who would fardels bear,
To grunt and sweat under a weary life,
But that the dread of something after death,—
The undiscovered country, from whose bourne
No traveller returns,—puzzles the will,
And makes us rather bear those ills we have,
Than fly to others that we know not of?

Shakespeare.

———◦◦———

METHOUGHT there were long ages come and gone—
Pale worlds were crumbling to their last decay,
Far in the East a coming glory shone,
  And morning broke—the morning of that day
Never again to set; a slanted ray
  Bridged earth and heaven with its quivering flame.
Thereon an angel trod his rushing way,
  And folding a white wing and flashing came,
  Sounded a golden blast, and hastened to proclaim,
"Glory to God, salvation and release!
    Tell it among the nations, tell it wide:
  Glory to God on high, on earth be peace."
    So shouted he; so sang from tide to tide.
  "Amen! amen!" the morning stars replied;
The winds were heralds of their minstrelsy,
    The clouds upbore it till the echoes died,
And utmost earth's acclaims formed meet antistrophe.

J. S. Gibson—Cambridge Prize Poem.

THERE is a grandeur in the soul that dares
   To live out all the life God lit within;
That battles with the passions hand to hand,
And wears no mail, and hides behind no shield;
That plucks its joy in the shadow of Death's wing,
That drains with ono deep draught the wine of life,
And that with fearless foot and heaven-turned eyes
May stand upon a dizzy precipice,
High o'er the abyss of ruin, and not fall.

Sara J. Clarke

———◦◦———

WHEN the cup is full, carry it even.

Scotch Proverb.

———◦◦———

IN many respects the *New York Herald* is the truest
   representative of American character and feeling of all
our newspapers; and this accounts for its success. It
reverences nothing; it has neither loves nor hates; it lives
in a sensational world; it is conscious of no ignorance; it
abhors all infirmity; it loves the strong, the capable, the
favorites of fortune; it wants results; it is bored with no
scruples; it has infinite audacity; it admires a great
scoundrel or a great saint with absolute impartiality; believes that this earth is a first-rate earth; is unterrified at
the invisible; goes in for any "big thing," and if a man
has money takes no interest in the inquiry how he came by
it. We doubt very much whether the *Herald* believes in the
spiritual world at all. There is something sublime in its
scorn of the right or wrong of a thing. It recognizes no
allegiance to any preter-earthly authority, and the rules
of conduct laid down between man and man are regarded
as purely artificial and founded on what can you make by
it! The moral sense at the *Herald* office is despised as
reactionary—not suited to this magnificent age—un-Ameri-

can, a .log on the wheels of progress. The duty of a people is "to go ahead," make railroads, stretch wires across
oceans, secure trade, make discoveries, beat Europe, increase the speed of ships, annex territory, follow in the wake
of Rome. **Richmond Enquirer.**

———•———

B LIND TOM'S mind is a beautiful opera written by the
finger of God in syllables of music.
Wheeling Paper.

———•———

T O love satisfies one half of our nature; to be loved satisfies the other half. But no human love can fully satisfy
us, because man is so constituted that nothing finite can
suffice him; he springs beyond the universe in search of an
ideal of beauty, a perfect object of love, hope and adoration,
and no human love for us can make us permanently happy,
for no human heart is fully attuned to ours—no human
heart can wholly understand or sympathize with our own.
God's love for us in Christ and our love for God in Christ—
here only can man's restless heart find eternal blessedness
and peace. Dr. A. A. H....n

———•———

F OR right is right, since God is God,
   And right the day must win:
To doubt would be disloyalty,
   To falter would be sin. **Anon.**

———•———

F OR forms of government let fools contest;
   Whatever's best administered is best.
For forms of faith let graceless zealots fight;
His can't be wrong whose life is in the right.

Pope.

A WEAPON that comes down as still
 As snow-flakes fall upon the sod,
Yet executes a freeman's will
 As lightning does the will of God;
Nor from its force, nor love nor locks
Shall turn us—'tis the ballot-box.

Anon.

 A MAN's best wealth ought to be himself.

William Austin.

SORROW is our John the Baptist, clad in grim garments,
 with rough arms, a son of the wilderness, baptizing us
in bitter tears, preaching repentance; and behind him comes
the gracious, affectionate, healing Lord, gathering the
wheat into the garner.

Huntingdon.

WHAT then is taste but these internal powers
 Active and strong, and feelingly alive
To each fine impulse? a discerning sense
Of decent and sublime, with quick disgust
From things deformed or disarranged or gross
In species? This, nor gems, nor stores of gold,
Nor purple state, nor culture can bestow;
But God alone, when first his active hand
Imprints the secret bias of the soul.

Akenside.

WHENCE is our love of fame?—a love so strong
 We think no changes great nor labors long;
By which we hope our beings to extend,
And to remotest times in glory to descend.

Anon.

WESTWARD the course of empire takes its way,
   The first four acts already past;
The fifth shall close the drama with the day:
   Time's noblest offspring is its last.

Bishop Berkeley.

ALAS! how faint,
How slow the dawn of Beauty and of Truth
Breaks the reluctant shades of gothic night,
Which yet involve the nations!

Anon.

IF a man is formed to be a poet, he watches the humanity in his own breast, in order to comprehend the infinitely changing play upon the wide theatre of the world; he subjects luxuriant fancy to the discipline of taste, and suffers the sober intellect to survey the banks between which the stream of inspiration is to leap and sparkle.

Schiller.

A MAN'S value and progress in this life must be measured, not by what he gets outwardly, but by what he gains inwardly. The beauty of a rose lies not in its encasements, but in the delicacy of its leaf-tinting and the delicious sweetness which rises out of its blushing bosom. So with man. It is the color and fragrance of his nature within, it is the richness of his inward experience, and not the grandeur and quality of his surroundings, which constitutes his real glory and charm.

Rev. W. H. H. Murray.

THE supreme happiness of life is the conviction that we are loved—loved for ourselves; say, rather, loved in spite of ourselves.

Victor Hugo.

BEFORE the wrought iron can become steel, it must be heated by means of charcoal, and made to pass through a process of cementation, until it is blistered by fire and freed from a portion of its carbon, and even then the merciless hammer must complete the work. Before the coal gas, that at night illumines and beautifies a city, is fit for use it must be freed from carbonic acid, tar, resinous compounds and other impurities which would dim its brilliancy, and this is accomplished by first subjecting it to intense heat, and then by passing it through water, cooling it in condensers and transmitting it through tubes and purifiers. And just so it is in the growth and progress of the soul. The friction and attrition, the purging and the purifying, the heating and the cooling, the sinning and repenting, to which we are subjected, the very difficulties and painful experiences we have to encounter in life, and of which we are so apt to complain, are the necessary conditions of our spiritual progress.

Anon.

———◦◦———

THE great hearts of the olden time
 Are beating with us full and strong;
All holy memories and sublime,
 And glorious, round us throng.

Anon

———◦◦———

GOD'S word can never die,
 Though fallen man
Oft dares its truth deny—
 Dares it in vain.

Anon.

———◦◦———

I LIVE not in myself, but become
 Portion of that around me.

Byron.

HER feet beneath her petticoat,
  Like little mice stole in and out,
    As if they feared the light;
But oh, she dances such a way,
No sun upon an Easter Day
    Is half so fine a sight.

                          Suckling.

HER lips were red, and one was thin,
  Compared with that was next her chin;
Some bee had stung it newly.

                          Suckling

ALAS! they had been friends in youth,
  But whispering tongues can poison truth;
And constancy lives in realms above;
  And life is thorny; and youth is vain;
And to be wroth with one we love
  Doth work like madness on the brain.

*   *   *   *   *   *

But never either found another
To free the hollow heart from paining—
They stood aloof, the scars remaining,
  Like cliffs which had been rent asunder;
A dreary sea now flows between,
  But neither heat, nor frost, nor thunder,
Shall wholly do away, I ween,
The marks of that which once hath been.

                  Coleridge's Christabel.

HE either fears his fate too much,
  Or his deserts are small,
Who fears to put it to the test,
  To win or lose it all.

                        Montrose.

IMMODEST words admit of no defence,
For want of decency is want of sense.

Roscommon

———◦◦———

THE lyre in breaking breathes a tone of power;
The fading lamp, while in its dying hour,
Flashes its parting ray of quivering light.

Anon.

———◦◦———

THERE are briers besetting every path,
Which call for patient care;
There is a cross in every lot,
And an earnest need for prayer;
But a lowly heart that leans on Thee
Is happy anywhere.

Mrs. Waring

———◦◦———

I LOVE contemplating—apart
From all his homicidal glory—
The traits that soften to the heart
Napoleon's story.

Campbell.

———◦◦———

TOUCH us gently, Time;
Let us glide adown thy stream;
Gently, as we sometimes glide
Through a quiet dream.

Barry Cornwall.

———◦◦———

THE deep affections of the breast,
That Heaven to living things imparts,
Are not exclusively possessed
By human hearts.

Campbell

SEEKEST thou great things for thyself? seek them not.

Jeremiah xiv. 5.

———◆◆———

LIBERTY! thou star of promise, hovering over the cradle where the Republic was born, and still burning on the front of the sky, we will follow thee wherever thy orbit may lead.

Hon. Daniel W. Voorhees.

———◆◆———

THE gnarled and twisted oak has its counterpart in the narrowed and stunted mind.

Rev. Herrick Johnson

———◆◆———

WE must force our minds to the study of that which is at first disagreeable to us.

Rev. Herrick Johnson

———◆◆———

HE that lacks time to mourn, lacks time to mend :
    Eternity mourns that.   'Tis an ill cure
For life's worst ills, to have no time to feel them.

Shakespeare.

———◆◆———

I WILL go to his grave, thinking of the value of civil government.

Prof. J. Black on the death of Capt. D. Acheson.

———◆◆———

'THE man who truly loves, loves humbly and fears not that another may be preferred, but that another may be worthier of preference than himself.

Miss Mulock.

———◆◆———

WERE it not for music we might, in these days, say the Beautiful is dead.

Disraeli

WHO knows whither the clouds have fled?
  In the unscarred heaven they leave no wake;
And the eyes forget the tears they have shed,
  The heart forgets its sorrow and ache.

Lowell.

———◇———

AND the night shall be filled with music,
  And the cares that infest the day
Shall fold their tents like the Arabs,
  And as silently steal away.

Longfellow.

———◇———

WANT of manliness is now the great danger among all
  people of all nations.   Henry Vincent.

———◇———

THE earth is full of tragedy and life is full of pathos.

Henry Vincent.

———◇———

THE age of coercion has not yet passed: the same thing
  is done as well in another way.

George Willy, Esq.

———◇———

OH these bodies of ours!   I wish I was disembodied!

Anon.

———◇———

THE vast cathedral of nature is full of holy scriptures
  and shapes of deep mysterious meaning, but all is solitary and silent there; no bending knee, no uplifted eye, no
lip adoring, praying. Into this vast cathedral comes the
human soul seeking its Creator, and the universal silence is
changed to sound, and the sound is harmonious and has a
meaning, and is comprehended and felt.

Longfellow's Hyperion.

SO near, so very near to God,
   Nearer I cannot be;
Near in the person of the Son,
   I am as near as he.

So dear, so very dear to God,
   Dearer I cannot be;
The love wherewith he loves the Son
   Is the love he bears to me.

Aron.

——◦◦——

COME then, Affliction, if my Father wills,
   And be my frowning friend.   A friend
That frowns is better than a smiling enemy.

Anon.

——◦◦——

AND how can a man die better
   Than facing fearful odds,
For the ashes of his fathers,
   And the temples of his gods.

Macaulay

——◦◦——

LET circumstance oppose him,
   He bends it to his will;
And if the floods o'erflow him,
   He dives and stems it still;
No hindering dull material
   Shall conquer or control
His energies ethereal—
   His gladiator soul!
Let lower spirits linger
   For hint and beck and nod—
He always sees the finger
   Of an onward-urging God.

M. F. Tupper

IN the yet to be, how much of joy or sorrow
   Awaiteth me, God knows alone:
How kindly hath he o'er the darkest morrow
   Hope's cheering mystery thrown!

While strength sufficient for the burden given
   He mercifully bestows,
I will not doubt his love though ties are riven;
   My need he knows!

Anon.

———•◦•———

WE will grieve not; rather find
   Strength in what remains behind,
In the primal sympathy,
Which having been must ever be.
In the soothing thoughts that spring
Out of human suffering,
In the faith that looks through death
In years that bring the philosophic mind.

Eclectic Magazine

———•◦•———

VOICES, sweeping through all time, peal
   Like the eternal thunders of the deep
Into my ears this truth: Thou livest for ever!

Byron

———•◦•———

GREAT truths are dearly bought. The common truth,
   Such as men give and take from day to day,
Comes in the common walks of easy life,
   Blown by the careless wind across our way.

Bought in the market at the current price,
   Bred of the smile, the jest, perchance the bowl;
It tells no tales of daring or of worth,
   Nor pierces even the surface of the soul.

Great truths are greatly won, not formed by chance,
   Not wafted on the breath of summer dream;
But grasped in the great struggle of the soul,
   Hard buffeting with adverse wind and stream.

Not in the general mart, 'mid corn and wine;
   Not in the merchandise of gold and gems;
Not in the world's gay hall of midnight mirth,
   Nor 'mid the blaze of regal diadems;

But in the day of conflict, fear and grief,
   When the strong hand of God, put forth in might,
Ploughs up the subsoil of the stagnant heart,
   And brings the imprisoned truth-seed to the light.

Wrung from the troubled spirit in hard hours
   Of weakness, solitude, perchance of pain,
Truth springs, like harvest, from the well-ploughed field,
   And the soul feels it has not wept in vain.

                       Blackwood's Magazine.

GO to work! Nothing is more salutary to the human soul than the direct work of saving men. There is a basis of fact. There is the next ground for action. Whatever your theory may be of this or that doctrine, there is man dying in his need, and there is a power which you may apply for his transformation. Therefore go to work upon men, and with men. And let me tell you, there is nothing that you could do that would be more satisfactory to your own soul. I speak what I do know when I say that there is nothing which brings men back from the desert of sandy and arid speculation, nothing which brings a man in again to the shore from the cheerless ocean of doubt, nothing which gives us such faith and certainty, as laying aside all reasoning and engaging in the practical work of the gospel.

I know that there is restorative influence in that work. I know that, whatever doubts I may have, once let my heart and hand join together in working with men for their salvation, and my doubts disappear; I know in whom I believe; I know the work to which I am appointed; and the sweetest that I ever had of God came to me in the act of laboring for my fellow-men. The most glorious views I ever had of man's interior life and of essential divine truths were ministered to me when I was working for the salvation of others.

H. W. Beecher.

————◆◆————

IN the day when our souls are beclouded,
   Merciful God!
When with legions of doubts they are crowded,
And our heaven of sadness is shrouded,
 We do seek thee, sin-press'd, and here,
Weeping—all penitent—O Jesus!
 Graciously pardon our hearts so drear.

For we that sin, oh we sin so grievous,
   Merciful God!
When a brother shall sue for our pardon,
Let the thought of the Cross and the garden
So soften us all with the spirit of heaven
That we may forgive e'en as we are forgiven.

Rev. Dr. J. B. Bittenger.

————◆◆————

   THEY have but
One answer to all questions, "'Twas His will,
And he is good." How know I that? Because
He is all-powerful, must all good, too, follow?
I judge but by the fruits—and they are bitter—
Which I must feed on for a fault not mine.

Byron's Cain.

BREAK, break, break,
   On thy cold gray stones, O sea!
And I would that my tongue could utter
   The thoughts that arise in me.

Oh well for the fisherman's boy,
   That he shouts with his sister at play!
Oh well for the sailor lad,
   That he sings in his boat on the bay!

And the stately ships go on
   To their haven under the hill;
But oh for the touch of a vanished hand
   And the sound of a voice that is still.

Break, break, break,
   At the foot of thy crags, O sea!
But the tender grace of a day that is dead
   Will never come back to me.

Tennyson.

———•◦•———

MINE be a cot beside the hill,
   A beehive's hum shall soothe mine ear,
A willowy brook that turns a mill,
   With many a fall, shall linger near.

Anon.

———•◦•———

THE twilight hours, like birds, flew by,
   As lightly and as free;
Ten thousand stars were in the sky,
   Ten thousand in the sea;
For every wave, with dimpled cheek,
   That leaped upon the air,
Had caught a star in its embrace,
   And held it trembling there.

Anon.

BREATHES there a man, with soul so dead,
   Who never to himself hath said,
"This is my own, my native land;"
Whose heart hath ne'er within him burned,
As home his footsteps he hath turned
   From wandering on a foreign strand?
If such there breathe, go, mark him well;
For him no minstrel raptures swell,
High though his titles, proud his name,
Boundless his wealth as wish can claim;
Despite those titles, power and pelf,
The wretch, concentred all in self,
Living, shall forfeit fair renown;
And, doubly dying, shall go down
To the vile dust from which he sprung,
Unwept, unhonored and unsung.

Scott.

IF your friend has got a heart,
   There is something fine in him;
Cast away his darker part,
   Cling to what's divine in him.

Eclectic Magazine

THE stars shall fade away; the sun himself
   Grow dim with age, and nature sink in years,
But thou shalt flourish in immortal youth,
Unhurt amidst the war of elements,
The wreck of matter and the crush of worlds.

Pollock.

A PEBBLE in the streamlet scant
   Has turned the course of many a river;
A dew-drop on the infant plant
   Has warped the giant oak for ever.

Anon.

A WOMAN'S heart, though delicate, is strong;
  Like virgin-gold it takes the furnace-heat,
Giving to history and immortal song
  A glow of heroism pure and sweet.

Great men have sought the battle in their pride,
  Hewing a path to glory as they fell,
But women, braver still, have grandly died
  In silent struggles fame may never tell.

               Silent Struggles.

OH let us carry hence, each one,
  Some kindly word, some look—
  Some tone—
Into his after-life, to be
  Treasured heart-deep and carried home—
An echo from the distant sea,
A thing of joy to memory
  In all the years to come.

               Anon.

I FALTER where I firmly trod,
  And falling with my weight of cares
  Upon the great world's altar-stairs,
That slope through darkness up to God,
I stretch lame hands of faith, and grope
  And gather dust and chaff, and call
  To what I feel is Lord of all,
And faintly trust the larger hope.

               Tennyson.

WHEN fools pretend to wit and sense,
  And wish to shine at your expense,
Defy them to the proof, and you
Will make them their own folly show.

               Anon.

WHY so pale and wan, fond lover?
    Prithee, why so pale?
Will, when looking *well* can't move her,
    Looking *ill* prevail?
    Prithee, why so pale?

Why so dull and mute, young sinner?
    Prithee, why so mute?
Will, when speaking well can't win her,
    Saying nothing do't?
    Prithee, why so mute?

Quit, quit for shame! this will not move,
    This cannot take her:
If of herself she will not love,
    Nothing can make her.

Suckling.

———◇◇———

SHE'S fair, she's wondrous fair,
    But I care not who knows it;
E'er I'll die for love, I fairly will forego it.

Suckling

———◇◇———

FROM every blush that kindles in thy cheeks
    Ten thousand little loves and graces spring,
To revel in the roses.   Rowe

———◇◇———

BEAUTY is but a vain and doubtful good,
    A shining gloss, that fadeth suddenly;
A flower that dies, when first it 'gins to bud;
    A brittle glass, that's broken presently;
A doubtful good, a gloss, a glass, a flower,
Lost, faded, broken, dead within an hour.

Shakespeare.

SUCH is life—a changing sky,
　Sometimes shadow, sometimes bright:
Morning dawns all gloriously,
　And despair shuts in the night:
But there is a quiet home,
　Far beyond the mortal range,
Where the loved in Christ may roam
　'Mid the flowers that know no change.

Catharine Mitchell

——◦◦——

THERE are white faces in each sunny street,
　And signs of trouble meet us everywhere;
The nation's pulse hath an unsteady beat,
　For scents of battle foul the summer air.

A thrill goes through the city's busy life,
　And then, as when a strong man stints his breath,
A stillness comes; and each one in his place
　Waits for the news of triumph, loss and death.

The "extras" fall like rain upon a drought,
　And started people crowd around the board
Whereon the nation's sum of loss or gain
　In rude and hurried characters is scored.

Perhaps it is a triumph-gleam—
　An earnest of our future recompense;
Perhaps it is a story of defeat,
　Which smiteth like a fatal pestilence.

But whether failure darkens all the land,
　Or whether victory sets its blood ablaze,
An awful cry, a mighty throb of pain,
　Shall scare the sweetness from the summer days.

21

God. how this land grows rich in loyal **blood,**
   Poured out upon it to its utmost length!
The incense of a people's sacrifice—
   The wrested offering of a people's **strength.**

It is the costliest land beneath the sun!
   'Tis priceless, purchaseless! and not a **rood**
But hath its title written clear and signed
   In some slain hero's consecrated blood.

And not a flower that gems its mellowing soil
   But thriveth well beneath the holy dew
Of tears, that ease a nation's straining heart,
   When the Lord of battles smites it through and through.

Louisville Journal.

H E dropped his plummet down the broad,
   Deep universe, and said, "No God!"
Finding no bottom.

Anon

HENCEFORTH it matters not
   If storm or sunshine be my earthly lot.
Bitter or sweet my cup, I only pray,
God make me pure, and nerve my soul
For the stern hour of strife.

Anon.

IS there not some chosen curse,
   Some hidden thunder, in the stars of heaven,
Red with uncommon wrath, to blast the man,
Who owes his greatness to his country's ruin?

Addison's Cato

THOU wert swift, O Morar! as a roe on the hill; terrible as a meteor of fire. Thy wrath was as the storm; thy sword in battle as lightning in the field. Thy voice was like a stream after rain, like thunder on distant hills. Many fell by thy arm: they were consumed in the flames of thy wrath. But when thou didst return from war, how peaceful was thy brow! Thy face was like the sun after rain; like the moon in the silence of night; calm as the breast of the lake when the loud wind is hushed into repose. Narrow is thy dwelling now, dark the place of thine abode. With three steps, I compass thy grave, O thou who wast so great before! Four stones, with their heads of moss, are the only memorial of thee. A tree with scarce a leaf, long grass whistling in the wind, mark to the hunter's eye the grave of mighty Morar.

Ossian.

IT must be so: Plato, thou reasonest well,
  Else whence this pleasing hope, this fond desire,
This longing after immortality?
Or whence the secret dread and inward horror
Of falling into naught? Why shrinks the soul
Back on itself, and startles at destruction?
'Tis the divinity that stirs within us;
'Tis Heaven itself that points out an hereafter
And intimates eternity to man.

Addison's Cato.

THE rose is fairest when 'tis budding new,
  And hope is brightest when it dawns from tears;
The rose is sweetest wash'd with morning dew,
  And Love is loveliest when embalm'd in tears.

Scott

FLOW on for ever, in thy glorious robe
  Of terror and of beauty.   God hath set
His rainbow on thy forehead, and the clouds
Mantled around thy feet; and he doth give
Thy voice of thunder power to speak of him
Eternally; bidding the lip of man
Keep silence, and upon thy rocky altar pour
Incense of awestruck praise.

Mrs. Sigourney's Apostrophe to Niagara

———◦◦———

BUT now he walks the streets,
  And he looks at all he meets,
    Sad and wan;
And he shakes his feeble head,
That it seems as if he said,
    "They are gone!"

The massy marbles rest
On the lips that he has pressed
    In their bloom;
And the names, he loved to hear
Have been carved for many a year
    On the tomb.

O. W. Holmes

———◦◦———

THERE is a time when all that grieves us
  Is felt with a deeper gloom:
There's a time when Hope deceives us,
  And we dream of bright days to come.

Thomas Haynes Bailey

———◦◦———

    THERE is strength
Deep bedded in our hearts, of which we reckon
But little till the shafts of heaven have pierced
Its fragile dwelling.

Mrs. Hemans.

O MEMORY! thou lingering murmurer
   Within Joy's broken shell,
Why have I not, in losing all I loved,
   Lost thee as well?

Anon

A M I mad, that I should cherish that
   Which bears such bitter fruit?
I will pluck it from my bosom, though my
   Heart be at its root.

Tennyson.

ALL thy vexations
Are but my trials of thy love, and thou
Hast strangely stood the test.

Shakespeare.

THY talk is the sweet extract of all speech,
   And holds mine ear in blissful slavery

Bailey's Festus.

'TIS not the babbling of an idle world,
   Where praise and censure are at random hurled,
That can the meanest of my thoughts control,
Or shake the settled purpose of my soul.
Free and large might their wild curses roam,
If all, if all, alas! were well at home!

Churchill.

MY Father! thou hast knowledge—only thou—
   How dreary 'tis for women to sit still
On winter nights, by solitary fires,
And hear the nations praising them far off,
Too far!

Mrs. Browning

AH, the key of our life, that passes all wards,
　　Opens all locks,
Is not I will—but I must—I must, I must,
　　And I do it!　　　　　　　　　　　**Anon,**

———◆◆———

I SAID, My heart, is all too soft:
　He who would climb and soar aloft
Must needs keep ever at his side
The tonic of a wholesome pride.
　　　　　　　　　　　　　　　　　Anon.

———◆◆———

FOR at my back I always hear
　Time's wingéd chariots hurrying near,
And onward, all before, I see
Deserts of vast eternity.　　　　　　**Anon**

———◆◆———

TROUBLE'S darkest hour
　Shall not make me cower
To the spectre's power—
　Never, never, never.

Then up, my soul, and brace thee,
While the perils face thee;
In thyself encase thee
　Manfully for ever.

Storms may howl around thee,
Foes may hunt and hound thee:
Shall they overpower thee?
　Never, never, never.　　　　　　**Anon**

THE heart, long worn by fierce
    Volcanic surges,
Feels its old world slow
Sinking from the sight,
Till o'er the wreck a home of
Peace emerges,
      Bright with unnumbered
      Shapes of new delight.

                                   Anon.

"STAND like an anvil!" when the stroke
    Of stalwart men falls fierce and fast;
Storms but more deeply root the oak,
    Whose brawny arms embrace the blast.

"Stand like an anvil!" when the sparks
    Fly far and wide, a fiery shower;
Virtue and truth must still be marks
    Where malice proves its want of power.

"Stand like an anvil!" when the bar
    Lies red and glowing on its breast;
Duty shall be life's leading star,
    And conscious innocence its rest.

"Stand like an anvil!" when the sound
    Of ponderous hammers pains the ear;
Thine but the still and stern rebound
    Of the great heart that cannot fear.

"Stand like an anvil!" Noise and heat,
    Are born of earth and die with time;
The soul, like God, its source and seat,
    Is solemn, still, serene, sublime.

                                 Bishop Doane.

TALKING is not simply a habit, but a matter of original constitution. Some persons have a talking endowment, and some have not. There is a positive faculty of expression, vocalization, of which silence is merely the negative. As cold is only the absence of heat, so silence may be not the result of prudence, but the want of a gift or impulse of spirit. There is a popular impression that great talkers are of course flippant, and that silent people are presumptively wise. To say of a man that "he talks a great deal," is equivalent to saying that he thinks but little. But will observation bear this out? It is true that some people are taciturn, but others, equally sagacious, are talkative. Some foolish people talk a great deal, but there are a great many foolish people who are very uncommunicative. A talkative man is seldom over-estimated; a silent man often is. There is great cunning in a judicious silence. To sit quietly while one talks, to look knowingly, to shake the head skillfully, to retire with grave features and silent tongue, gives one the reputation of being wise, considerate and self-contained. Commend me, however, to one who uses speech or silence as the instruments of his will. Some there be who discern your moods and occasions. Know when silence will soothe or when speech will cheer.   Henry Ward Beecher.

———◇———

A TALENT for conversation has an extraordinary value for common, every-day use of life. Let any one who has the gift enter into a social circle anywhere. How every one's face brightens at his entrance! How soon he sets all the little wheels in motion!—encouraging the timid, calling out unostentatiously the resources of the reserved and shy, subsidizing the facile, and making everybody glad and happy. The talent for conversation, more almost than anything else in life, requires tact and discretion. It requires one to have most varied knowledge, and then have it at instant and absolute disposal, so that he can use just so much or just so little as the occasion demands. It requires the ability to pass instantly and easily from the playful to the serious, from books to men, from the mere phrases of courtesy to the expressions of sentiment and passion. **Essays on Social Subjects.**

I LOOK along the columned years
  And see life's riven fane,
Just where it fell, amid the jeers
Of scornful lips, whose mocking sneers
For ever hiss within my ears,
  To break the sleep of pain.

I can but own my life is vain,
  A desert void of peace;
I missed the goal I sought to gain,
I missed the measure of the strain
That lulls Fame's fever in the brain,
  And bids earth's tumult cease.

Myself! alas for theme so poor,
  A theme but rich in fear!—
I stand a wreck on Error's shore,
A spectre not within the door,
A houseless shadow evermore,
  An exile lingering here.
Adah Isaacs Menken.

JESUS! thy blood and righteousness
  My beauty are, my glorious dress:
'Midst flaming worlds, in these arrayed,
With joy shall I lift up my head.
Wesley.

SOME hearts go hungering through the world,
   And never find the love they seek:
Some lips with pride or scorn are curled,
   To hide the pain they may not speak.
The eye may flash, the mouth may smile,
   The voice in gladdest music thrill,
And yet beneath them, all the while,
   The hungry heart be pining still.

O eager eyes which gaze afar!
   O arms which clasp the empty air!
Not all unmarked your sorrows are,
   Not all unpitied your despair.
Smile, patient lips so proudly dumb:
   When life's frail tent at last is furled,
Your glorious recompense shall come,
   O hearts that hunger through the world!

Anon

IN the still air music lies unheard,
   In the rough marble beauty lies unseen:
To wake the music and the beauty needs
   The master's touch, the sculptor's chisel keen.

Great Master! touch us with thy skillful hand—
   Let not the music that is in us die;
Great Sculptor! hew and polish us, nor let,
   Hidden and lost, thy form within us lie.

Spare not the stroke; do with us as thou wilt;
   Let there be naught unfurnished, broken, marred;
Complete thy purpose, that we may become
   Thy perfect image, O our God and Lord!

Anon.

A BATTLE-CRY is in that word;
    A force to wield on deadliest field,
      Which he who grasps shall feel
As if his hand had drawn a sword,
    And triumph were forestalled and sealed,
      With the first battle-peal!

A royal word! a conquering word!
    Which none could speak with lips so weak
      But straight they should grow strong;
As if in knowing they had heard
    The mighty host of victors speak,
      And echoed the new song.

The grand word! the eternal word!
    Given us whereby to glorify
      This daily work and care,
Building our temples to the Lord
    After the heavenly house on high,
      Where the city lies four-square.

The Right.

A SHIP was sailing in the southern waters on the Atlantic, when those on board saw another vessel making signals of distress. They bore down toward the distressed ship and hailed it:

"What is the matter?"

"We are dying for water," was the response.

"Dip it up, then!" was answered; "you are in the mouth of the Amazon river."

There those sailors were thirsting and suffering and fearing, and longing for water, and supposing that there was nothing but the ocean's brine around them, when, in fact, they had sailed unconsciously into the broad mouth of the mightiest river or the globe, and did not know it. And though to them it seemed that they must perish with thirst, yet there was a hundred miles of fresh water all around them, and they had nothing to do but "dip it up." Jesus Christ says, "If any man thirst, let him come unto me and drink." "And the Spirit and the Bride say, Come, and let him that heareth say, Come, and whosoever will, let him come and take of the water of life freely." Thirsting soul, the flood is all around you; "dip it up!" and drink and thirst no more for ever.

The Earnest Christian.

A SPANISH artist was once employed to paint the "Last Supper." It was his object to throw all the sublimity of his art into the figure and countenance of the Lord Jesus; but he put on the table in the foreground some chased cups, the workmanship of which was exceedingly beautiful. When his friends came to see the picture on the easel, every one said, "What beautiful cups!" "Ah!" said the artist, "I have made a mistake; these cups divert the eyes of the spectators from the Lord, to whom I wished to direct the attention of the observer." And he forthwith took up his brush and blotted them from the canvas, that the strength and vigor of the chief object might be prominently seen and observed. Thus all Christians should feel their great study to be Christ's exaltation; and whatever is calculated to hinder man from beholding him in all the glory of his person and works, should be removed out of the way! "God forbid that I should glory, save in the cross of our Lord Jesus Christ."

Anon.

HE who could not sit
And sing contented in a desert isle,
His audience the mute trees and wandering winds,
His joy the grace and beauty of his song,
Should never lift his voice 'mong mortal men.

Alexander Smith

I HAVE done at length with dreaming:
   Henceforth, O thou soul of mine,
Thou must take up sword and gauntlet,
   Waging warfare most divine.
Life is struggle, combat, victory!
   Wherefore have I slumbered on,
With my forces all unmarshaled,
   With my weapons all undrawn?
Oh how many a glorious record
   Had the angels of me kept,
Had I done, instead of doubted,
   Had I walked, instead of crept!
Yet, my soul! look not behind thee,
   Thou hast work to do at last:
Let the brave toil of the present
   Overarch thy crumbling past;
Build thy great acts high and higher,
   Build them on the conquered sod
Where thy weakness first fell bleeding,
   Where thy first prayer was to God.

Anon.

ONE autumn day I stood upon the sea-coast, where the waves, stirred by a recent tempest, dashed furiously upon the rocks. The great ocean waves, rolling in with full sweep from the Atlantic, leaped upon the coast with terrific roar. In one place rushing into a cavern, the surge, through an opening in the top, sprang in a column of spray and foam a great height in the air. The sight was so sublime that many persons came from the neighboring city to witness it. While looking upon the scene exhibiting the ocean in such power and grandeur, I observed that the rocks, even those upon which the surf broke with such fury, were covered with multitudes of very small shells. So, in the

very presence of the stormy sea, smitten every instant by
the thundering surf, the little shells, clinging with trustful
fingers to the great rocks, found shelter and life.   There
was the great ocean in its wrath, the symbol of restless
might, rushing upon the cliff as though it would break
over its ancient barriers.   Here were creatures, symbols
of frailty, having no strength of their own, finding complete safety and refuge by clinging to the immovable
rock.   So, thought I, it is between God and man; our
own safety is in clinging to him.   Are you tried by the
fierce onset of many difficulties?   Cling the closer to the
Rock of your strength.   Does the world allure you? does
Satan endeavor to overcome you?   Cling to the Rock
of your strength.   Nothing can pluck you from God's
hand if you place your trust in him.   Even the gates of
hell shall not prevail against you if your hopes are fixed
upon the Rock of Ages.   God is our refuge and our strength,
a very present help in trouble.   **Anon.**

———◦◦———

I SANG an old song; it was plain and not long—
   I had sung it very oft when they were small;
And long ere it was done they wept every one;
   Yet this was all the song—this was all:

The snow lies white, and the moon gives light:
   I'll out to the freezing mere,
And ease my heart of one little song,
   For none will be nigh to hear.
And its O my love, my love!
   And it's O my dear, my dear!
It's of her that I'll sing till the wild woods **ring,**
  When nobody's nigh to hear.

My love she is young, is young,
　When she laughs the dimple dips;
We walked in the wind, and her long locks blew
　Till sweetly they touched my lips.
And I'll out to the freezing mere,
　Where the stiff reeds whistle so low,
And I'll tell my mind to the friendly wind,
　Because I have loved her so.

Ay, and she's true, my lady is true;
　And that's the best of it all;
And when she blushes my heart so yearns
　That tears are ready to fall.
And its O my love, my love!
　And it's O my dear, my dear!
It's of her that I'll sing till the wild woods ring,
　When nobody's nigh to hear.

Jean Ingelow.—An Old Wife's Song

WITHIN a few years many poems of great beauty, sweetness and pathos have appeared in England, written in the Dorset dialect. The following, from an English magazine of recent date, serves to illustrate the capacities of that quaint dialect for the purposes of poetry:

WHILST I, a lonesome kind o' man,
　Wie'in my chimney-corner zit,
No vriend or dog do bide wie' me,
　Zo I be vorced to think a bit.

The bells ring in the wuld church-tower,
　The lime trees shiver in the blast;
But oh the aching sense o' loss
　That haunts me as I scan the past.

Last year it wur a cheerful tone
   The bells rang out zo zharp and **clear;**
But now my bonnie Jean is dead,
   My child is gone, and I be here.

Her pattens stand beneath the clock—
   No more they echo on the stoane;
O God! I pray for patience still,
   But I be left here all aloane!

She wur a spracker soul than I,
   And well I mind her litsome look,
As she my letters taught o' nights—
   And now her gravestone is my book.

And looking in the churchyard now,
   The letters "zacred" I can see;
'Tis whoaly ground wherein she lies—
   God knows how zacred 'tis to me.

A cradle stands right auverhead,
   And there a mouse ha' built her nest;
For thoaghts of him that's gone to her,
   And never could thick mouse molest.

The sparrows twitter in the perch,
   And yett the crumbs she used to gi'e;
I hear the parson read in church,
   "Better than many such are ye."

He taks o' heaven and happy zouls—
   And we ha' zouls I doan't deny—
But sparrows scease be varden's-wurths,
   And they be happier than I.

The bells clang in the wuld church tower,
   The yew tree spreads her branches wide;
Her aged limbs will vall at last—
   Lord, how much longer must I bide?

I treasure every word o' her
   Beneath that tree who takes her rest;
"God's will be done," she often zaid;
   "Bide patient, Jem, and do thy best."

Patience! the lesson's hard to learn;
   Christ taught it, and she practiced it;
The wind ha' kind o' stole her voice—
   "Be patient, Jem, and bide a bit."

To-morrow brings another year;
   God's plans surpass all human wit;
I thank thee, Lord, for they sweet words—
   "Be patient, Jem, and bide a bit."

Oh gi'e me strength to do thy will,
   To vollow her as best I can;
But she's a saint in glory now,
   And I'm a lonesome zort o' man.

R ꞓ

———◆———

THEY say that song is laid in Byron's grave!
   As long as lightning glimmers on the hills,
Song shall be heard as long as fields are green,
And skies are blue, and woman's face is fair.
     Life is enriched and multiplied by song;
     Song recreates the people of the past;
     For one immortal moment we are they,
     And one blood beats in all.
               Alexander Smith.

THE following poem, "*The Closing Scene,*" by T. Buchanan Read, is pronounced by the *Westminster Review* to be unquestionably the finest American poem ever
written :

Within the sober realms of leafless trees
   The russet year inhaled the dreamy air,
Like some tanned reaper in his hour of ease,
   When all the fields are lying brown and bare.

The gray barns looking from their hazy hills
   O'er the dun water's widening vales,
Sent down the air a greeting to the mills
   On the dull thunder of alternate flails.

All sights were mellowed and all sounds subdued,
   The hills seemed farther, and the streams sang low,
As in a dream the distant woodman hewed
   His winter log with many a muffled blow.

The embattled forests, erewhile armed with gold,
   Their banners bright with every martial hue,
Now stood like some sad, beaten host of old
   Withdrawn afar in Time's remotest blue.

On sombre wings the vulture tried his flight,
   The dove scarce heard his sighing mate's complaint ;
And like a star slow drooping in the light,
   The village church-vane seemed to pale and faint.

The sentinel cock upon the hillside crew—
   Crew thrice, and all was stiller than before ;
Silent till some replying warder blew
   His Alpen horn, and then was heard no more.

Where erst the jay within the elm's tall crest
   Made garrulous trouble round her unfledged young;
And where the oriole hung her swaying nest,
   By every light wind like a censer swung.

Where sung the noisy martens of the eaves,
   The busy swallows circling ever near,
Foreboding, as the rustic mind believes,
   An early harvest and a plenteous year.

Where every bird that waked the vernal feast,
   Shook the sweet slumber from its wing at morn,
To warn the reaper of the rosy East—
   All was now sunless, empty and forlorn.

Alone from out the stubble piped the quail,
   And croaked the crow through all the dreary gloom,
Alone, the pheasant, drumming in the vale,
   Made echo to the distant cottage loom.

There was no bud, no bloom upon the bowers;
   The spiders wove their thin shrouds night by night,
The thistledown, the only ghost of flowers,
   Sailed slowly by—passed noiselessly out of sight.

Amid all this, in the most dreary air,
   And where the woodbine shed upon the porch
Its crimson leaves, as if the year stood there,
   Firing the floor with its inverted torch,—

Amid all this, the centre of the scene,
   The white-haired matron, with monotonous tread,
Plied the swift wheel, and with her joyless mien,
   Sat like a Fate, and watched the flying thread.

She had known sorrow.　He had walked with her,
　Oft supped and broke with her the ashen crust,
And in the dead leaves still she heard the stir
　Of his thick mantle trailing in the dust.

While yet her cheek was bright with sunny bloom,
　Her country summoned and she gave her all;
And twice War bowed to her his sable plume,
　Regave the sword to rust upon the wall;

Regave the sword, but not the hand that drew,
　And struck for liberty the dying blow;
Nor him who, to his sire and country true,
　Fell 'mid the ranks of the invading foe.

Long, but not loud, the droning wheel went on,
　Like the low murmur of a hive at noon;
Long, but not loud, the memory of the gone
　Breathed through her lips a sad and tremulous tune.

At last the thread was snapped, her head was bowed,
　Life dropped the distaff through her hands serene,
And loving neighbors smoothed her careful shroud,
　While death and winter closed the autumn scene.

———◇———

THE future hides in it
　Gladness and sorrow;
We press still thorow,
Naught that abides in it;
Daunting us—onward.

And solemn before us,
Veiled, the dark Portal,
Goal of all mortal;
Stars silent rest o'er us!
Graves under us, silent!

While earnest thou gazest,
Comes boding of terror,
Comes phantasm and error,
Perplexes the bravest
With doubt and misgiving,

But heard are the voices—
Heard are the sages—
The world and the ages;
"Choose well; your choice is
Brief, and yet endless.

"Here eyes do regard you
In eternity's stillness;
Here is all fullness,
Ye brave, to reward you.
Work, and despair not!"

Goethe.

———◦◦◦———

At the end of every road there stands a wall,
    Not built by hands—impenetrable, bare.
Behind it lies an unknown land, and all
    The paths men plod tend to it, and end there.

Each man, according to his humor, paints
    On that bare wall strange landscapes; dark or bright,
Peopled with forms of fiends or forms of saints—
    Hells of Despair or Edens of Delight.

Then, to his fellows, "Tremble!" or "Rejoice!"
    The limner cries, "for lo, the Land beyond!"
And, ever acquiescent to his voice,
    Faint echoes from that painted wall respond.

But, now and then, with sacrilegious hand,
   Some one wipes off those painted landscapes all,
Muttering, "O fools, and slow to understand,
   Behold your bourne, the impenetrable wall!"

Whereat, an eager, angered crowd exclaims,
   "Better than yon dead wall, though pale and faint,
Our faded Edens! Better fiends and flames,
   By Fancy painted in her coarsest paint.

"Or the blind, bald, unquestionable face
   Of that obstruction, than its cold, unclad,
And callous emptiness, without a trace
   Of any prospect, either good or bad."

And straightway the old work begins again
   Of picture-painting. And men shout and call
For response to their pleasure or their pain,
   Getting back echoes from that painted wall.

                              Anon.

'TIS midnight! round the lamp which o'er
   My chamber sheds its lowly beam,
Is widely spread the varied lore
   Which feeds in youth our feverish dream.

We dream—the thirst, the wild desire,
   Delirious, yet divine, to know;
Around to roam, above aspire,
   And drink the breath of heaven below!

From ocean, earth, the stars, the sky
   To lift mysterious Nature's pall;
And bare before the kindling eye
   In man the darkest mist of all!

Alas! what boots the midnight oil?
  The madness of the struggling mind?
Oh, vague the hope and vain the toil
  Which only leaves us doubly blind!

What learn we from the past?   The same
  Dull curse of glory, guilt and gloom;
I asked the Future, and there came
  No voice from its unfathomed womb.

The sun was silent, and the wave;
  The air but answered with its breath:
But Earth was kind, and from the grave
  Arose the eternal answer—Death.

And this was all!   We need no sage
  To teach us Nature's only truth;
O fools! o'er wisdom's idle page
  To waste the hours of golden youth!

In Science wildly do we seek
  What only withering years should bring—
The languid pulse, the feverish cheek,
  The spirits drooping on their wing!

To think is but to learn to groan,
  To scorn what all besides adore,
To feel amid the world alone,
  An alien on a desert shore;

To lose the only ties which seem
  To idle gaze in mercy given!
To find Love, Faith and Hope a dream,
  And turn to dark Despair from heaven.

Bulwer.

THE dreams we loved in early life
   May melt like dreams away;
High thoughts may seem, 'mid passion's strife,
   Like Carthage in decay.

And proud hopes in the human heart
   May be to ruin hurled,
Like mouldering monuments of art
   Heaped on a sleeping world.

Yet there is something will not die,
   Where life hath once been fair;
Some towering thoughts still rear on high—
   Some Roman lingers there.
                           Anon.

THE heights by great men reached and kept
   Were not attained by sudden flight,
But they, while their companions slept,
   Were toiling upward in the night.
                           Longfellow.

FICTION hath in it a higher end than fact,
   'Tis the possible when compared with the merely posi-
     tive.
                           Anon.

MAIDENS, like moth, are caught by glare,
   And Mammon wins his way where seraphs would
     despair.
                           Byron.

PREPARE for rhyme: I'll publish right or wrong;
   Fools are my theme, let satire be my song.
                           Byron

FAREWELL! a word that hath been and must be—
A sound which makes us linger; yet farewell.

Byron.

AS nightingales do upon glow-worms feed,
So poets live upon the living light of Nature and Beauty

Bailey's Festus.

NATURE never did betray
The heart that loved her; 'tis her privilege
Through all the years of this our life, to lead
From joy to joy; for she can so inform
The mind that is within us, so impress
With quietness and beauty, and so feed
With lofty thoughts, that neither evil tongues,
Rash judgments nor the sneers of selfish men
Shall e'er prevail against us, or disturb
Our cheerful faith that all which we behold
Is full of blessing.

Wordsworth.

DARE to be right! dare to be true!
You have a work that no other can do;
Do it so bravely, so kindly, so well,
Angels will hasten the story to tell.

Dare to be right! dare to be true!
The failings of others can never save you;
Stand by your conscience, your honor, your faith,
Stand like a hero, and battle till death!

Anon

'TIS midnight's holy hour, and silence now
Is brooding, like a gentle spirit, o'er
The still and pulseless world.

G. D. Prentice.

IF in the world one heart does beat,
 Does beat for me and only me,
Oh, then 'twere sweet, dear love, how sweet!
 To breathe—to be.

If in the world one voice alone,
 Does call for me, for only me,
How precious has this poor life grown,
 To be implored of thee!

Anon

———◦———

FLAG of the free heart's hope and home,
 By angel hands to valor given!
Thy stars have lit the welkin dome,
 And all thy hues were born in heaven.

J. R. Drake.

———◦———

LEAVES have their time to fall,
 And flowers to wither at the north wind's breath,
And stars to set; but all—
 Thou hast all seasons for thine own, O Death!

Mrs. Hemans.

———◦———

SO live that when thy summons comes to join
 The innumerable caravan which moves
To that mysterious realm, where each shall take
His chamber in the silent halls of death,
Thou go not, like the quarry-slave at night,
Scourged to his dungeon; but, sustain'd and sooth'd
By an unfaltering trust, approach thy grave,
Like one that draws the drapery of his couch
About him, and lies down to pleasant dreams.

Bryant

EMPIRES rise,
Gathering the strength of hoary centuries,
And rush down, like the Alpine avalanche,
Startling the nations; and the very stars,
Yon bright and glorious blazonry of God,
Glitter a while in their eternal depths,
And, like the Pleiad, loveliest of their train,
Shoot from their glorious spheres, and pass away
To darkle in the trackless void; yet Time—
Time, the tomb-builder, holds his fierce career,
Dark, stern, all pitiless, and pauses not
Amid the mighty wrecks that strew his path,
To sit and muse, like other conquerors,
Upon the fearful ruin he hath wrought.

G. D. Prentice,

AND they call her cold! God knows
Underneath the winter snows,
The invisible hearts of flowers
Grow ripe for blossoming;
And the lives that look so cold,
If their stories could be told,
Would seem cast in gentle mould,
Would seem full of love and spring.

Anon.

IF there be memory in the world to come,
If thought recur to some things silenced here,
Then shall the deep heart be no longer dumb,
But find expression in that happier sphere;
It shall not be denied their utmost sum
Of love to speak without or fault or fear,
But utter to the harp, with changes sweet,
Words that, forbidden still, then heaven were incomplete

Jean Ingelow.

Gɪᴠᴇ sorrow words: the grief that doth not speak
   Whispers the o'erfraught heart and bids it break.

Shakespeare

Aʜ! when will all be ended? If the dead
   Have unto them some little memory left,
Of things that while they lived fate from them reft,
Ere life itself was reft them at last,·
Yet would to God these days at least were past,
And all be done that here must needs be done!
Ah! shall I, living underneath the sun,
I wonder, wish for anything again,
Or ever know what pleasure means, and pain?

William Morris.

Aɴᴅ History,
A mournful follower in the track of man,
Whose path is over ruin and the grave,
May linger for a moment in the place
Beside a worn inscription, and be sad.

Alexander Smith.

Sʜᴇ was like
A dream of poetry, that may not be
Written or told—exceeding beautiful!—
And so came worshipers.

Anon

Lᴇᴀɴ not on one mind constantly,
   Lest where one stood before, two fall;
Something hath God to say to thee
   Worth hearing from the lips of all.

Owen Meredith

LOVE not told,
And only born of absence and by thought,
With thought and absence may return to naught.

Jean Ingelow

———◦◦———

MY nerveless will
Is like a traitorous second, and deserts
My purpose in the very gap of need.

Alexander Smith.

———◦◦———

DEXTROUS men
Change but their voices, and are virtuous!

Alexander Smith.

———◦◦———

THE surest way of making a dupe is to let your victim suppose that you are his.

Bulwer.

———◦◦———

THE future seemed barred
By the corpse of a dead hope.

Owen Meredith.

———◦◦———

WHEN we see the dishonor of a thing, then it is time to renounce it.

Plutarch.

———◦◦———

PASSION is akin to pain. Love never yet penetrated an intense nature and made the heart light: sentiment has its smiles, its blushes, its brightness, its words of fancy and feeling, readily and at will; but when the internal sub-soiling is broken up, the heart swells with a steady and tremendous pressure till the breast feels like bursting; the lips are dumb, or open only to speak upon indifferent themes. Flowers may be played with, but one never yet cared to toy with flame.

Miss Anna E. Dickinson.—What Answer?

THERE are some deeds so grand
That their mighty doers stand
Ennobled, in a moment, more than kings.

Baker

----•◦•----

THERE are souls that are created for one another in the eternities, hearts that are predestined each to each, from the absolute necessities of their nature; and when this man and this woman come face to face, these hearts throb and are one.

Miss Anna E. Dickinson.

----•◦•----

FRIENDSHIP is excellent, and friendship may be called love; but it is not love. It may be more enduring and placidly satisfying in the end; it may be better and wiser and more prudent for acquaintance to beget esteem, and esteem regard, and regard affection, and affection an interchange of peaceful vows; the result, a well-ordered life and home. All this is admirable, no doubt; an owl is a bird when you can get no other; but the love born of a moment, yet born of eternity, which comes but once in a lifetime, and to one in a thousand lives, unquestioning, unthinking, investigating nothing, proving nothing, sufficient unto itself—ah, that is divine; and this divine ecstasy filled these two souls.

Miss Anna E. Dickinson.

----•◦•----

CONTACT with a high-minded woman is good for the life of any man.

Henry Vincent.

----•◦•----

I AM not one of those who do not believe in love at first sight, but I believe in taking a second look.

Herry Vincent.

----•◦•----

A FOOL cannot look nor stand nor walk like a man of sense.

La Bruyere.

HE that will believe only what he can fully comprehend, must have a very long head or a very short creed.

Colton.

———◦◦———

WHEN you are on good terms with any one, friendly, ay, even affectionately, think how it would be if you fell out with each other or were at enmity with each other.

Auerbach.—"On the Heights."

———◦◦———

THE only correct actions are those which require no explanation and no apology.

Auerbach.—"On the Heights."

———◦◦———

IT is only the drop which falls from the clouds which is free from intermixture; and it is only the pure thought which can be exactly perceived in its consequences.

Auerbach.—"On the Heights."

———◦◦———

HE who cannot wish that the whole world may think and act like himself, he has no right to call himself an honest and free man.

Auerbach.—"On the Heights."

———◦◦———

To live out oneself—that is everything.

Auerbach.—"On the Heights."

———◦◦———

I LOVE all men. I know that at bottom they cannot be otherwise; and under all the false and overloaded and glittering masquerade, there is in every man a noble nature beneath, only they cannot bring it out; and whatever they do that is false and cunning and evil, there still remains the sentence of our Great Example, "Forgive them, for they know not what they do."

Auerbach.—"On the Heights."

HE who has once despised the laws of nature, and has soared above them, has no right to live.

Auerbach.—" On the Heights."

THE highest punishment is not hell; it is not the place of condemnation, where other guilty ones suffer with us. No—to be condemned and to stand by some pure, happy one, feeling perfect innocence—that is the hell of hells.

Auerbach.—" On the Heights."

ON eagle-wings immortal scandals fly,
While virtuous actions are but born and die.

Pope.

HOW much the heart may bear, and yet not break!
How much the flesh may suffer, and not die!
I question much if any pain or ache
Of soul or body brings our end more nigh:
Death choses his own time; till that is worn
All evils may be borne.

We see a sorrow rising in our way,
And try to flee from the approaching ill;
We seek some small escape, we weep and pray;
But when the blow falls, then our hearts are still:
Not that the pain is of its sharpness shorn—
But think it can be borne.

We wind our life about another life—
We hold it closer, dearer than our own;
Anon it faints and falls in deadly strife,
Leaving us stunned and stricken and alone;
But ah! we do not die with those we mourn—
This also can be borne.

Behold, we live through all things—famine, thirst,
    Bereavement, pain; all grief and misery,
All woe and sorrow; life inflicts its worst
    On soul and body; but we cannot die,
Though we be sick and tired and faint and worn;
    So all things can be borne.   **Good Words.**

———◦◦◦———

EVERYTHING in the world—even respect—is to be bought
          Auerbach.—" On the Heights.'

———◦◦◦———

A LITTLE learning is a dangerous thing:
    Drink deep or taste not the Pierian spring;
There shallow draughts intoxicate the brain,
And drinking largely sobers us again.
        Pope.

———◦◦◦———

WHEN he shall hear she died upon his words,
    The idea of her life shall sweetly creep
Into his study of imagination,
And every lovely organ of her life
Shall come apparel'd in more precious habit,
More moving, delicate and full of life,
Into the eye and prospect of his soul,
Than when she lived indeed.
        Shakespeare

———◦◦◦———

THE Pagan kissing, for a step of Pan,
    The wild goat's hoof-print on the loamy down,
Exceeds our modern thinker, who turns back
The strata, granite, limestone, coal and clay—
Concluding coldly with, "Here's law? Where's God?"
        Mrs Browning

23

CANST thou not minister to a mind diseased,
    Pluck from the memory a rooted sorrow,
Raze out the written troubles of the brain,
And with some sweet, oblivious antidote
Cleanse the stuffed bosom of that perilous stuff
Which weighs upon the heart?

                                        Shakespeare

A THING of beauty is a joy for ever;
    Its loveliness increases; it will never
Pass into nothingness; but still will keep
A bower quiet for us, and a sleep
Full of sweet dreams, and health, and quiet breathing.
Therefore on every morrow are we wreathing
A flowery band to bind us to the earth,
Spite of despondence, of the inhuman dearth
Of noble natures, of the gloomy days,
Of all the unhealthy and o'erdarkened ways
Made for our searching; yes, in spite of all,
Some shape of beauty moves away the pall
From our dark spirits.

                                        Keat's Endymion.

GOD has made this world very fair. He fashioned it in
    beauty when there was no eye to behold it but his own.
All along the wild forest he has carved the forms of beauty.
Every cliff and stem and flower is a form of beauty. Every
hill and dale and tree and landscape is a picture of beauty.
Every cloud and mist-wreath and vapor-veil is a shadowy
reflection of beauty. Every spring and rivulet, every
river and lake and ocean, is a glassy mirror of beauty.
Every diamond and rock and pebbly beach is a mine of
beauty. Every sea and planet and star is a blazing face
of beauty. All along the aisles of earth, all over the

arches of heaven, all through the expanse of the universe, are scattered in rich and infinite profusion the life-germs of beauty. All natural motion is beauty in action. From the mote that plays its little frolic in the sunbeam, to the world that blazes along the sapphire spans of the firmament, are visible the ever-varying features of the enrapturing spirit of beauty.

Anon

LEARN to wait—life's hardest lesson,
　　Conned, perchance, through blinding tears,
While the heart-throbs sadly echo
　　To the tread of passing years.

Learn to wait Hope's slow fruition;
　　Faint not, though the way seem long;
There is joy in each condition—
　　Hearts, though suffering, may grow strong.

Constant sunshine, however welcome,
　　Ne'er would ripen fruit or flower;
Giant oaks owe half their greatness
　　To the scathing tempest's power.

Thus a soul, untouched by sorrow,
　　Aims not at a higher state;
Joy seeks not a brighter morrow:
　　Only *sad* hearts learn to wait.

Human strength and human greatness
　　Spring not from life's sunny side;
Heroes must be more than driftwood
　　Floating on a waveless tide.

Anon

THERE are buds that fold within them,
   Closed and covered from our sight,
Many a richly-tinted petal,
   Never looked on by the light.
Fain to see their shrouded faces,
   Sun and dew are long at strife,
Till at length the sweet buds open—
   Such a bud is life.

When the rose of thine own being
   Shall reveal its central fold,
Thou shalt look within and marvel,
   Fearing what thine eyes behold;
What it shows and what it teaches
   Are not things wherewith to part:
Thorny rose! that always costeth
   Beatings at the heart.

                                Jean Ingelow.

IT is only when Time, with reckless hand, has torn out half the leaves from the book of human life to light the fires of passion with from day to day, that man begins to see that the leaves which remain are few in number, and to remember, faintly at first, and then more clearly, that upon the earlier pages of that book were written stories of happy innocence, which he would fain read over. Then comes listless irresolution and the inevitable reaction of despair, or else the firm resolve to record upon the leaves that still remain a more noble history than the child's story with which the book began.   **Longfellow's Hyperion.**

I HAVE been spared to see the end of giant wrongs which I once deemed invincible in this country, and to note the silent upspringing and growth of principles and influences which I hail as destined to root out some of the most flagrant and pervading evils that yet remain. I realize that each generation is destined to confront new and peculiar perils—to wrestle with temptations and seductions unknown to its predecessors; yet I trust that progress is a general law of our being, and that the ills and woes of our future shall be less crushing than those of the bloody and hateful past. So, looking calmly, yet humbly, for that close of my mortal career which cannot be far distant, I reverently thank God for the blessings vouchsafed me in the past; and with an awe that is not fear, and a consciousness of demerit which does not exclude hope, await the opening before my steps of the gates of the eternal world.

Horace Greeley.—Reminiscences of a Busy Life.

THERE is a legend among the dwellers by the Rhine that on one night in every year, when the moon is at the full, the great Imperial Charles emerges from his tomb, and again visits the scenes that he loved on earth. When the moonbeams fall on the noble river, and fling from bank to bank a bridge of light, upon that bridge of moonbeams the monarch walks, calling down a benediction on all the German land. He blesses the earth, the corn-fields, the cities, the towns, the hamlets; he blesses the sleeping people of them all, and, his loving mission ended, he retires softly to his resting-place in La Chapelle.

Who knows but what such things may be true? I would rather trust the simple traditions of the people than one-half the theories of the philosophers; and if it may be that the dead can be again alive, if there can again exist on earth a tie so pure that death itself cannot break its bonds, pardon it as an idle fancy, forgive me if I say that in this city, on this night, the Founder of your Republic walks

His great spirit comes to revisit us; he comes to renew in every heart that still holds his memory dear some of the patriotism that fired his own, and to bless again, by his benignity and love, that now contentious land for which every hope of his noble life was spent.

Richard O'Gorman.

———◦◦◦———

AFTER the ocean has been swept by angry tempests, that have engulfed gallant fleets and strewed the shores with wrecks and the bodies of the dead, comes a calm; the mountain waves sink to gentle billows, the fierce gale lulls to a prosperous breeze, the sun shines forth in splendor, and the surviving mariners, with joyful hearts, again spread their sails, resume their course and speed away to their destined haven. So with our country, when peace, reconstruction and resumption have come. It had been swept and rent by the storms of civil war; the land was strewn with the dead, and everywhere are visible the vestiges of the conflict. But peace has come, and with it reconstruction. The bright sun of prosperity shines forth in a cloudless sky. Industry, trade and commerce again flow in their accustomed channels with accelerated currents. The tide of emigration, rising higher and higher, sweeps across from the Old World. The wilderness of the West yields up its golden treasures and "blossoms as the rose," and our country moves on gloriously to its great and final destiny.

Senator Morton.

———◦◦◦———

On every height there lies repose.

Goethe.

———◦◦◦———

A MAN is responsible for how he uses his *common sense* as well as his *moral sense*.

Beecher

THE friends of my adversity I shall always cherish most. I can better trust those who helped to relieve the gloom of my dark hours than those who are so ready to enjoy with me the sunshine of my prosperity.

Gen. Grant

THE extension of suffrage will not forbid the supremacy of intelligence.

Gen. Grant.

THE first thing about Parisian Positivism that strikes the Yankee mind is that it is Frenchy; that it smells of European mouldiness; that its ritual, for instance, indicates a reaction against Popery and an attempt to rival it. Reaction against a bad thing is very sure to be bad itself. Owen's "Communism" produced Warren's "Individual Sovereignty." Slavery gave us fighting anti-slavery—chills alternate with fever. A true thing does not come by reaction from evil, but by diving into good. We know that all men are affected, and the great thinkers as well as the rest, by the religious and political atmosphere which they breathe; and it is to be expected that systems coming from European thinkers should be tinctured with European reactions.

N. Y. World.

ELOQUENCE is made up at once of individuality and of sympathy; to live much in ourselves, to live much in others—such is the double condition of powerful speaking.

Vinet.

IN the different confessions we have a guarantee against fanaticism, and also a confirmation of the belief that a man can be to some extent independent of the outward forms of religion.

Auerbach.

AN extraordinary fallacy is the dread of night air. What air can we breathe at night but night air? The choice is between pure night air from without and foul night air from within. Most people prefer the latter—an unaccountable choice! An open window most nights in the year can never hurt any one.

Florence Nightingale.

———◇———

IMAGINATION is the greatest despot.

Auerbach.

———◇———

THE key of my inner life has changed from minor to major.

Auerbach.

———◇———

IT is now universally admitted that *literary* ability is *general* ability.

N. Y. World.

———◇———

THERE is a canon of common sense which should rule in everything.

Dr. T. A. Starkey, Cleveland.

———◇———

MAN

For a few years abandonment to lust—
Prodigious venture!—risks eternal flames.

Bickersteth.

———◇———

DESPAIR, as hope, breeds counsels. I have found Anguish no sluggish spur to thought.

Bickersteth.

———◇———

AN idle word may be seemingly harmless in its utterance, but let it be fanned by passion, let it be fed with the fuel of misconception, of evil intention, of prejudice, and it will soon grow into a sweeping fire that will melt the chains of human friendship, that will burn to ashes many cherished hopes, and blacken more fair names than one. What burns deeper than a bitter word? What is more desolating and destructive than a malicious tongue? There is no keener pain than that which bitter words inflict. The human tongue is as sharp as a knife, and it stings like a scorpion. "It is set on fire of hell." This is strong. If it were man's declaration, it would seem severe. Our natural tongues—our tongues unbridled by grace—our evil tongues are "set on fire of hell!" Oh fearful thought! A faggot of hell within our mouths! flames of Satan's kindling issuing from our mouths! No wonder they are desolating. No wonder they burn within and without. No wonder they occasion so much pain and misery. If we could bring ourselves to consider when we are speaking with an evil tongue that it is a flame of hell that is burning within us, would we not be more likely to close our mouths and quench the flame? would not the dread forethought strike us dumb? would not such a consideration lead us to sincere repentance for evil thus already done, and induce us to apply the balm of heaven where we had injured others with the burnings of hell?

Rev. Chas. A. Dickey, Allegheny City, Pa.

———◆◆◆———

PROVIDENCE is noiseless as it is irresistible. In the midst of the thunder of human conflict, and upon fields where the groans of the sufferers mingle with the shouts of noisy victory, God in silence launches great ideas, which sweep over the nations to mould the life of generations, just as the sun rises in silence to awake to busy life a sleeping continent.

. . . . It was reserved for the people of this generation to witness one of the grandest tragedies of time—one in which the actors numbered thirty millions, and in every scene there stood a silent figure—a figure without voice save at the mercy-seat. When the tragedy began he was a chattel, bought and sold in the market and worth so much. The blood flowed, and for a thousand miles the cannon thundered. At the end of the first act the silent figure took one step forward, and was announced to the world a chattel still, but one of a peculiar character, dangerous in he hands of an enemy, and so was written in history—"*a contraband.*" The tragedy went on till the blood of the slain baptized a hundred battle-fields, and at the end of the second act the voiceless figure moved again. Upon a paper proclamation, which fell silent as the withered leaf, he was heralded as man! The blood still flowed, and the wail of sorrow arose from a million of hearthstones, while the nations paused to wonder, when at the end of the third act the silent figure took one more step and stood as the highest type of a man—a citizen-soldier, fighting the battles of liberty and nationality. Laugh at the African if you will, and deny him a voice; God will make him his demonstration that Providence needs no voice. In the sublimity of silence will He who distills the dew and opens the flowers lift him up.   Rev. S. C. Logan, Pittsburg, Pa.

YOUNG gentlemen of the graduating class! as you now go from your college studies to enter upon your work in the world, I would warn you specially against four heresies which you will now have to combat:

1. The modern *cry against classical education*, as being impracticable. This is the cry of ignorance and of materialism. All knowledge is solid, practical, useful, especially the knowledge of the classics.

2. The *clamor for woman suffrage.* The Bible is against this. It places man at the head of the family, and the

family is the unit of the Church and State. Man is strong and bold in outline and endowment, fitted for work and endurance. Woman is tender, delicate, gentle in disposition and manner, but mighty in the extent of her influence. Let our "daughters be like cornerstones, polished after the similitude of a palace!"

3. The demand for the *abrogation of capital punishment.* This is the forerunner of lawlessness and anarchy.

4. The increasing *indifference to the religion of Christ.* Christianity is now confronted by (1) *Sensuality*—including intemperance, debauchery, gluttony and a degraded and prostituted art; (2) by *Rationalism*—including skepticism and materialism; and by (3) the Papacy—Rome and Ritualism. Combat these dangerous tendencies to the last, and be true to your instruction, to woman, to the majesty of law and the supremacy of Christ.

Dr. J. Edwards, Pres't of Washington and Jefferson College, to the Class of 1868

————•◦•————

WE sometimes meet with men who seem to think that any indulgence in an affectionate feeling is weakness. They will return from a journey, greet their families with a distant dignity, and move among their children with the cold and lofty splendor of an iceberg surrounded by its broken fragments. There is hardly a more unnatural sight than one of those families without a heart. A father had better extinguish a boy's eyes than take away his heart. Who that has experienced the joys of friendship, and values sympathy and affection, would not rather lose all that is beautiful in Nature's scenery than be robbed of the hidden treasure of his heart? Cherish, then, your heart's best affections. Indulge in the warm and gushing emotions of filial and fraternal love.

Miss Mulock.

STYLE is the intimate and inseparable fact of the personality of the writer—it is the verbal body of the man's moral and mental life—it holds his emotions and experiences, and is charged with his sensations—it is, in simplest words, his manifestation, refined and polished by his artistic faculty. Only men of peculiar or strong personality attain a style which distinguishes them, and imposes itself as a model upon the groping and undecided or formless writers whose work seems not to make immortal models, but to imitate them.

N. Y. Evening Mail.

————◦◇◦————

THE *year* passes quick, though the *hours* tarry, and time bygone is a dream, though we thought it never would go while it was going.

Newman.

————◦◇◦————

WHEN a man does a noble act, date him from *that*. Forget his faults. Let his noble act be the standpoint from which you regard him. There is much that is good in the worst of men.

Dr. Bellows.

————◦◇◦————

THERE are times when the pulse lies low in the bosom and beats low in the veins; when the spirit sleeps the sleep, apparently, that knows no waking in its house of clay, and the window shutters are closed, and the door is hung with the invisible crape of melancholy—when we wish the golden sunshine pitchy darkness, and are very willing to "fancy clouds where no clouds be." This is a state of sickness where physic may be thrown to the dogs, for we will have none of it. What shall raise the sleepless Lazarus? What shall make the heart beat music again, and the pulses dance to it through all the myriad thronged halls in our house of life? What shall make the sun kiss the eastern hills again for us, with all his old awakening gladness, and the night overflow with "moonlight music, love and flowers?" Love itself is the great stimulant—the most intoxicating of all—and performs all these miracles; but it is a miracle itself, and is not at the drug store, whatever they say. The counterfeit is in the market, but the winged god is not a money-changer, we assure you.

Men have tried many things, but still they ask for stimulant—the stimulant in use but requires the use of more. Men try to drown the floating dead of their own souls in the wine-cup, but the corpses will rise. We see their faces in the bubbles. The intoxication of drink sets the world whirling again, and the pulses playing music, and the thoughts galloping, but the fast clock runs down sooner, and the unnatural stimulation only leaves the house it fills with the wildest revelry—more silent, more sad, more deserted, more dead.

There is only one stimulant that never fails, and yet never intoxicates—*Duty*. Duty puts a blue sky over every man—up in his heart may be—into which the sky-lark, Happiness, always goes singing.

George D. Prentice.

WEARY human nature lays its head on the bosom of the divine Word, or it has nowhere to lay its head. Tremblers on the verge of the dark and terrible valley which parts the land of the living from the untried hereafter, take this hand of human tenderness yet of godlike strength, or they totter into the gloom without stop or stay. They who look their last look upon the beloved dead, listen to this voice of soothing and peace, or else death is no uplifting of everlasting doors, and no enfolding in everlasting arms, but an ending as appalling to the reason as to the senses—the usher to a charnel-house whose highest faculties and noblest feelings lie crushed with the animal wreck, and an infinite tragedy, maddening and sickening— a blackness of darkness for ever.

Reply to Essays and Reviews

———◦✦◦———

GOD has given understanding to man, to be employed for his glory in promoting the happiness of his creatures; and in nothing that belongs to earth can the human understanding be more worthily employed than in the researches of science and in the works of invention. Science and Invention may be called, perhaps not unfitly, the creators and the servants of civilization. Sometimes Invention, by a sort of intuition of principles, has grasped results and seemed to anticipate Science. More usually Science, by the patient investigation of truth and the discovery of principles, has prepared the way for the triumph of Invention. All Invention is realized Science, and this is especially true of the telegraph.

Chief-Justice Chase.

———◦✦◦———

MY imagination goes down to the chambers of the middle sea, to those vast depths where reposes the mystic wire on beds of coral, among forests of tangle, or on the bottom of dim blue gulfs, strewn with the skeletons of the drowned. Through these watery solitudes, among the fountains of the great deep, the abode of perpetual silence, never visited by living human presence and beyond the sight of human eye, there are gliding to and fro, by night and by day, in light and in darkness, in calm and in tempest, currents of human thought, borne by the electric pulse which obeys the bidding of man. That slender wire thrills with the hopes and fears of nations; it vibrates to every emotion that can be awakened by any event affecting the welfare of the human race.

William Cullen Bryant.

PEACE is not always produced by talking about it. Statesmen ought, I should imagine, to endeavor to discover what is most likely to engage men's interests, and to convince them that a state of peace is necessary to their well-being and to their moral and material comfort. What can be more likely to effect this than a constant and complete intercourse between all nations and individuals in the world? But statesmen are not always scientific men, and it is to Science that we are indebted for the means of communication. Steam was the first olive-branch offered to us by Science.

Mr. Thornton, the British Minister.

THERE is no such thing as human history. Nothing can be more profoundly, sadly true. The annals of mankind have never been written, never can be written; nor would it be within human capacity to read them if they were written. We have a leaf or two torn from the great book of human fate as it flutters in the storm-winds ever sweeping across the earth. We decipher them as we best can with purblind eyes, and endeavor to learn their mystery as we float along the abyss; but it is all confused babble—hieroglyphics of which the key is lost.

Motley.

UNLESS we hold fast to the fact that in human, as in physical history, Nature is ever patiently producing her effects through long lapses of time, by causes which have been in operation since the beginning, history is but another word for despair. But history is never hysterical, never proceeds by catastrophes and cataclysms; and it is only by remembering this that we can comprehend its higher meaning.

Motley.

SINCE the invention of gunpowder, and the development of all the many consequences to the human race which have flown from it, there are, perhaps, no three men who have contributed so much to the means of war as Fulton, Stephenson and Morse. As the great end of modern civilized war is to reach a state of peace in the soonest possible time, any invention which facilitates or hastens military operations is a step in advance of the olden time, when war was the normal state of the human race; and of the modern additions to the means at the command of the admiral afloat and the general on land the greatest unquestionably is the application of steam and electricity. It is a fundamental condition of all human progress that man should have peace; and he who gives us the means of sooner bridging over the chasms of war, and making still shorter those now happily brief contests which we do not seem to be able, as yet, to dispense with, is, in the highest sense, a benefactor to his kind.   **General McDowell.**

——◦——

THE main token of a strong character is not to make known every change and phase in thought and feeling, but to give the world the finished results.

Berthold Auerbach.

——◦——

IT is a postulate with many writers of this day that the late war was the result of two opposing ideas, or principles, upon the subject of African slavery. Between these, according to their theory, sprung the "irrepressible conflict" in principle, which ended in the terrible conflict of arms. Those who assume this postulate, and so theorize upon it, are but superficial observers.

That the war had its origin in opposing principles which, in their action on the conduct of men, produced the ultimate collision of arms, may be assumed as an unquestionable fact. But the opposing principles which produced these results in physical action, were of a very different character from those assumed in the postulate. The conflict in principle arose from differing and opposing ideas as to the nature of what is known as the General Government. The contest was between those who held it to be strictly federal in its character, and those who maintained that it was thoroughly national. It was a strife between the principles of Federation, on the one side, and Centralism or Consolidation on the other. Slavery, so called, was but the question on which these antagonistic principles, which had been in conflict from the beginning on divers other questions, were finally brought into actual and active collision with each other on the field of battle.

Alexander H. Stephens.

WHAT is this world but a world of progress? and what is the statesman worth who is afraid to fight in the front ranks? The liberty of the world is not yet effected. Half the world is yet in chains, half the world is yet under kingly government. We must go ahead; and, though I can do but little, I shall do what I can; and if, when I am dead, there sprouts any vigor from my bones and my grave to help forward posterity, to proclaim the same doctrines of universal liberty and universal suffrage and universal disenthrallment from kings, I shall be satisfied. The Goddess of Liberty is represented in ancient statues as a very nice little goddess, but very small. I want her to grow—to put on the habiliments of mature age—until she can embrace within her folds every nation, and every tribe, and every human being within God's canopy. I care not what you say of negro equality; I care not what you say of radicalism; these are my principles; and with the help of God I

shall die with them.   I ask no epitaph—I shall have none;
but I shall go with a pure consciousness of having tried to
serve the whole human race, and never having injured a
human being.   Thaddeus Stevens.

———◦◦———

THE ancients believed in a serene and beautiful genius
which ruled in the affairs of nations—which, with a
slow but stern justice, carried forward the fortunes of certain
chosen houses, weeding out single offenders or offending
families, and securing at last the firm prosperity of the
favorites of Heaven.   It was too narrow a view of the
Eternal Nemesis.   There is a serene Providence which rules
the fate of nations, which makes little account of time,
little of one generation or race—makes no account of dis-
asters, conquers alike by what is called defeat or by what
is called victory, thrusts aside enemy and obstructions,
crushes everything immoral, and obtains the ultimate triumph of the race by the sacrifice of everything which resists the moral laws of the world.   It makes its own instruments, creates the man for the time, trains him in poverty,
inspires his genius and arms him for its task.   It has given
every race its own talent, and ordains that only that race
which combines perfectly with the virtues of all shall
endure.   Emerson

———◦◦———

BUT Protestant Christianity we are not to regard as an
assemblage of statistics, an array of churches or denominations, and stop there.   Not at all; it is something more and
beyond—something deeper.   It is not so much an aggrega-
tion of sects as a profound religious movement, borne on by
an inner divine law, the opposite poles of which are freedom
and authority, sweeping through the nations and the ages,
and only in part appearing in the churches and sects.   Its

genius, its soul, is contracted and committed to no one of them; it is something larger and diviner than any one of them, or all of them combined, for it has not only produced each, and adopted it, as by a celestial instinct, for its subordinate mission, but it has in its fruitful capacity untold resources to meet future exigencies—the fertility, the flexibility, the power of adaptation—by means of which it puts itself, in some ·new and unheralded development, in direct contact with the various phases of human progress and want, pursuing humanity as a loving, divine presence; and holding to its lips, in every unexpected condition, the bread of life, is one of its leading and most promising characteristics. It keeps along with the great caravan, and is not found, after that has struck its tents and moved on, solemnly guarding the ashes of its forsaken camp-fires. Never before, or elsewhere, since apostolic days, has there been seen on the earth a religion so flexible, or so eager in the pursuit of man. When one of its organs becomes exhausted, stiffened, fixed, unable to keep up with the moving throng, the Protestant spirit leaves it and passes on. It does not cling to the dead limb, but enters into one—a new one or old one elsewhere— that has flexible and vital movements. There is no danger therefore, that Protestantism and the race will be severed. The same fecundity which produced Puritanism when it was needed, and Presbyterianism and Methodism and Evangelism, and domestic missions and lay preaching, and which now seeks to approach man in every condition of woe, with numberless other arrangements and supplementary enterprises, will produce any movement that may be necessary to meet the future wants of the thronging procession. Yet it will be the same Protestant Christianity; for this, we must remember, is not an organization, but a movement—a spirit, a life, underlying organizations and producing them at will on the call of need. If it were not this, but an organization, or something requiring a fixed organization, its vitality would be entangled in that and in the doings of that—in forms, rules, decrees, creeds; its freedom would be embarrassed; and soon, as in the case of all outward religions, it would be in one place and the race in another. But as it is, its many-sided life is free and irresistible, and if hindered at one point, reappears elsewhere, ever accompanying and blessing man. Protestant Christianity has no more reached its finality, exhausted its resources and adaptations, and become a fixture, than a growing child that is every day meeting the exigencies of life with unexpected capacities and powers. What the future forms of manifestation and working of this mighty presence, vainly trying to lodge in tabernacles which human hands assist in pitching, will be we know not, any more than we know what the future man will be from the child; but as we know it will be the same person in the one case, so we know it will be the same religion in the other.

Rev. J. E. Dwinell, D.D., of Sacramento.

———◦◦◦———

CHRISTIANITY has been confounded with the *doctrinal forms* which it has assumed. I find no fault with those who attempt to throw the facts of Christianity into a doctrinal form. The process is inevitable. But then one should not confound his philosophic rendering or solution of facts with the facts themselves. One should not confound Christianity with the purely human process of *reasoning upon* the facts of Christianity. Religious doctrinal systems will change after every great development in the philosophy of the human mind. They have changed hitherto, they are changing, and they will continue to change, because they are the result of mere human reasoning. Controversies that seemed to good men to threaten the very destruction of

Christianity, we can now see, as we look back upon them in history, only set Christianity, as a spirit, as a power, as a divine philosophy, free from the cerements that had been wrapped around it by the imperfection of human reason. Now when, in any age, careless men, who have confounded the spirit of Christ and of Christianity with the human doctrines of religion, see those doctrines attacked and modified, it is not strange that they should say, "Religion is passing away." But the external form that a principle assumes may change without in the slightest degree changing the principle itself.

Christianity has been confounded also with the *instruments* through which it has acted on this world. As a pure truth, it is impossible that Christianity should be universally and continuously powerful. It raised up for itself, therefore, institutions. The Church is one of them. Those institutions were relatively adapted to nationalities, to the civilizations of the world, to the necessities of the times in which they were developed. All forms of religious associations— the vehicles through which religious influence has been brought with power upon the world—are apt to be confounded with religion itself. Now, not undervaluing instruments, which are indispensable in this world, we are never to confound religion itself with the ordinances and institutions, the books and sermons it employs. These are separate from the thing itself, just as much as my hand is separate from my mind, though it is the indispensable instrument of the mind in working any manual craft. Christianity is a soul-power—an invisible, immutable power in the world. It employs ordinances and organizations, and men properly change and modify them from age to age, according to the exigencies of the civilization that exists; but religion does not change because its instruments do. Justice employs at one period of the human race one kind of laws: at another period justice changes those old laws and employs others. Laws change from generation to generation, and from nation to nation, not for the sake of destroying public welfare, but for the sake of maintaining it. The vehicles and instruments of religion are changing, but the spirit and the letter are never to be confounded.

There are many who seem to have the impression that the developments of science in our day, in mental philosophy, in sociology, in civil government, in political economy, in natural history, in all those elements which show the divine conception in the development of the physical world, are superseding Christianity. They speak of religion with respect. They say it has done an admirable work; that it has filled an interregnum; that before we could come to these higher knowledges it was an invaluable aid to human development; that it deserves all honor; that there are many elements in it which ought to be preserved; but they hold it is to be dispossessed by the developments of science. On the other hand, my own belief is that science is itself, however reluctantly in its first strides, ultimately to come round into perfect subjection to the law that is in Christ Jesus; and He that hath ruled over priests, over kings and over nations for ages past, is just as much in days to come to rule over laboratories and lecture-rooms and professional chairs and all that belongs to scientific knowledge. In our day there are apparent collisions, seeming discrepancies, but they are only apparent. Or, if they are real discrepancies, it will be found that they lie in that human element which has been wrapped around the exposition of religion. Religion itself, set free from imperfect human handling, is to emerge and be brighter than ever it was before, because it will be purer.

H. W. Beecher.

NO other book is more intensely *realistic* than the Word of God. It teaches us to honor life, men, society, occupation and the homely virtues which have their sphere in secular duties; and surely it cannot be so inconsistent with itself as then to undervalue all these things.

H. W. Beecher.

IT is not hard to die. It is harder a thousand times to live. To die is to be a man. To live is only to try to be one. To live is to see God through a glass darkly. To die is to see him face to face. To live is to be in the ore. To die is to be smelted and come out pure gold. To live is to be in March and November. To die is to find midsummer where there is perfect harmony and perfect beauty.

H. W. Beecher.

ALL high and grand emotions scorn the tongue, that lies as helpless in the mouth as would be artillery to express the sound and grandeur of mountain thunders in tropical storms.

H. W. Beecher.

WHEN a man stands in darkness and poverty and contempt; when he sees the whole community swept like a tide away from him; when he sees his friends turn their backs on him and leave him, and yet he never loses his courage or temper, and is as sweet-minded as ever, and says, "I am as happy as ever I was, and as hopeful and cheerful, for God is my support, he is my lover; he fulfills his promises to me, and he gives me the hidden manna, and also the white stone, on which my well-understood love-name is written," *there* is a testimony that the world cannot mistake; there is something mysterious and awful in this.

H. W. Beecher.

IT is a bad thing for a man, in looking at himself, at his
neighbors and at communities, to look at the side of
fault, and failing, and meanness, and imperfection, and
wickedness, and rottenness.   These things will force themselves upon his notice full enough—more than enough for
his good.   H. W. Beecher.

———◇———

BY sorrow men learn that they need to be fed with higher
food; that they must rest on stronger supports; that
they must have other friends and friendships; that they
must live another life; that there must be something that
neither time, nor chance, nor accident can undermine and
sweep away.   When men have learned the interior lesson
of sorrow, they look upon the trouble not as being less
troublous than it was, but as, from the higher point to
which they have risen, unreal and dreamy.
                                             H. W. Beecher.

———◇———

A MAN can bear
A world's contempt when he has that within
Which says he's worthy.   Alexander Smith

———◇———

THE saddest thing that can befall a soul
Is when it loses faith in God and woman.
. . . . Lost I those gems,
Though the world's throne stood empty in my path,
I would go wandering back into my childhood,
Searching for them with tears.   Alexander Smith

———◇———

THIS world is very lovely: O my God,
I thank thee that I live.   Alexander Smith

THE past is past. I see the future stretch
All dark and barren as a rainy sea.

Alexander Smⁱth.

I SPEARED him with a jest; for there are men
Whose sinews stiffen 'gainst a knitted brow,
Yet are unthreaded, loosened by a sneer,
And their resolve doth pass as doth a wave.

Alexander Smith.

HASTE is not always speed. We must learn to work
and wait. This is like God, who perfects his works
through beautiful gradations. We must have faith in duty.

Anon.

WHAT our enemies say ought not to be taken as
evidence.

Olive Logan.

THOUGH it be true that life is short and the world full
of vanity, yet God's work must be done diligently and
to the last.

Conybeare and Howson's Life of Paul.

VIEWED in connection with the corruptions by which
it is surrounded, the germ of life implanted in the
heart by the Holy Spirit at conversion is like a spark of
fire in the midst of the ocean! That the spark does not go
out is a very miracle, but it is kept by Almighty power,
until it warms and convulses and burns with purifying heat
the very extremities of the soul. The mighty work once
commenced in the heart will be carried on till the day of
God.

Rev. John T. Pressly, D D

WHEN I look out upon the world, the great problem to me is, How can Christianity be made to reach every individual man in his peculiar condition and characteristics? There is an infinite variety of men and women, differing in temperament and education, with peculiar prejudices and temptations and failings. Now as Christ tasted death for every man, so can his grace reach every individual case, and save the worst of men from their besetting sins. Young man! you think your case is peculiar and hopeless, but do not despair: Jesus Christ can save you; his power can rescue you. And it may be that *you,* saved from such fearful depths, will be the brightest star in his crown of redemptive glory. Now what will be the result of this morning's service? How greatly aggravated will be your guilt if you turn away from such offers of mercy!

Bishop Simpson.

SEEK thyself only in Christ, and not in thyself; so wilt thou find thyself in him for eternity.

Luther.

THE Cross is the prism that reveals to us the beauties of the Sun of Righteousness.

Dr. Goulburn.

ÆSTHETICS is now studied more than ethics.

Anon.

ASIA is the continent of origination; Europe the continent of differentiations, and America the continent of reunions.

Gulzot.

WE take no unimportant step here, viewed in the light of eternity.
Rev. Hanna, Pittsburg.

———◦◦———

EVERY man has a work to do proportionate to his abilities and opportunities.
A. A. Hodge, D. D.

———◦◦———

I REGARD this superstitious, unsmiling Christianity as a relic of the old Vandal times.
H. W. Beecher.

———◦◦———

THE history of religion is in one sense a history of language. Many of the ideas embodied in the language of the Gospel would have been incomprehensible and inexpressible alike if we imagine that, by some miraculous agency, they had been communicated to the primitive inhabitants of the earth. Even at the present day, missionaries find that they have first to educate their savage pupils, before the words and ideas of Christianity assume any reality to their minds, and before their own native language becomes strong for the purpose of translation.
Max Müller.

———◦◦———

ON the shores of the Adriatic, the wives of fishermen, whose husbands have gone far out upon the deep, are in the habit at eventide of going down to the seashore, and singing, as female voices only can, the first stanza of a beautiful hymn; after they have sung it, they listen till they hear borne by the wind across the desert sea the second stanza, sung by their gallant husbands as they are tossed by the gale upon the waves. Perhaps, if we could listen, we too might hear on this desert world of ours some sound, some whisper borne from afar, to remind us that there is a heaven and a home.
D . John Cumming.

I KNOW no method to secure the repeal of bad or obnoxious laws so efficient as their stringent execution.

Grant's Inaugural.

———◦◦◦———

ALL vegetable decompositions are poisonous and injurious to the human system. They are the descending elements of nature, and when taken into the system, in the shape of spirits, they inevitably cause the imbiber to descend also.

Dr. Chas. Jewett.

———◦◦◦———

1. MATHEMATICS (Numbers, Geometry, Mechanics).
2. Astronomy.
3. Physics.
4. Chemistry.
5. Biology.
6. Sociology, or the Social Science.
7. Anthropology, or the Science of Individual Man.

M. Comte's Classification of the Sciences.

———◦◦◦———

"THERE is a law above all the enactments of human codes—the same at all times and in all circumstances. It is the law written by the finger of God on the heart of man; and by that law, unchangeable and eternal, whilst men despise fraud, loathe rapine and hate blood, they will reject with indignation the wild and guilty phantasy that man can hold property in man" (Chatham). On the platform of this law we take our stand against *Utilitarianism*. Standing on the fundamental and palpable truth that man is possessed of a *moral nature*, we can, with equal authority say, that whilst men "do *by nature* the things contained in the law," whilst they *by nature* approve of virtue and condemn vice, they will reject the wild and guilty phantasy that the end and intention alone determine the morality of the man; and the no less wild and the no less guilty phantasy that happiness is a nobler thing than holiness— that it is the sole end of human action, and the only test and standard of virtue.   Robert Watts, D. D.

————◦⋄◦————

ALL things have something more than barren use,
    There is a scent upon the brier,
A tremulous splendor in the autumn dews;
    Cold morns are fringed with fire.

The clodded earth goes up in sweet-breathed flowers,
    In music dies poor human speech;
And into beauty blow those hearts of ours
    When Love is born in each.

Life is transfigured in the soft and tender
    Light of Love, as a volume dun
Of rolling smoke becomes a wreathéd splendor
    In the declining sun.   Alexander Smith.

————◦⋄◦————

BE true to your convictions!
                Miss L. L. F.

————◦⋄◦————

EACH time we love,
We turn a nearer and a broader mark
To that keen archer, Sorrow, and he strikes.
                Alexander Smith

————◦⋄◦————

MAN, as exercising will, is the subject of ethics; and this will, which is directed to the object of willing, and which affirms that object, and feels itself in harmony with it, is love.   Harless.

WHEN music grieves, the past
Returns in tears.   Alexander Smith

———◦◦◦———

A H, year by year life's fire burns out,
   And year by year life's stream runs dry;
The wild deer dies within the blood,
   The falcon in the eye;
And Hope, who sang miraculous songs
   Of what should be, like one inspired,
How she should right the ancient wrongs,
   (The generous fool!) grows hoarse and tired,
And turns from visions of a world renewed.
   We cheat ourselves with our own lying eyes,
We chase a fleeting mirage o'er the sand,
   Across a grave the smiling phantom flies,
O'er which we fall with a vain-clutching hand.

                                     Alexander Smith.

———◦◦◦———

A VERY old German author discourses thus tenderly of
   Christ:

My soul is like a hungry and thirsty child, and I need
his love and consolation for my refreshment; I am a wandering and lost sheep, and I need him as a good and faithful shepherd; my soul is like a frightened dove pursued by
the hawk, and I need his wounds for a refuge; I am a
feeble vine, and I need his cross to lay hold of and wind
myself about; I am a sinner, and I need his righteousness;
I am naked and bare, and need his holiness and innocence
for a covering; I am in trouble and alarm, and I need his
solace; I am ignorant, and I need his teaching; simple
and foolish, and I need the guidance of his Holy Spirit.
In no situation and at no time can I do without him. Do I
pray? he must prompt and intercede for me. Am I arraigned

by Satan at the divine tribunal? he must be my advocate. Am I in affliction? he must be my helper. Am I persecuted by the world? he must defend me. When I am forsaken he must be my support; when dying, my life; when mouldering in the grave, my resurrection. Well, then, I will rather part with all the world, and all that it contains, than with thee, my Saviour; and, God be thanked! I know that thou too art not willing to do without me. Thou art rich, and I am poor; thou hast righteousness, and I sin; thou hast oil and wine, and I wounds; thou hast cordial and refreshments, and I hunger and thirst. Use me then, my Saviour, for whatever purpose and in whatever way thou mayst require. Here is my poor heart, an empty vessel; fill it with thy grace. Here is my sinful and troubled soul; quicken and refresh it with thy love. Take my heart for thine abode; my mouth, to spread the glory of thy name; my love and all my powers, for the advancement of thine honor and the service of thy believing people; and never suffer the steadfastness and confidence of my faith to abate, that so at all times I may be enabled from the heart to say, "Jesus needs me, and I him, and so we suit each other."

THE religion of the day is an easy-minded religion, without conflict and wrestling with self-denial and sacrifice—a religion which knows nothing of the pangs of the new birth at its commencement, and nothing of the desperate struggle with the flesh and with the devil, day by day, making us long for resurrection deliverance, for the binding of the adversary and for the Lord's return. It is a second-rate religion—a religion in which there is no largeness, no grandeur, no potency, no noble-mindedness, no all-constraining love. It is a hollow religion, with a fair exterior, but an aching heart—a heart unsatisfied, a soul not at rest, a conscience not at peace with God; a religion marked, it may be, by activity and excitement, but betraying all the while the consciousness of a wound hidden and unhealed within, and hence unable to animate to lofty doings, or supply the strength needed for such doings. It is a feeble religion, lacking the sinews and bones of hardier times, very different from the indomitable, much-enduring, storm-braving religion, not merely of apostolic days, but even of the Reformation. It is an uncertain religion; that is to say, it is not rooted on certainty; it is not the outflowing of a soul assured of pardon and rejoicing in the filial relationship between itself and God. Hence, there is no liberty of service, for the question of personal acceptance is still an unsettled thing; there is a working for pardon, but not from pardon. All is thus bondage, heaviness, irksomeness; there is a speaking for God, but it is with a faltering tongue; there is a laboring for God, but it is with fettered hands; there is a movement in the way of his commands, but it is with a heavy drag upon our limbs. Hence the inefficient, uninfluential character of our religion. It does not tell on others, for it has not yet fully told upon ourselves. It falls short of its mark, for the arm that drew the bow is paralyzed.   H. Bonar.

———◦◇◦———

WE are all very busy—busy writing epitaphs. We do not let a day pass without doing something in this line, and we are all busy, not in writing epitaphs for others, but in writing our own. And we are making it very sure that people will read what we have written when we are gone. Shall we not be remembered? If not by many, we certainly shall by a few, and that remembrance we are making sure of by the tenor of our lives. Our characters are the inscriptions we are making on the hearts of those who know, and who will survive us. We do not leave this office to others. We are doing it ourselves. Others might falsify and deceive by what they might say of us. But we are telling the truth. The actions of our passing life are facts visible, plain, undeniable. We engrave them on the minds of all observers. How interesting the question, What kind of epitaphs are we writing? Will they be read with joy or sorrow? Remember the epitaphs we write are not for the marble that tells where we lie, but for the memory of every one that knew us.

Congregationalist.

———◦◦———

WITH the almost numberless opportunities for good and for evil that a city life presents, it is for each one, and especially for every young person, to choose at first which path he will pursue, which current to carry him along. New facilities will continually open before him for good, if he choose the good; for evil, if he drifts into that path which no one deliberately chooses, but where so many are wrecked for want of a firm moral principle to resist evil. Religion is a great safeguard in cities. Sincere and earnest religious principle is needed, both to avoid the dangers and improve the opportunities of a city life. He who mainly seeks the selfish accumulation of money, or the more social but not less dangerous pleasure of luxury and dissipation, only takes advantage of the worst elements of city life, and can only reap the natural results in a debased and degraded character. But he who, choosing wisely, resists evil in all its alluring shapes, and presses forward in the path of known duty, will receive from his city life a balance of mind, a comprehensiveness of purpose and a power of action that could not be developed in any other sphere.

Philadelphia Ledger.

25

A NATION cannot last as a money-making mob; it can-not with impunity—it cannot with existence—go on despising literature, despising science, despising art, de-spising. compassion, and concentrating its soul on pence. "Mighty of mind"—"mighty of mind"—"magnanimous" —to be this indeed is to be great in life; to become this in-creasingly is indeed to "advance in life"—in life itself, not the trappings of it. He only is advancing in life whose heart is getting softer, whose blood warmer, whose brain quicker, whose spirit is entering into living peace; and the men who have this life in them are the true lords or kings of the earth—they, and they only.

Ruskin.

———◦◦◦———

IT is a difficult thing to talk aright; so much so that "if any man offend not in word, the same is a perfect man;" and it is said to be easier to tame every species of animals— birds, fishes, and even serpents—than to tame the tongue. It is a wheel that catches fire by its own motion, and burns with increasing fierceness, and sets on fire the very course of nature. As one says: "The fire of a forest, fierce as it is, will burn out one day, but you cannot arrest the pro-gress of that cruel word you uttered carelessly yesterday: it will go on slaying, poisoning, burning, embittering, beyond your control for ever and for ever."

Rev. Dr. Kirk, Boston.

———◦◦◦———

LOVE is as gold in the rock. The mountain is but stone, and the gold is rare and scarce, and is found in veins here and there. So in this life it is in loving. We are too proud, too coarse, too selfish, too ungenerous; we are not magnanimous enough. Love runs in veins through us; and we are to take the experiences of love when it is in its most perfect moments in its ecstatic state, as it were purified gold, seven times purified and made clean—we are to take these as our ideas. Then we are to lift up, by the imagination, our conceptions to a state in which our character will turn on this feeling—not occasionally, but as an ordinary experience. Nay, we should rise up so completely into the influence of the purity and disinterestedness of this feeling as that it shall control all the other feelings, and harmonize them, till the conscience, and the reason, and the moral sentiments all are penetrated with the summer of love, as the whole atmosphere is, at times, penetrated by the warmth, and fragrance, and beauty of nature. And when we have thus by loving raised the ideal of loving, that very ideal comes back to rebuke, to correct, to restrain. It does not diminish and undervalue love; it augments the value of it. It teaches us how small it is; how it should be developed; and how pure, how unselfish, how generous, how noble it ought to be.

H. W. Beecher.

MISS DORA GREENWELL, in remarking that the success of Christian activities is measured by the depth of individual Christian life, says:

We hear so much around us of doings, so much of Christian exertion and charitable endeavor, that in witnessing the comparatively small result of much devoted labor, I have been led to believe that we work too much upon the surface. We have more than enough of systems—of machinery, which, whether more or less perfect, will not go of itself. We may have done all that of ourselves we can do, and the moving spring may yet be wanting—"The spirit of the living creatures in the wheels." God is a spirit and man is also a spirit, and all work that is done between God and man must be done in the spirit—must be wrought from the centre outward. The life that lies at the circumfer ence of its guiding idea lies there but in faint outline, feebly drawn, like the outermost ripple on disturbed waters. We are anxious to *spread* the knowledge of God. This is *our work*, the end to which Christian exertion is chiefly directed, but before we can pursue it to any true result, God must also work a work within us, upon the deepening of which the extension of Christ's kingdom naturally, inevitably, depends. For they who are rooted in God will in him bud and blossom, and fill the earth with fruit. All who have ever been strong for God have been strong *in him*, and have known too where the secret of their strength lay—in a dependence out of which they have been consciously weak as other men.

——◦◦◦——

SIT not like a mourner, brother! by the grave of that dear Past.

Throw the Present! 'tis thy servant only when 'tis overcast.

Give battle to the leagued world: if thou'rt worthy, truly brave,

Thou shalt make the hardest circumstance a helper or a slave;

As when thunder wraps the setting sun, he struggles, glows with ire,

Rifts the gloom with golden furrows, with a hundred bursts of fire,

Melts the black and thund'rous masses to the sphere of rosy light,

Then on edge of glowing heaven smiles in triumph on the night.

Alexander Smith

IF there be one man before me who honestly and contentedly believes that, on the whole, he is doing that work to which his powers are best adapted, I wish to congratulate him. My friend, I care not whether your hand be hard or soft; I care not whether you are from the office or the shop; I care not whether you preach the everlasting Gospel from the pulpit, or swing the hammer over the blacksmith's anvil; I care not whether you have seen the inside of a college or the outside—whether your work be that of the head or of the hand—whether the world account you noble or ignoble; if you have found your place, you are a happy man. Let no ambition ever tempt you away from it by so much as a questioning thought. I say, if you have found your place—no matter what or where it is—you are a happy man. I give you joy of your good fortune; for if you do the work of that place well, and draw from it all that it can give you of merriment and discipline and development, you are, or you will become, a man filled up, made after God's pattern, the noblest product of the world—a self-made man. Dr. Holland.

HOLD on, my heart, in thy believing—
  The steadfast only wins the crown;
He who, when stormy winds are heaving,
  Parts with his anchor, shall go down;
But he who Jesus holds through all,
Shall stand, though heaven and earth should fall.

Hold in thy murmurs, Heaven arraigning—
  The patient see God's loving face;
Who bear their burdens uncomplaining,
  'Tis they that win the Father's grace;

He wounds himself who braves the rod,
And sets himself to fight with God.

Hold out! There comes an end to sorrow:
  Hope from the dust shall conquering rise;
The storm foretells a summer's morrow;
  The cross points on to Paradise;
The Father reigneth! cease all doubt;
Hold on, my heart, hold on, hold out!

Golden Words.

THE longer I live, the more I feel the importance of adhering to the following rules, which I have laid down for myself in relation to such matters:

1. To hear as little as possible what is to the prejudice of others.

2. To believe nothing of the kind until I am absolutely forced to.

3. Never to drink in the spirit of one who circulates an ill report.

4. Always to moderate, so far as I can, the unkindness which is expressed toward others.

5. Always to believe that, if the other side were heard, very different accounts would be given of the matter.

An Old Scotch Writer.

IF the country is to be saved, to be reconstructed on a basis of holiness, purity, Christianity, the Christian young men of the country are to have a hand in the work; and the sooner they put hand, heart, pen and speech to the work, the better.

Young man! if God has given you brains, heart and voice, speak out. There are great reforms to be carried on. The whole nation needs awakening. Speak out, sir, and your speech will be welcome, wherever and on whatever particular branch of reforms you choose to make yourself heard. Lift up your voice for that which is "honest, lovely and of good report." Not in mere wordy harangue, not in windy palaver, not in grandiloquent spouting, nor yet in weary, drawling verbosity—not in the jabbering garrulity which is heard only when the speaker *must* be delivered of a speech. But in words of true, sanctified earnestness, opening your mouth because you have something useful to say, saying it with the genuine, unstudied eloquence which comes right from the heart, and in all cases closing your mouth the moment you have done.

Gough.

------◦◦------

I FEEL when I have sinned an immediate reluctance to go to Christ. I am ashamed to go. I feel as if it would do no good to go—as if it were making Christ a minister of sin to go straight from the swine-trough to the best robe —and a thousand other excuses; but I am persuaded they are all lies from hell. John argues the opposite way: "If any man sin, we have an advocate with the Father." And a thousand other Scriptures are against it. I am sure there is neither peace nor safety from deeper sin but in going directly to the Lord Jesus Christ. This is God's way of peace and holiness. It is folly to the world and the beclouded heart, but it is the way. I must never think a sin too small to need immediate application of the blood of Christ. If I put away good conscience concerning faith, I make a shipwreck. I must never think my sin too aggregated, too presumptuous—as when down on my knees, or in preaching, or by a dying bed, or during dangerous illness—to hinder me from fleeing to Christ. The weight of my sins should act like the weight of a clock—the heavier it is, it makes it go the faster.

McCheyne.

A MAN is first startled by sin; then it becomes pleasing, then easy, then delightful, then frequent, then habitual, then confirmed. Then man is impenitent, then obstinate, and then he is damned.

Jeremy Taylor.

———◦◦◦———

THE root that produces the beautiful and flourishing tree, with all its spreading branches, verdant leaves and refreshing fruit—that which gains for it sap, life, vigor and fruitfulness—is all unseen; and the farther and the deeper the root spreads beneath, the more the tree expands above. Christian, if you wish to prosper, if you long to bring forth all the fruits of the Spirit, strike your roots deep and wide in *private prayer*. That faith and support, that strength and grace, which you seek of God in secret, that it may be exercised in the hour of need, God will in that hour give it you before men.

Bickersteth.

———◦◦◦———

IN the moral life *conscience* predominates.

Rev. Phillips Brooks, Philadelphia.

———◦◦◦———

MANY a splendid genius was the despair of a good father when young. But all of a sudden he awoke and went into action like a soldier into battle, and made a name that will live for ever.

Rev. Day K. Lee, New York City.

———◦◦◦———

AN old-school deacon was asked: What is the difference between old divinity and new? Answer: Old divinity sends the prodigal son home in rags and utter poverty— new divinity brings him back with money enough to pay his expenses.

Presbyterian.

DO not hesitate to say that the outgrowths of the dance. the masquerade and the theatre are adultery, seduction, murder and death.

Rev. W. G. W. Lewis, Poughkeepsie, N. Y.

———◦◦◦———

IF the world goes against truth, then Athanasius goes against the world.

Athanasius.

———◦◦◦———

OUR very liberty will be our greatest danger in this country, should Christianity decay and the Sabbath come to be disregarded; for we have no law establishing Christianity as the national religion, and no class of men who are interested in its maintenance and success from political and ambitious motives.

Dr. Schaff.

———◦◦◦———

I WOULD not give five shillings for all Southey has written.

Wordsworth.

IS it his low estimate of Southey, or his esteem for the five shillings? Southey will long survive his reputation.

Byron.

———◦◦◦———

A WANT of individuality is the most dangerous sign in modern civilization.

John S. Mill.

———◦◦◦———

SIN may be clasped so close we cannot see its face.

Trench

———◦◦◦———

SIN, like a poisonous weed, resows itself, and becomes eternal by reproduction.

Beecher

AH! real thing of bloom and breath,
    I cannot love you while you stay,
Put on the dim, still charm of death,
    Fade to a phantom, float away,
    And let me call you yesterday.

Let empty flower-dust at my feet
    Remind me of the buds you wear;
Let the bird's quiet show how sweet
    The far-off singing made the air,
    And let your dew through frost look fair.

In mourning you I shall rejoice:
    Go; for the bitter word may be
A music—in the vanished voice;
    And on the dead face I may see
    How bright its form has been to me.

Then in the haunted grass I'll sit,
    Half tearful in your withered place,
And watch your lovely shadow flit
    Across to-morrow's sunny face,
    And vex her with your perfect grace.

So, real thing of bloom and breath,
    I weary of you while you stay;
Put on the dim, still charm of death,
    Fade to a phantom, float away,
    And let me call you yesterday.

"To-Day"—A Poem, from the Atlantic Monthly

ENOUGH!
        Last word of Lamartine

HE is too gushing to be useful.

James McCormick, Jr.

THE honorable gentleman is indebted to his memory for his wit and to his imagination for his facts.

Edmund Burke to an Antagonist in Parliament.

* * *

THE Catholics will in time get possession of America, for the "regulars always beat the militia."

De Tocqueville.

* * *

PROBABILITY is the guide of life.

Bishop Butler.

* * *

THROW dirt enough, and some will *stick*.

Archbishop Whately.

* * *

—WILL *stick*, but not *stain*.

Dr. John Henry Newman

* * *

THE strangeness of foreign life throws one back into himself.

Dr. John Henry Newman.

* * *

LIVING movements do not come of committees. No great work was ever done by a system, whereas systems rise out of individual exertions. The very faults of an individual excite attention; *he* loses, but his *cause* (if good and he powerful) gains. This is the way of things. We promote truth by self-sacrifice.

Dr. John Henry Newman.

* * *

INWARD bleeding is worse than any outward wound.

Saturday Review.

* * *

MAN legislates—woman ornates.

Eugene Benson.

ULTIMATE, saving truth is personal in the person of Christ, and demands personal fidelity.

Anon.

EVERY breath of air and ray of light and heat, every beautiful prospect, is, as it were, the spirits of their garments, the waving of the robes of those whose faces see God.

Dr. J. Henry Newman on the Angels.

PERSISTENCE in a given belief is not sufficient test of its truth; but departure from it is at least a slur upon the man who has felt so certain about it.

Dr. John Henry Newman.

FAITH in Christ justifies us before God—obedience to Christ justifies us before the world.

Rev. Dr. Bell, Allegheny City.

THERE is no antagonism between God's will and man's highest happiness.

Rev. Dr. Bell, Allegheny City.

IN following the details of a description or argument always give the "order of dependence."

Mrs. Howe Smith.

THE war exploded the prejudice against West Point discipline in favor of common-sense generalship.

N. Y. World.

RATIONALIST is a term of contempt, and means not one who is really reasonable, but one who would like to pass for such.

Dr. Ruckert.

THE deepest ice that ever froze
    Can only o'er the surface close;
The living stream lies quick below,
And flows, and cannot cease to flow.

Byron.

———◦◦◦———

HUMAN agencies achieve their legitimate results without regard to the motives that give them impulse.

Hurst.

———◦◦◦———

SCIENCE is nothing less than the latest and truest interpretation of the order of the world at which the human mind has arrived. It is the perfected mode of thinking in its application to all the phenomena of nature, physical and mental, which can become the subjects of thought.

Appleton's Journal.

———◦◦◦———

OUR Government needs an *educational* department as much as a legislative or executive.

Rev. Thomas Beecher.

———◦◦◦———

THE bitterest opponents of Jesus Christ are those who think they are so excellent as to deserve the love of God.

Rev. M. B. Riddle, Newark.

———◦◦◦———

THE true aim of life is not so much the accumulation and study of facts as it is the development and exercise of the powers and capacities of the soul.

Anon.

———◦◦◦———

I MADE a vow to God to look upon every child as one that would have a right to complain against me at the great day if I did not do all I could to afford each an adequate education for the work of life.

Prof. Eder, of Germany.

OUR greatest danger now in this country is corporative wealth.

Wendell Phillips.

———◦◦◦———

MY being a sinner is no reason why I should not trust in Christ. This is the very reason why I should trust. If my sins are great, Christ is a great Saviour. This was all Luther could say, even in death: "I have a great Saviour; this is all I know."

Rev. Dr. A. A. Hodge.

———◦◦◦———

THE most difficult thing in life is to keep the heights which the soul has reached.

Rev. David Riddle.

———◦◦◦———

THE American conflict was simply the burning of the dirtiest chimney that was ever set on fire.

Carlyle.

———◦◦◦———

UNPOPULARITY or popularity is utterly worthless as a test of manhood's worth.

F. W. Robertson.

———◦◦◦———

LISTEN to *conscience* more than to *intellect.*

F. W. Robertson.

———◦◦◦———

A SUNNY, cheerful view of life, resting on truth and fact, co-existing with practical aspiration ever to make things, men and self better than they are—this is the true, healthful poetry of existence.

Robertson.

———◦◦◦———

EVERY life that is based on deep principle tends to isolation. A great thought is always a protest. Thoreau's "Walden" is a minority report on the universe.

Galaxy.

EVERY day convinces me more and more that there is one thing, and but one, on earth worth living for, and that is to do God's work, and gradually grow into conformity to his image by mortification, self-denial and prayer.

Robertson.

———◆◆———

THERE is but one easy place in this world, and that is the grave.

Beecher.

———◆◆———

WE cannot vote right into wrong or wrong into right.

Froude.

———◆◆———

LEARN to concentrate thought.

Robertson.

———◆◆———

THERE are three things essential to success in life—*conscientiousness, concentration, continuity.* In extremity it is *character* that saves a man. To one object the lines of life should converge. This should be the focal-point of thought and feeling. We must not scatter our powers. Continuity is not incompatible with change; it is the reverse of a fragmentary and desultory mode of life. Every true life is a unit, an organic whole. There is advantage in continuity of place as well as of purpose.

President Smith, of Dartmouth, 1869.

———◆◆———

ALTHOUGH this is an æsthetic age, and men have fallen in love with the beautiful, yet all educated persons demand neatness and simplicity in every form of religious worship. Earthly beauty suggests and leads on to the infinite beauty and loveliness of the Son of God; simplicity enters largely into the beauty of holiness.

Edinburgh Review on Ritualism

EVERY wind is fair
When we are flying from misfortune.

Sophocles.

———◦◦———

ALL is distress and misery when we act against our nature and consent to ill.   *Sophocles.*

———◦◦———

GENERAL GRANT'S "Let us have peace," was the
still, calm voice that succeeded the whirlwind and
storm of war.   *Rev. Stewart St. Clairsville.*

———◦◦———

NATURAL religion contains all that is stated in the
dogmas.   *Emerson.*

———◦◦———

OUR best things are near us,
Lie close about our feet.

Anon.

———◦◦———

DR. NEWMAN says: "Once deny that the Church is
the medium between God and man, and you strike at
the idea of any mediation or Mediator whatever." How
absurd! As if the soul needed a Church as well as Christ
between it and God. The Church is only a help—not a
mediator.   *Anon.*

———◦◦———

IT is important that we should know what God has intended us for, but we must not spend our lives in trying
to find out. When God makes plain his will to us, we
ought to be willing to obey it. Instead of this, we persist
often in having our own way after God has plainly indi-
cated to us a different course.

W. K. Jennings, Esq.

WE glorify the supremacy of a first love, as if the heart did not require a training as varied as the intellect.

Galaxy.

———◦◦———

THE tears which destroy the beauty of the outward man, channel his cheek, cut his features with the marks of anguish, are doing a glorious work on the spirit within, which is becoming fresh with all young and living feelings.

F. W. Robertson.

———◦◦———

THERE is much that is wrong in our modern education. It teaches a man to be a gentleman; it does not enable him to make a living. It crams him with facts and words and images and theories; it does not unfold or develop the faculties of his mind; it does not perfect his individual manhood. It is too general, whereas it should be practical and specific, bearing on the wants and activities and hard necessities of life. Education is not so much the accumulation of *facts* as the development of *capacities*.

Anon.

———◦◦———

GRIEF is always conceited. It always thinks its case peculiar and unmatched.

Beecher.

———◦◦———

THE greatest men of a nation are those which it puts to death.

Renan

———◦◦———

HARD is his fate on whom the public gaze
Is fixed for ever to detract or praise;
Repose denies her requiem to his name,
And folly loves the martyrdom of fame.

Byron.

I LIVED in times of doubt and strife,
　When childlike faith was forced to yield;
I struggled to the end of life,
　Alas! I did not gain the field.

De Wette

————◦◦◦————

RAPTURES are troubled pleasures.

De Quincey.

————◦◦◦————

SCIENCE may be learned by rote; wisdom not.

Sterne.

————◦◦◦————

BLAME not fate
For sorrows which thyself did first create.

Anon.

————◦◦◦————

THE saddest country in the world is perhaps the region about Jerusalem.

Renan.

————◦◦◦————

EVERY idea loses something of its purity when it aspires to realization.

Renan.

————◦◦◦————

THEOLOGICAL seminaries turn out preachers as foundries turn out stoves—all of the same cast and pattern.

Rev. Alexander Clarke.

————◦◦◦————

SOME preachers ought to be judged as much by the number of those they repel from church as by the number of those they attract.

Rev. Alexander Clarke.

————◦◦◦————

THE tendency to suppress feelings may result in the extinction of feeling. Intellectual life destroys the purely sentimental life.

Hawthorne.

THERE is no saving a soul except by making it feel its need of being saved.

Spurgeon.

———◦◦———

THE world does not give a minister a court in which his case may be heard.

Rev. H. B. Fry.

———◦◦———

THE world does not express any surprise when it sees a skeptical man fall into immorality.

Beecher.

———◦◦———

WE should go through life as the traveler goes through the Swiss mountains. A hasty word may bring down an avalanche; a misstep may plunge us over a precipice.

Philadelphia Presbyterian.

———◦◦———

CHRISTIANITY is a battle—not a dream

Wendell Phillips.

———◦◦———

A TRUTH polemically stated loses half its effect.

Emerson.

———◦◦———

HE must be a strong man who can conceal his inclination.

Emerson.

———◦◦———

BROKEN men are indolent. Despondency cripples effort. Despair is fatal to exertion. Hopelessness leads to inaction.

Rev. Stuckenberg.

———◦◦———

THE first clash of innocence with guilt is a memorable crisis in one's life.

Saturday Review.

I ASK no favors and shrink from no responsibilities.

General Taylor.

———◇◇———

TO understand the present we must study the productive influences of the past.

Hurst.

———◇◇———

IF Nature abhors a vacuum, she has a great deal of abhorring to do. Space is not all occupied.

Ecce Cœlum.

———◇◇———

NEWSPAPERS are teachers of disjointed thinking.

Dr. Rush.

———◇◇———

PERSONAL religion is the life of God in the individual soul.

Goulburn.

———◇◇———

WE should go into the world with small expectations and infinite patience.

Good Words.

———◇◇———

'TIS the little rift within the lute
That by and by will make the music mute,
And, ever widening, slowly silence all.

Anon.

———◇◇———

HERE lies one whose name was writ in water.

Keat's Epitaph.

———◇◇———

I HAVE never seen anything in the world worth getting angry about.

Henry J. Raymond.

———◇◇———

FALSEHOOD may have its hour, but it has no *future.*

Pressense

HENRY, if each time you do as well as you can, your efforts will average about right.

Dr. Lyman Beecher to his son Henry.

———◦———

RATIONALISM has indirectly aided the cause of religion, for it has shown that Christianity does not rest entirely on tradition and authority, but also upon the profoundest convictions of man's inner reason and conscience.

Schaff.

———◦———

CHRIST awakened the world's thought, and it has never slept since.

Rev. Dr. W. D. Howard.

———◦———

A MAN may slander me to God for ever, and He will not hear.

Rev. Dr. W. D. Howard.

———◦———

AN old divine once wrote from the frontier to the students of Princeton: "We want strong oxen here; we have plenty of roots."

R. A. McConnell, Esq.

———◦———

ALAS for love, if thou wert all
And naught beyond, O earth!

Mrs. Hemans.

———◦———

OH how rarely do men learn the true enjoyments of this unstable life! Ever anticipating or procrastinating, while some, like idle children, strip from the fair young tree of hope its blossoms, and then weep because they gather no fruit; others are found to pass their whole existence in watching the growth of some centennial plant whose scentless blossoms they can never hope to behold.

Helen McCartney.

HOLD thou the good—define it well,
  For fear divine Philosophy
Should push beyond her mark, and be
  Procuress to the Lords of Hell.

Tennyson.

———◦◦◦———

BEHOLD the child, by Nature's kindly law,
  Pleased with a rattle, tickled with a straw;
Some livelier plaything gives his youth delight,
A little louder, but as empty quite.

Pope.

———◦◦◦———

A MAN cannot choose his own life. He cannot say, "I
  will take existence lightly, and keep out of the way of
the wretched, mistaken, energetic creatures who fight so
heartily in the great battle." He cannot say, "I will stop
in the tents while the strife is fought, and laugh at the
fools who are trampled down in the useless struggle." He
cannot do this. He can only do, humbly and fearfully,
that which the Maker who created him has appointed for
him to do. If he has a battle to fight, let him fight it
faithfully. But woe betide him if he skulks when his name
is called in the mighty muster-roll! woe betide him if he
hides in the tents when the tocsin summons him to the
scene of war!

M. E. Braddon.

———◦◦◦———

AT certain periods of life we live years of emotion in a
  few weeks, and look back on those times as on great
gaps between the old life and the new. You do not know
how much you suffer in those critical maladies of the heart
until the disease is over and you look back on it afterward.
The day passes in more or less of pain, and the night wears
away somehow.

Thackeray.

HE who, in obedience to the dictates of a false world, silences the purer instincts of his nature but garners up for his future years a harvest of disappointment and remorse.

Helen McCartney.

AMONG the pitfalls in our way
  The best of us walk blindly;
So, man, be wary, watch and pray,
  And judge your brother kindly.

Alice Carey.

IT is a dear delight for the soul to have trust in the faith of another. It makes a pillow of softness for the cheek which is burning with tears and the touch of pain. It pours a balm into the very source of sorrow. It is a hope undeferred, a flowery seclusion, into which the mind, when weary of sadness, may retreat for a caress of constant love; a warmth in the clasp of friendship for ever lingering on the hand; a consoling voice that dwells as with an eternal echo on the ear; a dew of mercy falling on the bruised and troubled hearts of this world. Bereavements and wishes long withheld descend sometimes as chastening griefs upon our nature; but there is no solace to the bitterness of broken faith.

Harper's Magazine, June, 1853.

A SOLID blow has in itself the elements of its rebound; it arouses the antagonism of the life on which it falls; its relief is the relief of a combat.

Miss E. S. Phelps—" Gates Ajar."

THE nerve which never relaxes, the eye which never blanches, the thought which never wanders,—these are the masters of victory.

" What Wins."

POETRY, being the concentrated richness and bloom of many seeds of thought gradually growing up into height and beauty, deserves to occupy the most prominent place in the garden of literature. Nor should it be considered merely as an object of curious loveliness, to be stooped over for a moment by an eye dazzled and fatigued with the contemplation of the surrounding beds. This flower, thus rising, as it were, upon the stem of grace, is not only precious for its wonderful mechanism of color and perfume, but it is precious also for the charm it works upon the intellectual eyesight. Like the fabled plant of antiquity, it purifies and brightens the vision of the understanding. To eyes sprinkled and enlightened by this flower no scene is barren and no tree is leafless. Every fountain shines with the form of its guardian naiad, and every wood is musical with the pipe of its sylvan spirit.

Eclectic Magazine.

———◦◦◦———

LOVE is a fire which the burnt child never dreads.

La Rochefoucauld.

———◦◦◦———

WHEN grasshoppers are so plenty as to make the pastures poor, gobblers grow fat.

Sam Slick.

———◦◦◦———

WHEN the greater malady is fixed,
The less is scarcely felt.

Anon.

———◦◦◦———

WITHOUT a friend, what were humanity?

Byron.

———◦◦◦———

RASHLY, nor ofttimes truly, doth man pass judgment on his brother.

Tupper.

A MAN is never astonished or ashamed that he doesn't know what another does, but he is surprised at the gross ignorance of the other in not knowing what he does

Sam Slick.

WHEN a man has no design but to speak plain truth, he isn't apt to be talkative.

George D. Prentice.

IF life to thee is but a constant care,
  Wed faith to hope—set both against despair.

Anon.

THE tie that binds the happy may be dear, but that which links the unfortunate is tenderness unutterable.

Anon.

THE best of men are but men. The agency that makes them holy leaves them human; there is nature in them as well as grace.

Tupper.

HE that stands upon a slippery place,
  Makes nice of no vile hold to stay him up.

Shakespeare.

BETWEEN two worlds life hovers like a star,
  'Twixt night and morn, upon the horizon's verge;
·How little do we know that which we are!
  How less what we may be! The eternal surge
Of time and tide rolls on, and bears afar
  Our bubbles; as the old burst, new emerge,
Lashed from the foam of ages; while the graves
Of empires heave but like some passing waves.

Byron

ALL of us pay a high price for the manhood we obtain—
nothing less than the sweet faith of childhood; all along
the way, from morning to high noon, robbers exact the toll
of life.
George D. Prentice.

———◦◦———

OUR doubts are traitors,
And make us lose the good we oft might win,
By fearing to attempt.

Shakespeare.

———◦◦———

ALAS! how oft does goodness wound itself,
And sweet affection prove the spring of woe!
Anon.

———◦◦———

BUT who shall so forecast the years,
And find in loss a gain to match?
Or reach a hand in time to catch
The far-off interest of tears?
Tennyson.

———◦◦———

ORNAMENT is but
The seeming truth which cunning times put on
To entrap the wisest.

Shakespeare.

———◦◦———

WHO would boast a victory that cost no strategy and
no careful disposition of the forces? But let a man
be very sure that the city is worth the siege.
Ike Marvel.

———◦◦———

THIS is the luxury of music. It touches every key of
memory and stirs all the hidden springs of sorrow and
of joy. I love it for what it makes me forget and for what
it makes me remember.
Belle Brittain.

NOTHING is humbler than ambition when it is about to climb.
Anon.

———◦◦———

PLEASURE and revenge
Have ears more deaf than adders to the voice
Of any true decision.
Shakespeare

———◦◦———

IF you want to strengthen an opinion, *tie it down.* Like the green bough bent with the finger, it will retain its altered position only while the hand of authority is applied to it, and will spring back again with a vigor increased by restraint when that hand is withdrawn.
Eclectic Magazine, June, 1844.

———◦◦———

LET it not be supposed that friendships are formed or even cemented by any similarity of character or of pursuit. This is a common mistake, and is the exact reverse of man's real course. We seek those who most differ from ourselves, and as stones can be more easily united together where cavities in the one correspond with asperities in the other, so character adapts itself to character by the very want in the one of those qualities which are prominent in the other.
Harper's Magazine, March, 1853.

———◦◦———

A BOLD surprise at a belief is sometimes the best argument against it.
London Quarterly.

———◦◦———

PEOPLE seem not to see that their opinion of the world is also a confession of character. We can only see what we are, and, if we misbehave, we suspect others.
Emerson.

A KNOWLEDGE of right and duty only renders one a greater hypocrite unless he have moral sense and moral life sufficient to conform to his own convictions.

J B. Walker Esq.

———◦◦———

CITY of the Dead! in the blessed Name wherein we are gathered together at this time, and in the presence that is here among us according to the promise, we will receive, and not dismiss, thy people who are dear to us. Lost friend, lost child, lost parent, sister, brother, husband, wife, we will not discard you. You shall hold your cherished places in our Christmas hearts and by our Christmas fires, and in the season of immortal hope and on the birth-day of immortal mercy we will shut out nothing. The winter sun goes down over town and village; on the sea it makes a rosy path, as if the sacred tread were fresh upon the waters. A few more moments and it sinks, and night comes on and lights begin to sparkle in the prospect. On the hillside, beyond the shapelessly-diffused town, and in the quiet keeping of the trees that gird the village steeple, remembrances are cut in stone, planted in common flowers, growing in grass, entwined with lowly brambles around many a mound of earth. In town and village there are doors and windows closed against the weather; there are flaming logs heaped high, there are joyful faces, there is healthy music of voices. Be all ungentleness and harm excluded from the temples of the household gods, but be those remembrances admitted with tender encouragement. They are of the time and all its comforting and peaceful reassurances; and of the history that reunited ever upon earth the living and the dead; and of the broad beneficence and goodness that too many men have tried to tear to narrow shreds.

Christmas as we Grow Older (Charles Dickens)

HAVE hope, my friend!   The future's voice
 Peals like a trumpet from afar;
It bids our drooping land rejoice
 And look to truth's eternal star.
Have hope!   The illumining hour draws near
 When love shall conquer pain and ill,
And all the hosts of hate and fear
 Go down before the might of will.

Have ever hope!   Though many a woe
 Hath darked thy life's disastrous day,
The tempest doth not always blow,
 The lightning rarely strikes to slay.
Sinks not in golden sheen from heaven
 The sun beneath his ocean tomb?
So shalt thou shine in manhood's even
 Ere thou descend to Hades' gloom.

The wise, the thoughtful know full well
 That God doth naught in vengeful ire;
But this deep truth all ages tell—
 He purifies his own by fire.
Woe to the man who knows not woe!
 Who never felt his soul grow dim!
Him threateneth dreadful overthrow—
 Heaven's love and care are not for him.

I, too, have borne unseen, alone,
 My own deep griefs—griefs writ on sand—
Until my heart grew like a stone;
 I struck it, and it hurt my hand.
My bitter bread was steeped in tears,
 Another Cain's mark marred my brow;
I wept for long my wasted years—
 Alas! too oft I weep them now!

           Anon

AMONG the elegant forms of insect life there is a little creature known to naturalists which can gather round it a sufficiency of atmospheric air, and, so clothed upon, it descends into the bottom of the pool, and you may see the little diver moving about dry and at his ease, protected by his crystal vesture, though the water all around and above be stagnant and bitter. Prayer is such a protector. A transparent vesture; the world sees it not, but, a real defence, it keeps out the world. By means of it the believer can gather so much of heavenly atmosphere around him, and with it descend into the putrid depths of this contaminating world, that for a season no evil can touch him; and he knows where to ascend for a new supply. Communion with God kept David pure in Babylon.

Dr. Hamilton on the Effect of Prayer.

———◦◦◦———

BE wise to win souls. Never despair of men, nor let men despair of themselves. Appeal to what is good and noble in man, and then there is that which is good and noble in the worst. Make use of each one's unsatisfying experience in life to lead him to the fullness of Christ. Men will become Christians when they see that it is the noblest and best thing for them.

Hints to Winners of Souls.

———◦◦◦———

EVERY act done in the great work of human progress will ever live. Every act which tends to the annihilation of error is a little rock started from the mountain-top, which gathers force on its way downward and starts others at every bound.

Anon.

———◦◦◦———

THE use of character is to be a shield against calumny.

Burke

I HAVE consulted our philosophers. I have perused their books. I have examined their several opinions. I have found them all proud, positive and dogmatizing, even in their pretended skepticism, knowing everything, proving nothing and ridiculing one another; and this is the only point in which they concur and in which they are right. Daring when they attack, they defend themselves without vigor. If you consider their arguments, they have none but for destruction; if you count their number, each one is reduced to himself; they never unite but to dispute; to listen to them was not the way to relieve myself from my doubts. I conceive that the insufficiency of the human understanding was the first cause of this prodigious diversity of sentiment, and that pride was the second. If our philosophers were able to discover truth, which of them would interest himself about it? Each of them knows that his system is not better established than the others, but he supports it because it is his own. There is not one among them who, coming to distinguish truth from falsehood, would not prefer his own error to the truth that is discovered by another. Where is the philosopher who, for his own glory, would not willingly deceive the whole human race? Where is he who in the secret of his heart proposes any other object than his own distinction? Provided he can but raise himself above the commonalty, provided he can eclipse his competitor, he has reached the summit of his ambition. The great thing for him is to think differently from other people. Among believers he is an atheist, among atheists a believer. Shun, shun, then, those who, under pretence of explaining nature, sow in the hearts of men the most dispiriting doctrines, whose skepticism is far more affirmative and dogmatical than the decided tone of their adversaries. Under pretence of being themselves the only people enlightened, they imperiously subject us to their magisterial decisions, and would fain palm upon us for the true causes of things the unintelligible systems they have erected in their own heads; while they overturn, destroy and trample under foot all that mankind reveres, snatch from the afflicted the only comfort left them in their misery, from the rich and great the only curb that can restrain their passions, tear from the heart all remorse of vice, all hopes of virtue, and still boast themselves the benefactors of mankind. "Truth," they say, "is never hurtful to man." I believe that as well as they, and the same, in my opinion, is a proof that what they teach is not the truth.   Rousseau.

TRUE science is the knowledge of things in those relations in which they exist in the actual constitution of things. Christianity, in the actual constitution of things, is like the sun in the firmament, that holds the earth with all things in it from falling away headlong into ruin. Science, then, which does not embrace the knowledge of Christianity is deficient in that which is the chief part of knowledge, and in relation to which all other parts should be regarded.
                    Rev. Dr. E. D. McMaster.

THE conscience will enforce no truth upon the soul, however perfect, unless it sees the authority of God in it.
                    J. B. Walker.

WHEN the intellect moves to the work of human elevation, the power which gives the impulse and secures permanency is generated in the heart and conscience.
                    J. B. Walker.

I AM about to take a leap in the dark.
                    Last words of Diderot.

THE only hope of the soul is, that " the blood of Christ, who through the Eternal Spirit offered himself without spot unto God, shall purge the conscience from dead works to serve the living God."

Dr. Adam Clarke.

———◦◦———

HAZEL eyes are the more usual indications of a mind masculine, vigorous and profound; just as genius, properly so called, is almost always associated with eyes of a yellow cast, bordering on hazel.

Lanater

———◦◦———

THE hope I dreamed of was a dream,
  Was but a dream; and now I wake
Exceedingly comfortless, and worn and old
  For a dream's sake.

I hang my harp upon a tree,
  A weeping willow in a lake;
I hang my silenced harp there, wrung and snapt,
  For a dream's sake.

Lie still, lie still, my breaking heart;
  My silent heart, lie still and break;
Life, and the world and mine own self are changed
  For a dream's sake.

Anon.

———◦◦———

IT is well!
God's ways are always right,
And love is o'er them all,
Tho' far above our sight.

Anon. ·

———◦◦———

IT is by a constant series of new starts that the spiritual life is carried on within us. Sanctity is not the work of a day, but of a life.

Goulburn

27

EARNEST work for Christ is the best means of spiritual culture.

Stephen H. Tyng.

———◆———

THESE tones of mercy are the after-notes of the law which the sinner has outraged, prolonged beyond its thunder, and sweetly sounding in the melody of the gospel.

Rev. Francis Vinton, D.D.

———◆———

IT is the province of the preachers of Christianity to develop the connection between this world and the next; to watch over the beginnings of a course which will endure for ever, and to trace the broad shadows cast from imperishable realities on the shifting scenery of earth.

New York Herald.

———◆———

WHAT is dogma but the true intellectual apprehension and the true verbal expression of the truths and facts of the divine revelation? What axioms are to science, dogma is to theology. As there can be no science without fixed principles and primary certainties, so there can be no knowledge of God, nor of his revelation, without fixed and primary truths.

Archbishop Manning.

———◆———

THAT it is the right and duty of all men to exercise their reason in inquiries concerning religion, is a truth so manifest that it may be presumed there are none who will be disposed to call it in question. Without reason, there can be no religion; for in every step we take in examining the evidences of revelation, in interpreting its meaning or in assenting to its doctrines, the exercise of this faculty is indispensable. When the evidences of Christianity are exhibited, an appeal is made to the reason of men for its truth; but all evidence and all argument would be perfectly futile if reason were not permitted to judge of their force. This noble faculty was certainly given to man to be a guide in religion as well as in other things. He possesses no other means by which he can form a judgment on any subject or assent to any truth; and it would be no more absurd to talk of seeing without eyes than of knowing anything without reason. Archibald Alexander.

THAT man lives twice who lives the first life well.
Herrick.

MY half-day's work is done,
  And this is all my part,
I give a patient God
  My patient heart.

And clasp his banner still,
  Though all the blue be dim;
These stripes, no less than stars,
  Lead after him.
Anon.

THE best thing in the world is to be a Christian.
Rev. Phillips Brooks, Philada.

I WOULD rather have one smile from Christ than to have the acclamation of a world. Beecher.

I WILL go forth 'mong men, not mailed in scorn,
  But in the armor of a pure intent.
Great duties are before me, and great songs,
And whether crowned or crownless when I fall,
It matters not, so as God's work is done.
Alexander Smith.

LEADING WRITERS.

THE following list of leading writers, with their assumed signatures, may be of service to those who are interested in literary matters:

PSEUDONYMS.	REAL NAMES.
A..	Matthew Arnold.
Agricola....................................	William Elliott.
Wilibald Alexis..........................	W. Haering.
Lucy Austin..............................	Lady Duff Gordon.
A. K. H. B.................................	Rev. A. K. H. Boyd, Country Parson
H. B..	Richard Doyle.
Samuel A. Bard..........................	E. G. Squier.
Miss Laura Barker......................	Mrs. T. Taylor.
Currer Bell...............................	Charlotte Brontë.
Cuthbert Bede...........................	Rev. E. Bradley.
Miss H. Beecher.........................	Mrs. H. B. Stowe.
Paul Beranger...........................	J. A. S. C. D. Collin.
Josh Billings.............................	Henry W. Shaw.
Miss M. Botham.........................	Mrs. M. Howitt.
Boz...	Charles Dickens.
Miss Buell................................	Sarah Josepha Hale.
Ned Buntline............................	E. T. C. Judson.
Miss A. Caldwell........................	Mrs. A. Marsh-Caldwell.
Mary Clavers............................	Mrs. C. M. Kirkland.
Davenant Cecil..........................	Rev. Derwent Coleridge.
Parson Chartist.........................	Rev. C. Kingsley.
Barry Cornwall..........................	William Proctor.

Alfred Crowquill..................................A. H. Forrester.
Alexander de Comyne.....................C. T. Browne.
The Married Critic...........................J. G. Janin.
Croaker..F. G. Halleck.

Delta..Thomas Aird.
P. B. Doesticks................................Mortimer Thompson.
Leon Durocher..................................M. R. L. Reybauld.

George Eliot.....................................Mrs. Marian J. (Evans) Lewes.

Fanny Fern..Wife of James Parton and sister of
                                                              N. P. Willis.
Miss A. M. Fielding.........................Mrs. A. M. Hall.
Gilbert Forrester.............................Miss M. E. Braddon.
Miss Francis....................................Mrs. L. M. Child.
Miss M. Francis..............................Mrs. M. Thornycroft.

Miss Garrow.....................................T. A. Trollope.
Miss M. Geddes...............................Mrs. Carpenter.
Howard Glyndon..............................Miss Laura C. Redden.
Miss Goward.....................................Mrs. Keely.
Lady G. Gower..................................Lady G. Fullerton.
Miss J. Griffin.................................Lady J. Franklin.

Gail Hamilton...................................Miss Abigail E. Dodge.
Miss Hehl...Mrs. Stirling.
Higgin..Rev. J. C. M. Bellew.
Miss E. Hughes................................Madame T. Cherr.
Burton Hunt......................................Miss M. E. Braddon.

Ianthe..Mrs. E. C. Embury.
Young Ireland..................................C. G. Duffy.
Isa..Isa Craig.
Iskander..Alexander Herzen.

Miss Johnstone...............................Mrs. H. Gray.
Miss C. Jones...................................Mrs. C. Chrisholm.
Jennie June......................................Mrs. Jennie Croly.

Orpheus C. Kerr..................Robert H. Newell.
Miss F. A. Kemble.. ....Mrs. Butler.
Edmund Kirk..................J. R. Gilmore.
Miss A. E. Kempe..............Mrs. A. E. Bray.
The Railway King..............G. Hudson.

Patty Lee.....................Alice Carey.
Luke Limner..................J. Leighton.
Miss E. Lynn.................Mrs. E. Linton.

Ike Marvel..................Donald G. Mitchel.
Miss E. C. Manley...........Mrs. E. C. Embury.
Adolf Meyer.................M. A. Goldschmidt.
Max Müller..................Frederick Maximilian Müller.
Meier.......................Louise Oston.
Owen Meredith..............Edward Robert Bulwer Lytton.
Miss E. L. Montague.........Mrs. T. R. Harvey.
Miss D. M. Mulock..........Mrs. Craik.

Petroleum V. Nasby..........D. R. Locke.

Edward Stevenson O'Brien.....Isaac Butt.
O'Keefe ....Madame A. S. L Belloc.
Jacob Omnium................M. J. Higgins.
Miss E. O'Neill.............Lady E. Beecher.
Miles O'Reilly.............Major Halpine.
Ouida......................Mrs. Montgomery Atwood.

Mrs. Parker................Amy Sedgwick.
Mrs. Partington............B. P. Shillaber.
Florence Percy.............Mrs. Elizabeth Aikers.
Jeemes Pipes...............Stephen Masset.
K. N. Pepper...............James M. Morris.
Phiz.......................H. K. Browne.
Miss J. Pinhorn............Mrs. J. Thomas.
De Prat....................Lamartine.
Miss Price.................Mrs. H. Wood.

Miss E. Rigby..............Lady Eastlake.
Miss A. Reviere............Lady A. Bishop.

Mrs. Robinson..................................Miss M. W. Freer.
Mark Rochester..............................Charles Kent.
Roso..Mad'lle Rosalie Bonheur.

Village Schoolmaster...................Chas. M. Dickinson.
Miss A. M. Scott..........................Mrs. A. M. Gatlv.
Miss C. E. Sheridan.....................Hon. Mrs. C. E. Morten.
Silverpen......................................E. Meteyard.
Mace Sloper, Esq.........................C. G. Leland.
Jacques Souffrant........................Louis Ulbach.
Mrs. S. L. Stephens.....................Y. M. L. Duvernay.
Miss S. Stickney..........................Mrs. Ellis.
Miss S. Strickland.......................Mrs. S. Moodie.
Mrs. Stirling................................Miss Fanny Clifton.
Felix Summerly...........................Henry Cole.

Timothy Titcomb.........................Dr. J. G. Holland.
Miss E. Tree.................................Mrs. C. Kean.
Miss L. Tramley..........................Mrs. L. Meredith.
Mark Twain..................................Samuel S. Clemens.

V..Mrs. C. Clive.
Louis de Vermond........................L. Enault.

Artemus Ward..............................Charles F. Browns
Miss Wigley..................................Mrs. C. Clive.
Miss S. I. Woolgar.......................Mrs. A. Mellon.

Sydney Yendys............................Sydney Dobell.

INDEX OF AUTHORS.

INDEX OF SUBJECTS.

[The figures refer to the pages. The letters to the number of the selection ; thus, 351 c denotes page 351 third selection.]

PAST:
    And future, 216 b.
    And present, 388 a.
    The remorseless, 75 b.
PATRIOTISM: Universal in America, 70 g.
PEACE:
    Approach of, 25 a.
    Promoted by science, 367 a.
PEOPLE:
    And schools, 207 a.
    Clever, 74 d.
    Formal, 69 f.
    Good and bad, 110 b.
    How distinguished, 202 d.
    Inquisitive, 114 e.
    Most difficult to know, 229 e.
    Relation to government, 189 b.
    Silent and talkative, 328 a.
    Sovereignty of, 225 c.
    Trust in, 106 a.
PERPLEXITY: 163 f.
PERSEVERANCE: Power of, 229 b.
PICTURES: Use of, 145 b.
PIETY: Healthy, 140 e.
PILOT: True, 71 a.
PITTSBURG:
    At night, 198 b.
    Its importance, 55 a.
PLEASURE:
    And revenge, deafness of, 411 b.
    Definition of, 213 i.
    Evanescence of, 297 g.
    Past and present, 296 h.
PHILOSOPHERS:
    Errors of some, 171 b.
    Skeptical, differ, 415 a.
POETICAL INSTINCT: Effect of, 129 c.

POETS:
    Description of, 23 b, 124 b.
    How inspired, 345 b.
    Nature of, 307 c.
POETRY:
    And prose, 36 c.
    And music, 129 d.
    Composition of difficult, 65 d.
    Defined, 408 a.
    In theology, 129 a–b.
    True, of existence, 398 g.
POEM:
    Finest American, 338 a.
    Of Dorset dialect, 335 a.
    On to-day, 394 a.
POLITENESS: Result of, 57 e.
POLITICAL:
    Convulsions, 142 b.
    Prosperity, supports of, 217 d.
POOR: Attention to the, 107 a.
POPE: Power of the, 179 e.
POSITIVISM:
    Parisian, 359 c.
POPULARITY and unpopularity, 398 e.
POWER: Latent, 56 e.
POWERS: Contraction of our, 220 f.
PRAISE AND CENSURE: 119 d.
PRAYER:
    At a marriage, 258 f.
    A protection, 414 a.
    For strength, 322 b.
    Nature of, 110 g.
    Private, necessity of, 392 b.
    Vocabulary of, 257 d.
PREACHING:
    And fiction, 302 c.
    Compared to lightning, 141 a.
    Effect of, 191 d.

CPSIA information can be obtained at www.ICGtesting.com
Printed in the USA
LVOW11s1950170813

348399LV00011B/305/P